A DIRTY WAR IN WEST AFRICA

LANSANA GBERIE

A Dirty War in West Africa

The RUF and the Destruction of Sierra Leone

HURST & COMPANY, LONDON

First published in the United Kingdom by
C. Hurst & Co. (Publishers) Ltd,
41 Great Russell Street, London WC1B 3PL
© Lansana Gberie, 2005
All rights reserved.
Printed in India

The right of Lansana Gberie to be identified as
the author of this publication has been asserted
by him in accordance with the Copyright, Designs
and Patents Act, 1988.

A catalogue record for this book is available from
the British Library.

ISBNs
1-85065-747-5 *casebound*
1-85065-742-4 *paperback*

CONTENTS

CONTENTS

PREFACE AND ACKNOWLEDGEMENTS

'We shall know nothing until we know whether we have the right to kill our fellow men or the right to let them be killed. In that every action today leads to murder, direct or indirect, we cannot act until we know whether or why we have the right to kill.'[1]

This study of Sierra Leone's decade-long war has been long in the making. It is the result of several years' observation of and writing about the war. The author was a journalist in Sierra Leone during the early years of the war, and left in 1996 to write a postgraduate thesis on it in 1997 at Wilfrid Laurier University in Canada. He returned several times, at the height of the conflict, to do research and write about the war for various publications. This book is, therefore, a combination of journalistic reporting and historical analysis. It does not pretend to be an aloof academic study. The author witnessed first hand some of the atrocities that marked the war, and felt the emotional pressures as a result. This accounts for the sometimes passionate tone of the book.

In 1997, following a seminal review of Paul Richards' *Fighting for the Rainforest: War, Resources and Youth in Sierra Leone* (1996), the first scholarly treatment of the war waged by the RUF (Revolutionary United Front), by Yusuf Bangura,[2] a lively debate ensued among Sierra Leonean scholars on the e-mail discussion forum Leonenet. Richards' book (see also Chapter 5), sought to analyse the RUF war as a rational rebellion against a failed and bankrupt patrimonial state by a group of 'embittered pedagogues' (his words)—'excluded intellectuals' who aimed to replace that state with a 'revolutionary egalitarian' one. Bangura's review tried to understand the RUF's predilection for terroristic violence against the very civilians whom it claimed it was fighting to 'liberate', and the debate that followed

---

[1] Albert Camus, *The Rebel*, New York: Vintage Books, 1956.
[2] Yusuf Bangura, 'Understanding the Political and Cultural Dynamies of the Sierra Leone War,' *Africa Development* (Dakar: CODESRIA), vol. XXII, nos 3–4, 1997, pp. 117–48.

the review—which was first published on Leonenet—took up from this point. Bangura had argued that the RUF's violence did not have 'only one logic, but several: there is obviously the logic of political violence…but this competes, coexists and interacts with the logics of banditry, hedonism and brutality.' The challenge, Bangura wrote, is to analyse 'crucial forms of RUF behavior that would [help] to shed…light on the character of the organization: the systematic rape of women, which most people know about…; the central issue of drug abuse…; the beheading and systematic maiming of victims…; and the problem of random looting of property.'[3]

. I was a participant in that debate, and the preoccupation was with the essential character of the RUF—its composition and its worldview. Although Bangura's trenchant review provided the starting point for the debate, the actual reference point was Ibrahim Abdullah's provocative thesis on the RUF: 'Bush Path to Destruction: the Origins and Character of the RUF', which built on the important work of Ismail Rashid (also a participant in the debate) on radical student politics in Sierra Leone in the 1970s and 1980s,[4] and was also first published on Leonenet. In it Abdullah traces the emergence of the RUF from the popular struggles of student radicals in the 1980s: a trip to Libya by some of them for 'ideological' and military training, the co-optation and dominance of '*lumpen*' (underclass, poor and often criminal) elements and ideas, and then the almost complete phasing-out of whatever 'intellectual' elements there were during the Libyan training even before the 'revolution' began. It was this *lumpen* dominance, Abdullah argues, that explains the character and behaviour of the RUF—'a revolutionary movement without revolutionaries', in his Strangelovian phraseology. Abdullah wrote:

There are no radical intellectuals in the RUF nor has the movement established any meaningful relationship with the peasantry based on the acceptance of a common programme produced within the context of a revolutionary dialogue. What marks the RUF is the chronic lack of cadres imbued with any revolutionary ideology. Its lumpen base has made it impossible for the movement to attract support from any social group.[5]

[3] Ismail Rashid, 'Subaltern Reactions: Lumpens, Students, and the Left', ibid., pp. 19–43.
[4] Ibrahim Abdullah, 'Bush Path to Destruction: The Origins and Character of the RUF', ibid., pp. 45–76.
[5] I. Abdullah *et al.*, 'Lumpen Youth Culture and Political Violence: Sierra Leoneans Debate the RUF and the Civil War', ibid., pp. 171–215.

During the debate I raised a number of questions which were never adequately addressed (to my mind) and which concerned wholly the violent pathology of the RUF:

Let me start by raising two points that may help us to understand the RUF's acts of barbaric violence and its ex post rationalization. The first relates to the movement's unremitting use of child combatants in carrying out atrocities. As a journalist, I visited Pujehun with a team of national electoral officers in late 1991 to observe former President Momoh's referendum on the one-party state shortly after the 'liberation' of the town from the RUF. I was shown graves that had been hastily dug by the streets in which were buried people who had been slaughtered by their own children (mostly pupils of St Paul's Secondary School). The children, I was told, were forced to commit these terrible acts by the RUF who liberally supplied them drugs. These young fiends ran away with the RUF combatants when ULIMO (United Liberation Movement of Liberia for Democracy) and the Sierra Leone government troops entered the town. It is clear that most of the RUF combatants (partly recruited in this way) are teenagers, even pre-teenagers, and are known to be most reckless with human lives. How does this use of children to commit atrocities reconcile with the view that the RUF war has been characterized by irresponsible acts of hooliganism and terror simply because it is led by lumpens? Isn't it the case that 'lumpens' are adults with some political aims, however odious or vague such aims may be?

The second point relates to Paul Richards' postulation...that among the cadre of RUF fighters who invaded the country from Liberia in 1991 were Burkinabes (and Liberians) who, he claims, were responsible for most of the terrorism of the early period. He suggests that such...murderous acts caused the defection of most of the more conscientious Sierra Leonean members from the RUF...How does this foreign element help us to understand the misdirected acts of terror by the RUF?[6]

The debate, as well as the articles written by Abdullah and Bangura and other Sierra Leonean contributors (including the present writer), were published in a special edition of the journal *Africa Development* (1997), and it is to date the most comprehensive and serious analysis of the RUF's war. This book expands and clarifies the limited focus of the special edition, and offers a more in-depth treatment of the RUF as an organisation and the processes of disintegration of the Sierra Leonean state. It also analyses the predatory and mercenary nature of the insurgent forces in a more concentrated and empirical manner.

---

[6] The 'Special Issue' was further expanded, with more chapters and authors added, and published as a book entitled *Between Democracy and Terror: The Sierra Leone Civil War* (Dakar: CODESRIA, 2003), edited by Ibrahim Abdullah.

I was a participant observer for most of the period that the war was fought, covering it as a journalist from 1991 to 1996, and visiting the country for extended periods in 1999, 2001 and 2002. As a journalist I was among the first to meet and interview the RUF leader Foday Sankoh (in Ivory Coast, in 1996), and over the years I have met and interviewed many other RUF commanders, soldiers, civil defence militia members, civilian victims of rebel atrocities, aid agency workers, government officials (including the current President and the former military leader Maada Bio) and many others directly or indirectly involved with the prosecution of the war.

Acknowledgements

My thanks go, first and foremost, to Professor Terry Copp, a military historian at Wilfrid Laurier University, who supervised my MA thesis on the war, and who has remained immensely supportive of my intellectual endeavours since then. I also thank Professor Martin Klein, my PhD supervisor at the University of Toronto, who first encouraged me to expand my MA thesis for possible publication. I also thank my colleagues at Partnership Africa Canada, especially Ian Smillie, Ralph Hazleton and Bernard Taylor, with whom I have worked closely over the past three years on research into African conflicts, and especially the links between some of these conflicts and extractive resource (mainly diamonds) predation. PAC paid for a number of research trips I undertook to various parts of West Africa, including many to Sierra Leone, as part of its Human Security and International Diamond Trade project. These trips immensely enriched my knowledge of the RUF and other players in the Sierra Leone war. I am extremely grateful to Stephen Ellis for his encouragement and for commenting extensively on the initial draft. Thanks are also due Stephen Rockel, also of the University of Toronto, and to Ismail Rashid (at Vassar College), Patrick Muana, Lansana Fofana and Zoe Dugal.

I must thank my very close friends Mohamed Swaray (who assisted tremendously with research for this book in Sierra Leone), Kingsley Lington (a longtime colleague in journalism), Timothy Sowa (who also assisted with research for this book), Alhaji M. S. Bah, Sharka Sannoh, Bondi Gevao, David Tam-Baryoh, Anthony Kola-Olusanya, Valentine Swaray, Khalilu Totangie and many others. I also thank Yusuf Bangura for his encouragement and support; Kofi Akosah-Sarpong, a longtime friend and a journalist colleague, whose encouragement was also important; and Peter Penfold, the former

British High Commissioner to Sierra Leone, whose interest in the project was important for its ultimate realisation. My very good friends Abibatu Koroma, Yemah Gebeh (who read an earlier draft and made very incisive comments), Miatta Gebeh, Patricia Luseni, Victoria Shears, Fatmata Ballah-Conteh, Nancy Bangura and Rhoda Mahawah Suffian-Kargbo deserve special thanks for their encouragement and support. I must, as anyone writing on contemporary Sierra Leone surely should, thank my friend Peter Andersen, who started and for many years ran the extremely useful Sierra Leone Web (at 'www.sierra-leone.org'), for his support.

December 2004 L. G.

ABBREVIATIONS

AFRC	Armed Forces Ruling Council
APC	All Peoples Congress
ARC	Anti-Corruption Revolutionary Council
BBC	British Broadcasting Corporation
CAST	Consolidated African Selection Trust
CAW	Children Associated with War
CDF	Civil Defence Force
CMS	Church Missionary Society
DFID	Department for International Development (UK)
Ecomog	ECOWAS Monitoring Group
ECOWAS	Economic Community of West African States
Eredcom	Eastern Region Defence Committee
EO	Executive Outcomes
FBC	Fourah Bay College
FCO	Foreign and Commonwealth Office (UK)
GGDO	Government Gold and Diamond Office
GNP	Gross National Product
GSG	Gurkha Security Guards
IA	International Alert
IMF	International Monetary Fund
INPFL	Independent National Patriotic Front of Liberia
ISU	Internal Security Unit (later SSD)
LURD	Liberians United for Reconciliation and Democracy
MODEL	Movement for Democracy in Liberia
MRD	Movement for the Restoration of Democracy
NCCP	National Coordinating Committee for Peace
NCDDR	National Committee for Disarmament, Demobilisation and Reintegration
NCSL	National Council of Sierra Leone
NDMC	National Diamond Mining Company
NPFL	National Patriotic Front of Liberia
NPRC	National Provisional Ruling Council

NRC	National Reformation Council
NSC	National Security Council
NUP	National Unity Party
NUSS	National Union of Sierra Leone Students
OAU	Organisation of African Unity
PAC	Partnership Africa Canada
PDP	Peoples Democratic Party
PPP	Peoples Progressive Party
RPG	rocket-propelled grenade
RUF	Revolutionary United Front
RUFP	Revolutionary United Front Party
SLA	Sierra Leone Army
SLAJ	Sierra Leone Association of Journalists
SLBS	Sierra Leone Broadcasting Service
SLPMB	Sierra Leone Produce Marketing Board
SLPP	Sierra Leone People's Party
SLST	Sierra Leone Selection Trust
SOFA	Status of Forces Agreement
SSD	Special Security Division
TRC	Truth and Reconciliation Commission
Ulimo	United Liberation Movement of Liberia for Democracy
UN	United Nations
Unamsil	UN Mission in Sierra Leone
Unomsil	UN Observer Mission in Sierra Leone
VSO	Voluntary Service Overseas (UK)
WFP	World Food Programme

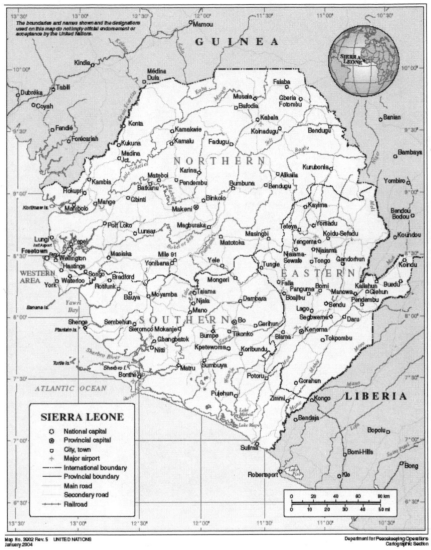

1

INTRODUCTION
THE RUF PHENOMENON

'War is, at first, the hope that one will be better off; next, the expectation that the other fellow will be worse off; then, the satisfaction that he isn't any better off; and finally, the surprise at everyone's being worse off.' (Karl Kraus[1])

They fought, the *Washington Post* dryly noted, 'for nothing, and that's what they got'.[2] The *Washington Post* was writing about individual Revolutionary United Front (RUF) militia fighters who were being disarmed by UN peacekeepers in Sierra Leone in late 2001. Shabby and broken, many able to call their own nothing but the tattered shirts on their backs and old denim jeans they were wearing, the militias, once dreaded for their brutality and daring, had finally submitted to a UN-supervised disarmament process in the diamond-rich district of Kono. There was little in their stupefied and vacant looks to indicate their awfully dreaded past. Whatever they had found in the alluvial diamond pits had been taken away by their leaders—mainly to Liberia—and now the disarmed fighters looked only to the meagre reintegration benefits which were being handed out by the UN and other agencies. Except that, as the *Washington Post* story made clear, some of the fighters, the hardcore ones who had been fighting since it all started in 1991, were Liberians, and would probably end up in their country and enlist in other militia groups. Many more of the hardcore RUF would follow them there and elsewhere in the volatile and crisis-ridden region. There

---

[1] In Jon Winokur, *The Portable Curmudgeon* (New York: Penguin, 1992), p. 282.
[2] Douglas Farah, 'They fought for nothing, and that's what they got', *Washington Post*, 1 September 2001.

1

would, it seemed, never be a tidy ending to this confused kind of warfare.

Sierra Leone's 'rebel' war formally ended on 11 January 2002, with the symbolic ceremonial closure of the last disarmament centre in Kailahun district, where the war had begun in March 1991, to be followed by the symbolic burning of arms in Makeni and Freetown. It was, in a sense, a fitting end for a war that was marked by an utter craving for drama: a war that was highly demonstrative, its military and 'political' efficacy depending almost wholly on shock or terror tactics, and which, in that sense, seemed to be guided by what the nineteenth-century evangelist of anarchism, Mikhail Bakunin, called the 'Propaganda of the Deed'.

In February 2002, a month after these events, the British Prime Minister Tony Blair made a brief stop in the country. Britain's support for the Sierra Leone government had been crucial in ensuring the disarmament; and Blair had made a commitment, unfashionable among world leaders in this age of *Realpolitik*, to support Sierra Leone's transition from war to peace for ostensibly humanitarian reasons. His commitment to Sierra Leone, he made clear on more than one occasion, was part of a broader commitment to help salvage Africa, a continent that had become 'a scar on the conscience of the world'. Blair believed that however deep Africa's problems are, 'If the world as a community focused on it (the continent of Africa), we could heal it. And if we don't, it will become deeper and angrier.'[3] Africa had to be helped to make the transition from destitution and war and diseases to a stable and prosperous future, which its vast resources should be able to sustain, and Sierra Leone was a good beginning. Blair's missionary tone—when he spoke about Africa—evoked the late eighteenth-century pronouncements by British liberals and abolitionists on the continent in view of the ravages caused by the Atlantic slave trade, and it is perhaps not so fortuitous that Sierra Leone, which in its modern form was created by the British as a place to resettle slaves freed mainly by them, would again be so central to a British government's declared commitment to an 'ethical foreign policy' and to help salvage an Africa that is, once again, crippled by wars and exploitation.

Blair did not, on that trip, actually enter Freetown, the seaside capital of the country, and one which, for much of the nineteenth century, had been the most important base of Britain's West African

---

[3] 'Blair's Speech: This is a battle with only one outcome, our victory', *Guardian*, 3 October 2001.

empire, a place that was both a colonial city and a city holding great hope for a resurgent Africa. It had West Africa's oldest Western-style university institution, Fourah Bay College, and was then known as the 'Athens of West Africa'. Freetown had been, in January 1999, seriously battered by rebel forces, with some of its best hotels badly vandalised and a few totally destroyed; which perhaps was the reason why Blair did not even visit the city. But at Lungi, a very small town which holds the country's main airport, Blair made his sentiment about the country clear: 'I wanted to say to you that my first introduction to Sierra Leone came many many years ago because my father used to come to Freetown to the University there to teach,' he told a cheering crowd. 'And I remember him telling me what a wonderful country it was and how friendly the people were. And if we think back to the past and the possibilities there, and if we look forward to the future now, then I think we can see that this dreadful process of conflict is not the true Sierra Leone. It is an aberration of the true Sierra Leone.'[4] All around the Prime Minister were palpable signs of the country's desperate state: a bare-knuckled airport, Bangladeshi troops (of the UN mission in the country) camped in tiny, makeshift huts; and next to these dusty little houses, shack dwellings, mango and orange trees growing out of badly trampled earth, their half-hearted promise of meagre bounty only adding to the impression of depression, poverty and nullity.

Shortly after Blair left the country, the man who started the 'aberrant' war, Foday Saybanah Sankoh—who, after getting a senior government post in the 1999 peace settlement and then seeking to revive his rebellion, had been arrested and detained by the Sierra Leone government with the support of British troops—was hauled before a Freetown court charged with murder. The charge related to an incident in May 2000 in which Sankoh's men, allegedly on his orders, opened fire and killed twenty-one peaceful demonstrators before his house in Freetown. Sankoh had always had a fearsome reputation, but his court appearance was steeped in bathos. 'Looking at his dreadlocked figure, slumped against the wall,' the BBC reported, 'it was hard to believe that this is a man who bears much responsibility for ten years of bloody civil war in Sierra Leone.'[5] It was a similar spectacle, of decrepit old men appearing in court helpless and innocuous but who had committed unspeakable acts

---

[4] Blair's speech as posted to the Sierra Leone Web, www.sierra-leone.org.
[5] Tom McKinley, 'Sankoh murder trial begins', http:/news.bbc.co.uk/hi/ English/Africa, 11 March 2002.

of cruelty and destruction, that moved Hannah Arendt, writing of Nazi Germany, to remark famously on the 'banality of evil'. Sierra Leone's decade-long war may have been aberrant and freakish, but it was started and managed by ordinary men whose motivations, as well as the conditions that made it possible for them to play out their terrible fantasies, need to be investigated and understood. This is the main purpose of this book.

Sierra Leone was settled by freed slaves brought there by the British navy in 1787, and became a Crown Colony in 1808. At the time, the Colony covered only the small coastal peninsular area around Freetown. The much larger hinterland of the Colony was declared a Protectorate in 1896, and together—Colony and Protectorate—Sierra Leone gained its independence from Britain in 1961. So the country's link to Britain is a very long one. The country, in 1961, was weak and poor, but it was promising. After independence, Sierra Leone passed through a succession of leaders, from the patrician and conservative Sir Milton Margai, a decent leader whose gradualist policy helped the country develop steadily in the 1960s, to the utterly corrupt and destructive Siaka Stevens, whose policies eroded the state's machinery and legitimacy and led to the collapse of much of its institutions, and then to Joseph Momoh, under whose ineffectual leadership the country was plunged into war in 1991. The war, which directly triggered three military coups—one in 1992, the National Provisional Ruling Council (NPRC) coup led by Captain Valentine Strasser, then another in 1996, a palace coup that led to Strasser's replacement by his deputy Brigadier Maada Bio, and then the most destructive, in 1997, a bloody putsch that temporarily terminated the democratically elected government of Tejan Kabbah—led to a complete normative collapse.

This book is a narrative and analysis of events during the period from 1991 to 2001, when the war engulfed the country with a destructive force. In that sense it is also a series of reflections by a witness—someone who, as a journalist, covered the war for several years and has been writing about it for a long time; the analysis is the result of insights gained in the process, and of my training as a military historian. It is not political science, and it avoids a lot of the theorising that can often create more confusion than clarity. The aim is to produce a historically accurate account of the war, to lay bare its true character, and thereby to dispel a lot of the mystifications which have come to surround such conflicts in Africa.

Wars like the one that devastated Sierra Leone—small, somewhat localised but highly destructive—are often portrayed by the Western media as the reality of the African continent. For the media Africa is compulsively a crisis-ridden continent sucked into savagery, with murderous despots and inter-tribal and religious conflicts the rule rather than the exception. This negative portrayal of Africa is not entirely without basis. The continent remains the poorest and most violence-prone in the world. Until recently, about a third of Africa's states were embroiled in localised or regional warfare (or both), and weapons proliferated among private citizens, including children, whose participation in such conflicts has become a metaphor for the continent's underdevelopment and the lunacy that passes for much of its social functioning. A large number of these conflicts—excluding the very significant ones in Angola and Sudan—began after the end of the Cold War and are of low intensity. They became so widespread in Africa that Michael Ignatieff, a prominent liberal writer on conflict issues, could find it convenient to make this evident exaggeration: 'War, like a virus, has worked its way into the very tissue of the Great Lakes regions, part of West Africa...It is the major employer, the chief economic activity. All power comes from the barrel of an AK-47.'[6] An earlier assessment by another liberal writer, Victoria Brittain of London's *Guardian* newspaper, put it in even more apocalyptic terms, speculating a future for the continent in which 'Conrad's *Heart of Darkness* will be read as straightforward description.'[7] Reading such accounts, one would be forgiven for concluding that this dismal condition of much of Africa is an almost deterministic process, a self-destruct tendency among Africans that is as incomprehensible to Westerners as it is unstoppable. An American journalist, Robert Kaplan, made precisely this point in 1994 in a notorious article to which I will return.[8]

The Sierra Leone war began in March 1991 ostensibly as a spill-over from Liberia, which had been wracked by a devastating civil war since an invasion on Christmas Eve 1989 by a small group of armed men, led by a former junior government minister named Charles Ghankay Taylor. Within a few years it had taken on a character of its own—but still maintaining its crucial Liberian links—and engulfed the country with destructive force. By the end of 1996

---

[6] Michael Ignatieff, 'The Gods of War', *New York Review of Books*, 9 October 1997.

[7] Victoria Brittain, 'Africa: a lost continent', *New Statesman*, 8 April 1994.

[8] See Robert Kaplan, 'The Coming Anarchy: how Scarcity, Crime, Over-Population and Diseases are Rapidly Destroying our Planet', *Atlantic Monthly*, February 1994.

more than 15,000 people had been killed and almost two-thirds of the country's population of 4.5 million displaced. The economy collapsed, with a negative annual growth rate—minus 6.24 per cent—between 1991 and 1995. By March 1996 an estimated 75 per cent of school-aged children were out of school, and 70 per cent of the country's educational facilities, already troubled by the time war started, were destroyed. Only 16 per cent of the country's health facilities were functioning by March 1996, and almost all of these were in the as yet untouched capital (i.e. untouched by war).

These grim figures were given in an incisive report in 1996 by Ian Smillie, a close colleague at Partnership Africa Canada, a small research group that was later to produce a report linking the continuation of the war to the RUF's access to the country's rich diamond mines—*The Heart of the Matter: Sierra Leone, Diamonds and Human Security*.[9] By the end of 1999 the casualty figure had risen, by most estimates, above 50,000, and Freetown had itself been partly destroyed in a devastating attack by the rebels and rogue government soldiers in January 1999. Thousands of civilians, including young babies, had their hands crudely amputated by the rebels in a campaign of insane terror.

The group spearheading this destruction, the Revolutionary United Front (RUF), was led by a dismissed army corporal and former cameraman, Foday Saybanah Sankoh, and it claimed that the aim was to overthrow Sierra Leone's 'corrupt' rulers, 'liberate' the country's derelict peasantry and the dispossessed, and institute 'genuine democracy'. The issues of corruption and bad governance, not to mention the historical dereliction and distress of rural Sierra Leone and the country's disadvantaged peasantry and urban youth population, were real and palpable issues, well discussed even by the country's sclerotic elite, as will emerge in this book in due course. But throughout its nearly eleven-year campaign of largely terroristic violence, the RUF targeted mainly those very dispossessed people, killing and mutilating them in an orgy of bewildering cruelty, while all the time looting the country's rich diamond reserves and maintaining an extremely profitable trade in them with outsiders, through Liberia's Charles Taylor.

Diamonds may not have been the cause of the war; the question of 'causes' can often seem wholly misdirected—Taylor, the real

[9] See Ian Smillie, 'Sierra Leone: NGOs in Complex Emergencies', unpublished paper, 1996; also Ian Smillie, Lansana Gberie and Ralph Hazleton, *The Heart of the Matter: Sierra Leone, Diamonds and Human Security*, Ottawa: Partnership Africa Canada, 2000.

mastermind, aimed at both revenge and pillage, as we will see, and his protégé Sankoh's grudges against the ruling All Peoples Congress (APC) party went beyond a simple wish to steal, with many among the country's despairing poor sharing his incoherent political sentiments. But diamonds were soon to become much more than a handy resource underwriting the RUF's campaigns: they became the principal motivation for the RUF and its outside backers. Throughout its campaigns, the RUF failed to articulate a coherent ideology or even practical political aims beyond its leaders' fulminations against the country's ever-changing and pedestrian leadership.

For some years now I have been trying to grapple with the RUF phenomenon—for it is a phenomenon. In 1997, having taken a break from journalism to pursue postgraduate studies in history, I wrote an MA thesis entitled 'War and State Collapse: The Case of Sierra Leone'. The thesis was a critique of Robert Kaplan's views of the conflict as expressed in his widely read *Atlantic Monthly* article 'The Coming Anarchy'. My thesis rejected Kaplan's sweeping and impressionistic views and instead focused on the progressive disintegration of the Sierra Leonean state, which was anyway a very fragile entity at its independence from Britain in 1961, from the imposition of the one-party system by the country's long-time plunderer, President Siaka Stevens, in 1978. It was state-centric (to use the glamorous word preferred by political scientists), and I wrote a few things in there that I now have cause, after more exhaustive research and after the whole RUF infrastructure came to full public view in 1997 and 1999, to disown. For example, I was too quick to reject David Keen's hard-nosed focus on the RUF's economic preoccupations;[10] and I gave too much credit to the view that youth disenchantment was at the root of the 'rebellion'. There was, in the final analysis, no rebellion; and I am now convinced that my political narrative gave too much credit to a form of warlordism which, however much encouraged by the inept and often criminal nature of state-civic relations in the country, should not be confused with even the colourful 'social bandit' described in Eric Hobsbawm's path-breaking study, *Bandits*.[11] Hobsbawm's banditry—'a form of

---

[10] See David Keen, 'War without Battles: The Strange Case of Sierra Leone', unpublished paper, 1996. Keen and I have been in close touch recently, and we have exchanged constructive views on the subject of the RUF and the war in Sierra Leone.

[11] Eric Hobsbawm, *Bandits*, London: Weidenfeld & Nicolson, 2000; first published 1969.

individual or minority rebellion within peasant societies'—was often much loved and admired and supported by the poor and disenfranchised people among whom it emerged. This unrepentant radical left historian wrote:

> The point about social bandits is that they are peasant outlaws whom the lord and state regard as criminals, but who remain within peasant society, and are considered by their people as heroes, as champions, avengers, fighters for justice, perhaps even leaders of liberation, and in any case as men to be admired, helped and supported. In cases where traditional society resists the encroachments and historical advance of central governments and states, native and foreign, they may be helped and supported even by the local lords. This relationship between the ordinary peasant and the rebel, outlaw and robber is what makes social banditry interesting and significant.[12]

One thinks immediately of Robin Hood of English folk memory, of the pranks of the likes of Musa Wo in Mende folk legend, and of the early anti-colonial peasant revolts in parts of Africa. The RUF phenomenon, however, falls in a different category altogether: it was more a case of organised mass delinquency. What is more, it was mainly aimed at criminal expropriation, not social protest. The spread of the violence and its durability clearly had more to do with the near-total collapse of state institutions, especially the army and the police, than with any support for the RUF among the wider populace.

On this issue, alas, a lot will have to be said, for how often have we not heard from apparently well-intentioned scholars and analysts the claim that an understanding of the phenomenon of the criminal warlord as politician in Africa requires an analysis of the African state itself as an instrument of criminality, which makes inevitable its own nemesis—the likes of Sankoh and Taylor? In other words, that a moral equivalence can be drawn between, say, a Foday Sankoh and a Joseph Momoh, Sierra Leone's ineffective President against whose rule Sankoh launched his war? The implied view that some of these corrupt leaders are little better than the armed bandits ravaging their countries for loot may have some justification, but it is largely exaggerated and even jaundiced. For the fact is that Momoh (for example), while corrupt, functioned within an infrastructure that continued to maintain, however unsatisfactorily, its social responsibilities, did not kill at random, certainly did not sanction arson, and generally allowed space for civil society to function.

[12] Ibid., p. 20.

In any case, why should a 'rebellion' against a corrupt system be so much more destructive and brutal to people it otherwise claimed to be geared towards 'liberating', and moreover be concerned primarily with pillaging the very resources it claimed were being squandered by the governing state? The question answers itself, while exposing the intellectual and moral frivolity of those who would confuse the categories. The likes of Foday Sankoh and Charles Taylor may have learned a thing or two from the sordid policies of the political leaders they took on, but they are certainly of a completely different mould from even the bloodthirsty paranoiac Samuel Doe, and it is high time for this point to be made as forcefully as possible. Indeed this point has gained great political salience recently, with calls from influential circles for a 'new imperialism' to tame what British Prime Minister Tony Blair's controversial foreign policy adviser Robert Cooper called the 'pre-modern world of failed states'. According to Cooper, this 'pre-modern' world, of 'barbarians, chaos and disorder', poses a grave threat to Western civilisation, for 'it can provide a base for non-state actors who may represent a danger to the post-modern world.' In Cooper's cavalier view,

The pre-modern world is a world of failed states which have lost legitimacy for or monopoly over the use of force; often both. Examples of total collapse are relatively rare, but the number of countries at risk grows all the time. Some areas of the former Soviet Union are candidates, including Chechnya. All of the world's major drug producing countries are part of the pre-modern world. Until recently there was no sovereign authority in Afghanistan; nor is there in up-country Burma or in parts of South America, where drug barons threaten the state's monopoly on force. All over Africa countries are at risk. In such areas chaos is the norm and war is a way of life. In so far as there is a government it operates in a way similar to organized Crime.[13]

This book rejects both the concept of a 'pre-modern state' and the calls for a 'new imperialism'. These hastily contrived concepts flow from a simplistic reading of current affairs, precipitated by the singular catastrophe of September 11, 2001, when a handful of rogue Middle Eastern militants, trained to pilot aircraft, hijacked American planes and crashed them into buildings, killing thousands. That Afghanistan, a so-called failed state, was a base for the spon-

---

[13] Robert Cooper, 'Reordering the World: the Long Term Implications of September 11', Foreign Policy Centre, www.fpc.org.uk. This quote is taken from an excerpt of the article published in the *Observer* as 'Why we still need empires' (*Observer*, 8 April 2002).

sors of these terrorists resulted from a set of historical circumstance almost peculiar to this jinxed polity: interminable warfare, Cold War intrigues, Islamic fundamentalism. The problems of much of Africa, where civil authority has been under threat from predatory armed groups, are totally different. Yet the nature of the state and its role in the perpetuation of violence bear serious analysis. By the time the RUF war began, in 1991, Sierra Leone was virtually a collapsed state, its ruling elite a corrupt, violent and effete class confined largely to the capital, with the writ of the state not running much beyond this capital. Poverty and despair rotted the society; violence and political thuggery became the norm in terms of governing and control of the civil populace. State institutions had withered away, and much of the countryside remained beyond the writ of the receded state. The educational and other social infrastructure in much of the country had collapsed, and evidence of governance or state presence in much of the country was almost non-existent. The government was bankrupt and in a state of near-paralysis.

The distinguished French political scientist J.-F. Bayart has argued persuasively that in much of Africa, where the state is hardly a social institution that provides services for its citizens, civil authority is often exercised through 'the strength of the networks', principally 'police raids and the truncheon of the commissariat'.[14] In Sierra Leone by 1991, however, even these raw 'networks' had been effectively downgraded: the police and army had become as corrupt and weak and bankrupt as the ruling elite. They were no longer functioning in any meaningful sense. So the truly disturbing question raised by the RUF war—how a self-interested and even criminal group could both recruit support and inflict such violence and terror on the civil population while the state and its agents appeared so ineffective in meeting the challenge—becomes fairly easy to answer by an analysis of a state which had been emasculated and corrupted, and which had alienated the majority of its citizenry through decades of misrule and political thuggery. We will analyse the nature of this state in Chapter 2.

This book aims to be a factual, unsentimental account detailing what happened during the period from 1991, when the first shots were fired, to the end of 2001, when a UN-supervised disarmament team announced that all the factional fighters had been disarmed and the war effectively ended. It will focus mainly on the character

---

[14] J.-F. Bayart, *The State in Africa: The Politics of the Belly*, London: Longman, 1993, p. 264.

of the RUF and its use of violence, although the excesses of other players, especially the often brutal and uncontrollable Sierra Leone army, as well as the more admirable but sometimes recklessly violent Civil Defence Force, will be discussed. I focus on the RUF because ultimate responsibility for the starting of the war, and therefore the atrocities that largely characterised it, rests with this group. To put it this way is not to argue that the violent excesses of (especially) the decrepit and totally unprofessional and corrupt Sierra Leone army—which often matched, and sometimes surpassed, those of the RUF—are not worthy of careful study and accounting; it is merely to acknowledge context. In this regard, I find Martin van Creveld's observation on the copy-cat trajectory of wars like the eleven years of violence in Sierra Leone particularly pertinent: 'War being the most imitative of all human activities,' he wrote, 'the very process of combating low-intensity conflicts will cause both sides to look alike unless it can be brought to a quick end.'[15]

Underlining my approach is a concern of great practical importance: to understand so-called rebel groups, increasingly the greatest challenge to African stability for over a decade now, for what they really are, rather than what they deem fit to represent themselves to be. West African rebel leaders, particularly the Liberian warlord Charles Taylor, and professional image-makers for the RUF showed throughout the 1990s a tremendous adeptness at projecting an image to international observers, the UN and Western political leaders that was completely at variance with their actual preoccupations and character. This helped to complicate attempts to mediate an end to the inter-connected crises in the region, and thereby prolong them. For example, the RUF's claim in the early 1990s that it was fighting to defeat corrupt dictatorships—first the scrofulous APC one-party state, later the NPRC junta—was believable to anyone who was concerned about the wretchedness of these regimes but otherwise took no account of the activities of the RUF and its leadership structure.

This situation posed a serious problem, especially during the 1996 peace talks in Côte d'Ivoire, which I attended. The talks were sponsored by the UN, ECOWAS and the OAU, and they brought together for the first time the leaders of the RUF and the NPRC junta (and later the elected government of President Tejan Kabbah). Almost everyone attending the talks knew about the corruption

---

[15] Martin van Creveld, *The Transformation of War*, New York: The Free Press, 1991, p. 225.

and unpopularity of the NPRC regime, but hardly anyone knew anything at all about the leadership of the RUF. Sankoh was, before his emergence for the talks, a mysterious figure, hidden in the rain-forests of eastern Sierra Leone; and the main instrument available for outsiders to judge his RUF—apart from his group's already notorious reputation for atrocities against civilians—was *Footpaths to Democracy*, hastily put together in London by Addai Sebo (a Ghanaian and formerly publicist for Charles Taylor) a few months earlier in 1995. Apart from its eloquent denunciations of the corrupt regime in Freetown, the document made strenuous appeals to Western liberal environmental and social activists, and was represented as a kind of manifesto for the RUF. It was all rhetoric, of course, bearing little relationship to the true character and preoccupation of the pillaging and brutal and largely illiterate RUF, but it was all that was available to many people in order to judge the RUF beyond the horrors of their warfare.

The result was that the RUF was treated as a serious political organisation with a social programme, however incoherent, and its crucial links with Taylor were ignored. Its preoccupation with criminal appropriation was similarly ignored. Sankoh's essential character—as a highly manipulative psychopath and a proxy for Taylor—was also ignored. As a result, the Abidjan Accord's programme of political transition, which would have seen the RUF transformed into a political party and its leadership amnestied, was doomed to failure: the RUF, an almost entirely military outfit reminiscent of the *écorcheurs* of early modern Europe, simply could not be transformed into a serious political organisation. It did not have the cadres and ideological orientation and political base. Not surprisingly, as we will see, it was planning to restart its military campaigns shortly after signing the Abidjan Accord that formally ended the war—not for the last time—in November 1996. Lillian Wong, of the UK Foreign and Commonwealth Office (FCO), who as part of the FCO's Africa Research Group followed these events, has written trenchantly in retrospect about the problem—the lack of any attempt to understand the psychology and real motives of the RUF and to factor these in dealing with them:

The psychology of rebel leaders, or warlords, is…important. Both Sankoh and Taylor had personal grievances, there was nothing ideological about either of them. They were criminals in alliance with each other. Documents found at Sankoh's house in Freetown in May 2000 demonstrate clearly their close relationship and the diamonds for arms deals. Sankoh has proved to be a cheat and a liar. He used the rank and file for his own purpose but concealed his money-making activities from them. Taylor too has an obsession with his personal wealth and personal security. Neither is interested in governing in any conventional sense. Taylor is infinitely better educated than Sankoh, and easily sold the idea to Sankoh of exporting rebellion from Liberia...to Sierra Leone... The clear lesson from this is that it is worth taking time to understand the true nature of the warlord to be able to assess his sincerity. This assessment will give vital clues to his likely behaviour in any peace negotiations. The RUF, composed of semiliterates at best and illiterates, could not articulate their grievances and demands at the Peace Talks in 1996 and 1999. Some concerned but well educated Sierra Leoneans attended the talks and interpreted what they believed the RUF stood for, but they were wrong. They put a romantic gloss on a very brutal group of people and both agreements failed to stop the conflict.[16]

The last sentence has a particular relevance for me and this book: I know some of these Sierra Leoneans personally, and in this book have engaged some of their sincerely mistaken views. But it was not just Sierra Leoneans who 'put a romantic gloss' on the brutal and mercenary RUF, as we will see. Some Western academics and so-called conciliators and some aid agency workers played their own nefarious roles in presenting the murderous RUF as something of a misunderstood and misrepresented rural rebellion against the failed 'patrimonial' state of Sierra Leone. Such views made even the sweeping and largely offensive views of Kaplan look more to the point, and my own analysis of the RUF's brutality and lack of serious political concern would often tend to jell with Kaplan's. But I disagree with him in fundamental ways, as will emerge. I also avoid, as much as possible, the confusions and generalities inherent in Paul Collier's 'greed versus grievance' thesis—which has now spawned a small but apparently growing academic industry on the back of the paltry argument that modern civil wars are caused by greed rather than grievance—in my analysis of the RUF and the Sierra Leone war, while broadly agreeing with Collier about the predatory nature of the RUF.

Since our (PAC) work on the role of diamonds in the Taylor-controlled wars in the Mano River region has been widely, if unjustly, cited as an amplification of the 'greed over grievance' thesis, it is important to state here at outset that diamonds did not cause

[16] Lillian Wong, 'Conflict in the Mano River Union—Causes, Solutions and Lessons: the Case of Sierra Leone', paper presented at the Conflict and Development Policy in the Mano River Region and Côte d'Ivoire, 'The Regional Stakes for Stability and Reconstruction', Paris, 13–14 May 2003.

the war in Sierra Leone. What diamonds did was to underwrite the RUF's war effort, and they were clearly a big motivation for the RUF's leaders as well as for their outside supporters, particularly Charles Taylor. It would be simplistic to say that the war was only about greed. Greed, in purely economic terms, became central to the rebels' thinking, but so was power, however crude their notions of it. Raw, unmediated power: that was a strong motivation too. And there were grievances, many of them. This book recognises those grievances, while emphasising that they played the role of correlate factors in an essentially mercenary enterprise.

Particular attention is paid, in this book, to the types of atrocities preferred by the RUF. Why did the group resort to mass amputations of civilians? Why amputations and not simply summary executions? Victims of rebel amputations report that the rebels would refuse to kill them even when they (the victims) begged them to do so, with the rebels asserting that they were only interested in 'chopping off' their hands. Why was this the case? There is no record or memory of such violations in any of the many cultures of Sierra Leone before the war. Where did ideas for such horrific atrocities come from? Renamo in Mozambique, also a brutal and mercenary force, carried out large-scale mutilations. Before that, the only record of mass amputations in Africa concerns the Belgian King Leopold's rubber bandits in the Congo in the late nineteenth century. Adam Hochschild's book *King Leopold's Ghost: A Story of Greed, Terror, and Heroism in Africa*[17] brilliantly examines this extreme depravity. Foday Sankoh had a stint as a UN peacekeeper in the Congo in the early 1960s. Did he learn the efficacy of such methods—as a highly potent terror tactic—while he was in the Congo? Memories of the brutality of Leopold's agents in the Congo were a powerful force in Congolese nationalism, as represented by Patrice Lumumba (a leader Sankoh greatly admired) in the 1960s. The question, while fascinating, will probably remain unanswered— Sankoh was in absolute denial about amputations in every interview he gave, and he died peacefully in 2003. But it deserves examination all the same.

What is clear is that although the RUF started the amputations at an early stage of the war, its mass amputations started only when the civil defence group, the Kamajors, started posing a serious challenge to the RUF by the mid-1990s. Various RUF commanders, who

[17] Adam Hochschild, *King Leopold's Ghost: A Story of Greed, Terror, and Heroism in Africa*, New York: Houghton Mifflin, 1999.

were uniformly in complete denial about the perpetration of this depraved type of violence, have however told me of their frustration at countering attacks from the Kamajors—who were a grass-roots militia force, operating in their own terrain and therefore largely 'invisible'—and how this led to more violent and indiscriminate attacks by the RUF against villagers they would no longer take for granted.[18] The tactic was adopted by renegade elements of the Sierra Leone Army, who joined forces with the RUF after the 1997 coup to form the so-called People's Army, and who in their anger and frenzy after their expulsion from Freetown by the Nigerian-led intervention force in 1998 undoubtedly carried out most of the atrocities, including mass amputations, after 1998.

Interviews I conducted among victims in Freetown and Kono district revealed that most of the amputations were carried out by former army personnel, and one of them gained particular notoriety for mass murder and amputations in the Kono district, and may have been responsible for the killing of hundreds of people in late 1998 in the district. A mass grave, actually a pond said to be the site of his murders and dumping ground for the victims, was sealed off by UN investigators at Tomboudou, about 15 kilometres from Koidu, the headquarters town in Kono district, in September 2002. Investigators believe that the site, where human skulls and bones were found, may contain the remains of 400 to 1,000 people murdered by the People's Army.[19] There was, in other words, a mark of desperation about the strategy: lacking any appeal among the citizenry, and without ideological motivations and political base of support, rejected by society, facing defeat, the rebels became wanton, the wantonness easily becoming neurosis and nihilism.

Among other things, the present work attempts to answer the questions I posed by focusing on the most distinctive and important feature of the RUF: its essentially mercenary character. The RUF's war, I argue, was driven not by local command and ideas and sensitivities—although there was a carefully-choreographed attempt to create this impression—but by outsiders, principally Charles Taylor of Liberia. This fact does not obviate the need to examine the conditions of pre-war Sierra Leone, the horrible neo-colonial failure

---

[18] Interview with the RUF's chief of security, Augustine Gbao, and with various other former RUF combatants, Freetown, September 2002.

[19] Richard Dowden, 'Justice goes on trial in Sierra Leone', *Guardian*, 3 October 2002.

which Basil Davidson[20] would describe as 'nation-statist'—the kind of entity where 'despair rots civil society, the state becomes an enemy', where a harsh and corrupt dictatorship ruled 'over people who distrust(ed) them' (this is how Davidson despairingly described much of sub-Saharan Africa in 1992, a year after Sierra Leone's war began), and where 'one dismal tyranny gives way to a worse one.' This state created the conditions for the development into a full-scale and highly destructive civil war and the emergence of a criminal warlord system with an invasion from Liberia by a petty army, largely foreign, which could easily have been crushed by any reasonably functioning state.

Chapter 2 examines this state, its history of decline and disintegration, and the violence and corruption that were its marked characteristics. Chapter 3 focuses on the 'making' of the RUF, the context in which it emerged and its development into a warlord-type insurgency. Chapter 4 discusses the explosion of the insurgency into a full-scale civil war, focusing on the role of the NPRC junta and its '*sobel*' army and later of mercenaries, and on the destructive guerrilla tactics of the RUF. Chapter 5 discusses the coup of 1997, an event that marked the almost complete collapse of formal state institutions, to be replaced by what I describe as 'street power' and criminal warlordism. Chapter 6 discusses the RUF's war methods, focusing on the amputations and other terror tactics. Chapter 7 discusses the UN and British military interventions and the disarming of the various militia fighters, and Chapter 8 examines the role of diamonds in the perpetuation of the conflict. An Epilogue reflects on the aftermath of the war: the transition from war to peace, the setting up of the two instruments of 'transitional justice'—the Special Court and the Truth and Reconciliation Commission (TRC)—and their impact, and the lingering threats to the fragile peace from within and without the country.

[20] Basil Davidson, *Black Man's Burden: Africa and the Curse of the Nation-State*, New York: Random House, 1992.

2

SIERRA LEONE

FROM INDEPENDENCE TO STATE RECESSION

'....in 1960 during the planning for independence, Sir Milton insisted that the hymn "Lead Kindly Light" be sung. After a brief silence the Archbishop of Sierra Leone spoke. "Mr P. M., do you think that's appropriate? Remember that the next line goes 'Amidst the encircling gloom'." Sir Milton looked around the table. "I think that there is a lot of encircling gloom." The hymn was sung.' (John Cartwright on Sierra Leone's first Prime Minister[1])

'Ah, so you want to know, just like the gold merchant almost one hundred and fifty years ago—except that in this case he was a robber of gold, not a maker. Age transforms everything, Garbage, so we do those things that the passage of time demands. One age is about to end in Malagueta, a new reign without honour but with the embellishment of falsehood, such as to make the dead tremble in their graves, is to about to begin, so we must say goodbye to the old ways by giving this ring to the old power.' (Syl Cheney Coker on Siaka Stevens' regime[2])

Sierra Leone is a small West African state about the size of the Canadian province of New Brunswick. In its modern form it began as a settlement for freed slaves who had served on the side of the British in the American War of Independence and later found themselves in England and Nova Scotia, Canada, as the so-called Black Loyalists. It was the period of anti-slavery agitation in Britain and, appalled by the destitute condition of the Black Poor, as the freed

---

[1] John Cartwright, *Political Leadership in Sierra Leone*, London, 1978, p. 99.
[2] Syl Cheney-Coker, *The Last Harmattan of Alusine Dunbar,* London: Heinemann, 1990, p. 304. The novel is a brilliant satire on Siaka Stevens' rapacious regime. Cheney-Coker is Sierra Leone's best known poet; this is his first and only novel to date.

slaves living on the mean streets of London were called at the time, a few British abolitionists, notably Granville Sharp and William Wilberforce, convinced the British government to help repatriate them to some place in Africa. Sierra Leone was chosen, and a settlement, 'intended...for the happy establishment of blacks and people of colour, to be shipped as freedmen...under the protection of the British government',[3] was started on land fraudulently acquired from a Temne chief and called Freetown, on the coast of the country.

True to its name, and to the idealistic intentions of the abolitionists, the aim of the settlement was high-minded: it was to be a self-governing state with 'a constitution, bound by social contract, rooted in history, in the institutions of Anglo-Saxon monarchy, and of Israel under the Judges'.[4] That was in 1787, in the heady period of abolitionism and liberalism in Britain, and the extravagant wording, penned by Granville Sharpe, was not meant lightly. However, reality was soon to make a mockery of them. The new settlement was soon beset by difficulties, including an outbreak of tropical diseases, food shortage and attacks by the defrauded Temne landholders. Some of the settlers, both black and white, facing imminent extinction, ran away and tried to make a living by working for slave traders on the coast. Reports of the slave trading activities by the settlers scandalised the abolitionists in London, and gave ammunition to pro-slavery activists who were already arguing that blacks were incapable of prospering in freedom.

The British government resolved the issue by declaring the settlement a Crown Colony—the first in West Africa—in 1808, and over the following years made it viable by an infusion of freed blacks from Jamaica and North America. Following the passage in England in 1807 of the Abolition Act, nearly 74,000 persons rescued by the British anti-slavery squadron—the Liberated Africans—were resettled in the colony. Largely through the efforts of the colonial government and the Church Missionary Society (CMS), the Liberated Africans were socialised into the foundational values of the colony, which were rooted in Anglican Christianity. The British regarded the Sierra Leone colony as an experiment in 'conversionism' which, in the words of the historian Leo Spitzer, was reflected in

....the belief that the social redemption and elevation of submerged groups would not occur through the removal of legal disabilities alone: that the

[3] W. S. Marcus-Jones, *Legal Development and Constitutional Change in Sierra Leone, 1787–1971*, London, 1981, p. 15.
[4] Ibid.

state or established religious, philanthropic or educational institutions, would be required to bring about the integration and social adjustment of the emancipated.[5]

As early as the 1840s there were higher proportions of children attending primary school in Freetown than in Britain,[6] and the emergent Creole community—for this was how the blend of early settlers and Liberated Africans came to be known—was highly educated and elitist, consisting at first of traders, then of lawyers, doctors, teachers, journalists and clergymen who even went to other parts of Africa on a 'civilising mission'.

However, this was true only of the small coastal colony. The rest of what came to constitute Sierra Leone was declared a 'Protectorate' of Britain in 1896, and it constituted at the time a diverse group of people already living under their own established traditions and speaking at least thirteen different languages. The largest groups were the Mendes in the south and east of the country and the Temnes in the north, each accounting for about 30 per cent of the population. The British did not encourage the development of a single unitary state and a sense of nation, describing the Protectorate as 'foreign countries adjoining the colony'; they justified its annexation as 'in the interest of the people'.[7]

The first attempt to bring all of Sierra Leone together in a political unit was the 1924 Constitution, which provided for a unicameral legislature with the Colony and Protectorate represented in the same chamber. The Colony was allocated five seats in the chamber, three representatives to be elected and two nominated from professional and other groups. The three representatives from the Protectorate, which was several dozen times bigger and more populated than the Colony, were to be chiefs. This disparity heightened tension between the two groups, but the Creoles determined to perpetuate it. The Western-educated Protectorate elites—there was now an emergent group of them—had a dual concern: they wanted to rectify the Legislative Council imbalance but they were also dissatisfied with the provision that chiefs, almost all uneducated and highly conservative, were chosen as representatives instead of them. From this struggle there eventually emerged two political parties reflecting the competing Colony/Protectorate interests: the National Council of Sierra Leone (NCSL), led by a blimpish and ageing

[5] Leo Spitzer, *Lives in Between*, Cambridge University Press, 1989, p. 24.
[6] Ibid.
[7] Christopher Fyfe, *History of Sierra Leone*, London, 1961, p. 541.

Creole conservative Bankole Bright (for the Colony), against the Sierra Leone Peoples Party (SLPP), led by Milton Margai, a dour British-trained medical doctor (for the Protectorate).

The SLPP, founded in 1951, emerged as a united front for most Protectorate educated people, from diverse ethnic and regional backgrounds, and through its agitation forced the colonial authorities to introduce the 1951 Constitution, which granted the Protectorate majority control. Milton Margai emerged as Chief (later Prime) Minister. Elections in 1957 confirmed the dominance of the SLPP in the Legislative Council, and Margai became Prime Minister of the country.

Margai's government was intensely conservative and pro-British, and the new Prime Minister had no time for the harsh anti-colonial rhetoric of African nationalist radicals like Ghana's Kwame Nkrumah and Guinea's Sekou Touré. Instead he favoured a gradualist approach, declaring that his country was too poor and underdeveloped to stand without the goodwill of powerful friends. Not for him Touré's nihilistic declaration in challenging the French: 'We prefer freedom in poverty to riches in slavery.'[8] It was under Margai—a leader who stoutly refused to articulate an ambitious vision for the country, even initially thinking that a Constitution for his party was unnecessary—that Sierra Leone became independent in 1961. For him there was nothing extraordinary about self-rule because 'life must go on all the same, with the same justice in our courts, the same taxes and other responsibilities...the significant change is that we are now in control of our destiny and for the formulation of our external as well as internal policies.'[9] It was his way of playing down any unwarranted expectations that might have been unleashed in the general euphoria which greeted self-rule, and it was hardly enough for the very essential task of mobilising his long-suppressed people for the task of nation-building.

Many since the awful 1990s have tended to portray the era immediately before and after Sierra Leone's independence as one of near-idyllic peace and prosperity, but this was hardly the case. A few years before independence, in November 1955 and March 1956, protests against the alleged oppressiveness of dishonest chiefs in the Northern Province led to widespread riots and many deaths.

---

[8] Lapido Adamolekun, *Sekou Toure's Guinea: an Experiment in Nation Building*, London: Methuen, 1976, p. 1.

[9] Joe A. D. Alie, *A New History of Sierra Leone*, New York: St. Martins Press, 1990, p. 280.

The riots began in Port Loko with more than 7,000 youths attacking property belonging to chiefs, and soon spread to other chiefdoms. The army was sent to the areas and by the time the riots were quelled, twenty-three people had been killed, three policemen were kidnapped and later murdered, and property damage estimated at nearly £1 million was done.[10] Similar riots, this time directed against allegedly corrupt local politicians including two future Prime Ministers (Albert Margai and Siaka Stevens) and then against almost anyone seen to be part of the governing Western-educated elite, had taken place in Freetown ten months earlier. A mob of over 1,000 young men and women, described by the pro-SLPP newspaper *Vanguard* as 'hooligans...unemployed...and the dregs of the working class,'[11] surged through eastern and central Freetown attacking and looting shops and the homes of prominent politicians. The army quelled the riots, killing eighteen people in the process and injuring 111.

Perhaps more ominous still, among the Westernised elite itself there were signs of serious problems. Siaka Stevens, a former minister in Margai's government, felt left out of the political power game as independence approached, and consequently launched a new political party, the All Peoples Congress (APC), which soon gained notoriety for its inflammatory rhetoric and subversive tendencies. After receiving credible threats that the APC was planning to carry out bomb attacks in Freetown on the eve of independence, the government had Stevens and a number of other APC activists detained until the celebrations were over.

In addition to this, there was the old schism between the Creole elites and Protectorate politicians. In spite of Margai's attempts to bridge this gap by disproportionately representing the Creoles in his government—at the time of independence Margai had five Creoles in his government, though Creoles were only 2 per cent of the population, so that they had a proportion of ministers higher than that of any other group[12]—this problem remained, at least for a while. Shortly after independence in 1961, a group of reactionary Creole notables, capitalising on the Protectorate Act of 1896 which defined the Protectorate as 'foreign countries adjacent to the

[10] John Cartwright, *Politics in Sierra Leone*, University of Toronto Press, 1970, p. 69.

[11] *Vanguard*, 18 February 1955.

[12] Martin Kilson, *Political Change in a West African State: a Study of the Modernization Process in Sierra Leone*, Harvard University Press, 1966, p. 232.

Colony', sued in an English court to have the Constitutional Order in Council, under which the country gained independence, declared invalid on the ground that the Colony and Protectorate were 'separate countries' which should not exist as one. The case was summarily thrown out of court by the Judge Lord Wilberforce, a descendant of the philanthropist who had assisted in having the Sierra Leone settlement established, as 'legally hopeless since it concerned the sovereignty of an independent nation'.

The Creole factor was very significant and controversial because of the lopsided nature of their 'development' compared to the rest of the country: Constituting less than 2 per cent of the population, they had a literacy rate of 80 per cent compared with 6 per cent for the rest of the country.[13] A development with a more profound and lasting impact on the country was happening away from the elite corridors of power, however; and it would totally change the nature of the Sierra Leonean state, and the nature of the country's politics. It had to do with the country's most important and valuable economic resource, diamonds, and the way they were to be mined and marketed.

Commercial exploitation of diamonds first started in Sierra Leone in 1931, after a prospecting party from the Gold Coast-based Consolidated African Selection Trust (CAST) arrived in the country and started work in the Kono district. CAST sent in the team in 1930 after a small geological survey group, led by N.R. Junner and J. D. Pollet, picked up a small crystal by the Gboraba stream, in Kono district, which turned out to be a diamond. CAST, which was British owned, was originally an independent company formed to work two diamond concessions in the Gold Coast (now Ghana) in the 1920s, but by the time of the Sierra Leone diamond discovery, the majority shares were held by Selection Trust Limited, also British and one of the largest companies of the day. De Beers, the world's diamond giant, had a strong interest in Selection Trust. In 1935 the Sierra Leone colonial authorities concluded an agreement with Sierra Leone Selection Trust Ltd, a subsidiary of Selection Trust, giving the company exclusive mining and prospecting rights over the entire land for ninety-nine years. The diamond mining fields were soon to cover an estimated area of some 7,700 square miles, a large chunk of Sierra Leone's overall 27,000 square miles of territory.

[13] Roy Lewis, 'Sierra Leone: Independence without Pains', *Africa Report*, April 1961.

Sierra Leone was an impoverished, barely self-sustaining colony by the time diamonds were discovered. The economy contained two productive sectors. The first and most important was agriculture, which was largely a subsistence activity, employing some 700,000 of Sierra Leone's then 2 million population. It accounted, however, for barely 30 per cent of GNP. The cash crops produced were palm kernels, palm oil, ginger and groundnuts. Extractive minerals, including iron ore and diamonds, were discovered only in the 1930s, and diamonds soon came to dominate the economy, alone accounting for three-fifths of the country's export earnings by the time of independence. So Sierra Leone's economy, like almost all colonial economies, was a wholly extractive one, producing raw materials for the metropolitan economy in Europe. As Walter Rodney observed,[14] such an economy was virtually condemned to 'underdevelopment', and worse, the creation of a parasitic local comprador class that would be even more mercenary and exploitative than the colonial state it replaced. Siaka Stevens, who took over the Sierra Leone state in 1967 as Prime Minister, became the embodiment of this class, and his activities verged on the criminal, leading to the gradual disintegration of the state and the emergence of what William Reno has called the 'shadow state'.[15]

Siaka Probyn Stevens started his career as a police constable before becoming a worker at the iron ore mines at Marampa in the 1930s. There he joined the workers' union, very soon becoming its spokesman. When the West African Youth League was launched by the Creole radical and Marxist trade unionist I.T.A. Wallace Johnson in 1938, Stevens, who possessed little formal education but much native intelligence, showed little enthusiasm for its anti-colonial rhetoric. Wallace-Johnson and his Youth League were repressed by the British during the Second World War—in 1940 he was detained, along with almost all of the Youth League executives, for the duration of the war—and political activity subsequently collapsed in the country. On the other hand Stevens, less militant, was consciously fêted by the British authorities, who later sent him to Ruskin College, Oxford, to help prepare him to become a more 're-sponsible trade unionist'.[16] Stevens became involved later in the

[14] Walter Rodney, *How Europe Underdeveloped Africa*, London: Bogle L'Ouverture, 1973.
[15] William Reno, *Corruption and State Politics in Sierra Leone*, Cambridge University Press, 1996.
[16] Stevens writes about his experience at Oxford in glowing terms in Siaka Stevens, *What Life has Taught Me*, London: Kensal Press, 1984.

more conservative SOS and later the SLPP, both of them launched by Milton Margai.

In 1951, after the SLPP emerged as the dominant party in the Legislative Council, Margai, then Chief Minister, made Stevens Minister of Mines, a very important portfolio for which Stevens was preferred because of his trade union experience. It was an era of agitation in the mining sector, and it was hoped that Stevens was the best person to handle the situation. All diamond mining areas of the country were legally under the control of Sierra Leone Selection Trust (SLST), but by the early 1950s there was a huge influx of illicit miners who nearly succeeded in overrunning the company's holdings. By the mid-1950s an estimated 75,000 illicit miners were in the Kono district, from all parts of the country and outside it, and they had the areas 'verging on anarchy, with armed bands of as many as 400 to 500 men raiding SLST...areas, and on occasion doing battle with the police'.[17] This was the era of the 'Great Diamond Rush' and Cartwright has indicated the extent of its socio-political and economic impact on the country as a whole with these figures: at the time of the Rush, the total number of persons calculated by the Labour Department to be in wage employment was between 75,000 and 80,000, which means that within a period of three years 'as many men (75,000) left (their homes)...to search for diamonds as had left it over half a century to seek wage employment.'[18] Rice production slumped, as many young men abandoned the rice fields for the more interesting and promising diamond fields. Sierra Leone soon began to import rather than export rice.

A Sierra Leonean writer, J. Sorie Conteh, has captured the social meltdown caused by the rush in his novel The Diamonds, which appeared in 2001. In the novel a successful peasant farmer, Gibao Semabu, leaves his village and rice farms for the more interesting and promising diamond mining town of Sewa. It is a totally different, graft-addled world, and Semabu quickly succumbs to the greed and corruption of diamond mining, and even takes things further: he commits ritual murder after being told by a local sorcerer that this will help him make big diamond finds. He is arrested and then hanged. The novel is a parable of the destruction of the bucolic and beautiful ordered society of rural Sierra Leone by the unregulated diamond mining and capitalism, and if Conteh's authorial voice concluding the novel may seem too earnest and fad-driven, it

---

[17] Cartwright (note 10), p. 69.
[18] Ibid.

nevertheless is accurate: '...what was to become a diamond boom became a curse on the nation. Herein lies the irony. The economic benefits of diamonds, which were meant to free people from the clutches of poverty, instead enslaved them in the clutches of greed.'[19]

However, the critical problem for the government at the time was the ravages of illicit miners in SLST's fields. A populist nationalist movement would simply have sided with the illicit miners against a foreign capitalist corporation. But it was not as simple as that for a party which was effectively ruling the country in partnership with the colonial power. And SLST was the major source of income for the government. The company was paying income tax at the rate of 27 per cent (later increased to 47 per cent) on its profits, in addition to a small 'Special Development' fund, mainly for the Kono region. Something, however, had to be done. A compromise was hammered out in 1956, mainly through the work of Stevens: it was the Alluvial Diamond Scheme, a semi-populist measure that won Stevens thousands of supporters in the diamond mines. The scheme scrapped SLST's monopoly and confined its operations to Yengema (in Kono district) and Tongo Field, an area of about 450 square miles, in return for £1 million in compensation. The Scheme also introduced mining and buying licenses for indigenous miners and dealers. All mining areas were declared government property, and inspectors of mines were appointed to grant the licenses for a small fee.

Shortly before independence, however, Stevens lost his parliamentary seat, and was dropped from the government. As a result he broke away from the SLPP, denounced the independence agreement, and alleged that the Margai government was still British-controlled. Stevens launched the All Peoples Congress and called for elections before independence. The party quickly showed a tendency towards violence. In February 1961 two of the party's stalwarts were arrested for allegedly inciting supporters to 'stop traffic, sink launches, stop trains and assault ministers'. Stevens himself was arrested in Britain in March, a few weeks before independence, on a Fugitive Offender's Warrant which accused him of 'criminal libel, sedition and conspiracy'. The Crown Counsel described his APC as 'a terrorist organisation believed to be financed by an outside power for the purpose of furthering subversive activities in this country'.[20] Stevens was then flown to Sierra Leone where he

---

[19] J. Sorie Conteh, *The Diamonds*, New York: Lekon Dimensions Publishing, 2001, p. 248.
[20] *Daily Mail* (Freetown), 9 March 1961.

remained in prison until after the independence celebrations. Independence was granted to the country on 27 April 1961, without great fanfare. The patrician Margai sent a bottle of brandy to Stevens to enjoy the celebrations behind the tranquil walls of Pademba Road prison.

The Prime Minister, for whom there was universal respect and adulation, could easily afford to ignore Stevens politically, but then he died in 1964 and in a controversial move was replaced by his younger brother Albert Margai. Stevens became more assertive, and appealing to Northern and Freetown sentiments, depicted the Albert Margai takeover as an attempt to perpetuate 'Mende hegemony' (the Margais were Mende). The message proved to be a potent one, as in succeeding his brother Albert Margai seemed to have robbed John Karefa-Smart (a Temne), who many believed was closer to the late Prime Minister, of the premiership. However, there were strong reasons for Albert's succession. In the first place he was the most senior and prominent member of the SLPP at the time and immensely popular among its rank and file. Stevens' resort to ethnic politics frightened Margai, a British-trained lawyer with an acute sense of order, into attempting, in a nation-wide campaign, to introduce a one-party state. Stevens—along with the highly educated Creole elite, whose animus against Margai had to do more or less with the new Prime Minister's policy of promoting Protectorate-born citizens for positions once considered the preserve of the Creoles—actively campaigned against the idea. Margai had to abandon the campaign in 1966, and promised not to raise the issue again. But the damage was done.

In the general elections that followed in March 1967 Margai appeared to have lost to Stevens' APC, but the army, led by a Margai-protégé Brigadier David Lansana, stepped in at the crucial moment and prevented the swearing-in of Stevens as the new Prime Minister.[21] Hinga Norman, who later emerged as an important figure during the RUF's war, was then a captain in the army, and he was the officer ordered by Lansana to arrest Stevens and the Governor-General.

---

[21] See Thomas Cox, *Civil-Military Relations in Sierra Leone: a Case Study of African Soldiers in Politics*, Harvard University Press, 1976, pp. 93–203, for a discussion of this turbulent period in Sierra Leone. The Dove-Edwin Commission of Inquiry set up later in 1967 concluded that Stevens' APC had clearly won the elections, but that did not settle the controversy surrounding them.

In his post-takeover broadcast, Lansana claimed that the Governor-General, a Creole, had acted unconstitutionally in announcing Stevens as the winner since the elections of chiefs, who constituted an integral block in Parliament, was still in progress. This argument was certainly sound on legal grounds, but it was even more pertinent for political reasons. The chiefs constituted a voting block, and there was no provision in Parliament that would prevent any one of them from even vying for the premiership. The argument that it was unnecessary to wait for the conclusion of the election of the chiefs because the chiefs traditionally voted for the winning party in Parliament, which has found its most recent enunciation in a pitiful book by a former APC Foreign Minister,[22] is bogus for two reasons. First, the 1967 elections were only the second nation-wide elections with any claim to seriousness, and voting patterns in only one or even two elections cannot constitute tradition. Second, there were good reasons for chiefs to prefer the SLPP because it was distinctly the more conservative and chief-friendly party.

Still, Lansana's ill-fated action created a destabilising trend of which he was, in fact, to be among the first victims. A day after he announced his coup a trio of majors in turn unseated him and then set up what they were pleased to call the National Reformation Council (NRC). The NRC was headed by Major Andrew Juxon-Smith, an eccentric and power-hungry soldier who was abroad at the time of the coup, but flew in immediately afterwards. Juxon-Smith appeared at his first press conference wearing a clownish Russian fox fur hat, and was in the habit of turning up at civil servants' offices very early in the morning and sacking anyone who was not at his or her desk when he called.[23] The NRC was in turn overthrown a year later by junior rank and file soldiers who set up the Anti-Corruption Revolutionary Council and then promptly handed over power to Stevens in April 1968. Stevens was later to have Lansana arrested (along with several others), charged with treason and executed, one of the first official state killings in Sierra Leone since the colonial authorities hanged over eighty anti-colonial rebels in 1898.

Stevens' first action in power, on the advice of the army, was to form a National Coalition government which included four SLPP

---

[22] Abdul Karim Koroma, *Sierra Leone: the Agony of a Nation*, Freetown: Afromedia Publications, 1996.

[23] Aminatta Forna, *The Devil that Danced on the Water: a Daughter's Memoir of her Father, her Family, her Country and a Continent*, London: HarperCollins, 2002, p. 96.

members and two Independents. The aim of this arrangement, he explained later in his ghost-written memoir *What Life has Taught Me*, was 'to project to the masses...that the new Government was a Government for chiefs and non-chiefs, a Government for rich and poor, and a Government for all tribes'.[24] Once he felt himself secure in power, however, Stevens quickly dismantled the coalition government and appointed an entirely APC government. Then he successfully reduced the SLPP membership in Parliament by mostly fraudulent election petitions, an action in which the judiciary, which was dominated by the Creoles, fully colluded.[25] The by-elections that followed were marked by a wave of violence spearheaded by APC 'youths'. Stevens declared a State of Emergency and had several SLPP leaders arrested. APC candidates were then declared unopposed in most of the constituencies affected by the violence.

In 1971 Stevens got a republican constitution enacted and declared himself executive President; two years later he conducted general elections, which were marked by violence and vote rigging, and which allowed him to reduce the opposition presence in Parliament still further. Stevens finally crushed formal political opposition after heavily rigged and violent elections in 1977: in 1978 he had a bill to establish a one-party state passed in Parliament without much debate, and a heavily rigged referendum that same year registered 97 per cent voter support for the one-party state. Stevens announced that all opposition was henceforth illegal, and many in the SLPP either retired from politics or joined his APC. Cyril Foray, who was Stevens' first Foreign Minister, later described the entire process of introducing a one-party state as 'legal violence'.[26]

In spite of the stark uniformity of the country's political colour, Stevens' one-party state remained what political scientists would call 'factional'. James Wunsch has described the main features of this kind of political system as 'extreme executive centralization and the erosion of formal institutions...(which) facilitate the rise of paternalistic bargaining political patterns.'[27] Acutely aware of the

---

[24] Stevens (note 16), p. 286.

[25] Alpha Lavalie, 'The SLPP in Opposition', *Sierra Leone Studies*, 1985.

[26] Cyril Foray, *The Road to the One-Party State: The Sierra Leone Experience*, Edinburgh: African Studies Centre, 1988.

[27] James Wunsch, 'Centralization and Development in Post-Independence Africa' in James Wunsch and Dele Olowu (eds), *The Failure of the Centralized State: Institutions and Self-Governance in Africa*, Boulder, CO: Westview Press, 1990, p. 245.

illegal nature of his rule, Stevens created extra-legal institutions and channels which came to supersede the formal state institutions and fatally undermined them. Distrusting the army, which he had reason to fear, Stevens starved it of much-needed resources and created a shadow army, the Internal Security Unit, ISU (later renamed the Special Security Division, SSD), with Cuban assistance in 1973. This force was recruited mainly from the slums of Freetown, and soon gained notoriety for thuggery and vandalism against political opponents. It was better armed than the army, and better cared for. He appointed a servile and mediocre officer from his Limba ethnic group, Joseph Momoh, head of the army and made him an unelected member of Parliament. Almost all other institutions of the state, including the police, the judiciary and the municipal councils were similarly corrupted, with Stevens making sure that heads of these important institutions were political appointees. Even the institution of chieftaincy, which in the past had been held almost sacrosanct by his predecessors, was not left untouched. Stevens had chiefs who were not supportive of his APC replaced by more pliable candidates from rival 'ruling houses'. But his most inventive forms of corruption were seen in his handling of the economy, and principally his tinkering with the important diamond mining and marketing sector.

William Reno has made the useful suggestion that African leaders, plagued by limited state capacity, and especially the constraints on the state's extractive powers, are forced to devise a strategy of 'elite accommodation' with 'inherited intermediaries'. This system necessarily bypasses inherited state institutions and involves the use of paternalism and forms of bribery, thus allowing the ruler to enhance his wealth-making capacity even as the state disintegrates and becomes dysfunctional. For Stevens the country's diamond reserves became the basis of his patrimonial order: the semi-literate dictator criminalised the industry and established a 'shadow state' which was both minimalist and highly autocratic.[28] The problem, in fact, is more ingrained than would seem from this lofty analysis: it is utterly fundamental, because it has its roots in the nature of the state itself, which is of colonial—and therefore illegitimate and exploitative—origin and function.

This problem came to prominence during the diamond rush of the 1950s. SLST and the colonial authorities, even after employing

---

[28] William Reno, *Corruption and State Politics in Sierra Leone*; also, more forcefully and with only a slight shift of emphasis, his *Warlord Politics and the African State*, Boulder, CO: Lynne Rienner, 1998.

armed private security forces and a large police force in Kono, found that they were unable to control illicit mining largely because—as a colonial investigator reported in an incisive report to the Minister for Lands, Mines and Labour, who happened to be Siaka Stevens, in 1956—'practically the entire population of the areas concerned appeared to be of the belief that the diamonds were in reality their property and were therefore sympathetic with the miners.' This feeling 'was also prevalent in the rank and file of both the police and the security forces, who in any case could not resist the corrupting influence of the large sums of money offered for silence.' It was felt that the whole SLST business was a big racket principally aimed at enriching foreigners by robbing the 'natives' of their legitimate resources, and anyone ripping them off was to be embraced rather than seen as a crook. The diamonds were mined in the Protectorate, in an area that before their discovery was hardly touched by the writ of the colonial state. The minerals were therefore considered not a state resource but 'the property of the indigenous population and under the control of the Paramount Chief and the Tribal Authority.'[29]

The colonial authorities tried to get around this problem first by co-opting the chiefs through bribery and other forms of influence peddling, and then by introducing the Alluvial Mining Scheme to placate ordinary citizens. Ensuring the co-operation of the chiefs was an enduring concern, and the colonial authorities overlooked serious breaches of the law by the chiefs in the area, including even murder and other forms of what would otherwise be considered crimes, like forced labour. Even in such a context, however, Stevens managed to achieve prodigies of excess and innovation. For good measure he had bigger fears of local strongmen than even the British colonial authorities, who in the final analysis could resort to a reliable armed force to put down organised resistance, if temporarily. Stevens had much more limited resources, and because of his anti-democratic temperament was unwilling to forge a new, more institutional relationship with chiefs and other local strongmen with a stake and political persuasion different from his own. Instead he forged what was, right at its conception, an almost criminal partnership with the Lebanese merchant community in the country.

The Lebanese had arrived in the country at the end of the nineteenth century as refugees fleeing from economic hardships such

---

[29] 'Interim Report on the Alluvial Diamond Mining Scheme 1956', confidential report, 18 June 1956 (document in author's possession).

as those caused by a silkworm crisis which struck Lebanon in the mid-nineteenth century, and several decades later had come to dominate the wholesale and retail business in Sierra Leone. After the discovery of diamonds in the 1930s they were among the first to get involved, on the illicit side, in the extremely profitable mining that ensued after SLST launched its operations. Diamonds soon became the linchpin of Lebanese business and a range of subterranean political activities. The Lebanese became the main sponsors of illegal mining operations, helping to fund the mining as well as being the main buyers of stolen gems. Before Stevens' emergence as Prime Minister and then President, however, they operated discreetly, mainly by bribing chiefs and other local strongmen, and by supplying mining 'gangs', through local intermediaries, with the simple equipment used to raid and mine SLST holdings. They would then purchase the diamonds from the small-time local buyers who dealt directly with the miners. Lebanese unfortunate enough to be caught in such illegal deals were punished: in 1959 one Lebanese trader, Jamil Sahid Mohamed, was sentenced to six months in gaol for illegal possession of diamonds. After Stevens took over power, Jamil (as he was popularly known) became the diamond tsar in the country.

Stevens had started his efforts to criminalise the diamond industry when he was in the opposition. As a minister in the SLPP government, he was known for his 'law and order' approach; once out of government, however, he took a populist stance, defending illicit miners and announcing that their activities, however illicit in the eyes of the authorities, represented 'the little man's only hope for wealth'. Because of his trade union background, and his intimate knowledge of the mining industry, he quickly recognised the potential political uses of the huge army of illicit diggers, and his new populism was clearly related to this. His rhetoric emboldened the miners and transformed their activities into a near-ideological battle that depicted SLST as a hated predatory foreign corporation stamping down the long suffering natives.

Soon after Stevens became Prime Minister in 1968, illicit mining, once largely contained, exploded again, with outright hijackings of SLST gravel trucks by armed illicit miners, some of them even digging up highways and airfields in a rapacious hunt for diamonds. SLST was forced to abandon all prospecting efforts as a result of the widespread, unchecked theft. Things only got worse. On 3 November 1969 part of the company's monthly haul of diamonds, valued locally at $3.4 million, was stolen at gunpoint as it was about to be flown out of the country at Hastings Airport. The daring thieves, who acted in a professional manner, were never caught, and the case died in the courts because almost everyone who should have cared, including the police and the judiciary (now heavily infiltrated by Stevens' cronies), appeared uninterested. The diamonds were later reported sold in Europe for $10 million.

Stevens effectively nationalised SLST in 1971 by forming a new company, the National Diamond Mining Company (NDMC), with the government having 51 per cent of the shares and SLST 49 per cent. A private individual clasp to Stevens was given 12 per cent of the government shares—which meant, in effect, that the mainstay of the country's economy was now personalised. More diamonds were smuggled than officially exported. Many were going to Liberia to be sold, as had long been the case. From a peak of over 2 million carats officially exported in 1970, legitimate diamond exports dropped to 595,000 in 1980 and 48,000 carats in 1988.[30]

His partnership with various Lebanese also allowed Stevens to acquire enormous wealth, as contracts awarded in preparation for the vulgarly extravagant hosting of the Organisation of African Unity (OAU) summit in Freetown in 1980 showed. The contracts, for construction of hotels and imports of luxury goods, were awarded mainly to Stevens' Lebanese friends and, in the words of William Reno, there was 'a 200 million dollars extravaganza of state spending, constituting half of budgeted outlays amidst further cutbacks on development and social services'.[31] Sierra Leone's economy had been, for all intents and purposes, criminalised and destroyed. As George O. Roberts has observed, Sierra Leone under Stevens was 'a coalition of constitutionally ordained and authorized components of law and order, carrying out illegal acts and condoning the violence perpetrated by the government'.[32]

Worse, there remained the extremely vexed phenomenon of what political scientists call 'urban bias'. State institutions and the country's limited social infrastructure were concentrated in Freetown, leaving the rest of the country in extreme poverty and wretchedness. A health survey published in 1978 was illuminating in this

[30] The story of the criminalisation of Sierra Leone's diamond industry is vividly told in Ian Smillie, Lansana Gberie and Ralph Hazleton, *The Heart of the Matter: Sierra Leone, Diamonds and Human Security*, Ottawa: Partnership Africa Canada, 2000.
[31] Reno, *Corruption and State Politics* (note 28), p. 137.
[32] George O. Roberts, *The Anguish of Third World Independence: the Sierra Leone Experience*, Washington, DC: University Press of America, 1984, p. 184.

regard: the infant mortality rate for Freetown was put at 20 per cent versus 33.3 per cent for the rest of the country; malaria parasites in the blood in Freetown were put at 4 per cent versus 36.2 per cent in the rest of the country; the proportion of chronically undernourished children in Freetown was 10.3 per cent versus 26.6 per cent for the rest of the country; and 'significantly underweight' children in Freetown were estimated at 18.3 per cent versus 32.4 per cent for the rest of the country.[33]

Government neglect was sometimes politically motivated, like the phasing out of the railway in the early 1970s. The railway, built by the British in the early 1900s, ran mainly through the Southern and Eastern Provinces from Freetown to Moyamba, Bo, Kenema and Pendembu, with a small spur line to Makeni in the north. The route was selected because the areas were the major producers of the country's cash crops—cocoa, coffee, piassava and palm kernels—and it stimulated significant economic and social activities in those areas. The Sierra Leone Produce Marketing Board (SLPMB) was established as a government parastatal to buy this produce from the (mainly) peasant farmers, and although the SLPMB itself became a huge racket, paying the farmers less than 45 per cent of world market prices for their goods, the maintenance of its offices in remote parts of the east and south of the country, and the cash infused into these rural areas, helped to create a sense of community with the capital as well as a moderate level of infrastructural development.

With the discovery of rich mineral deposits in the 1930s and later the fall in prices of the cash crops, the commercial importance of the railway somewhat diminished: it was, to begin with, small-gauge, too small and too slow, and therefore very inconvenient for passenger transport. By the 1960s, it was costing the government a deficit of £500,000 a year simply to maintain it. But its strategic importance—as the main link connecting the capital to vast and strategic rural areas—was never lost on the SLPP government, which balked at the World Bank's purely economistic suggestion to phase it out.

When Stevens took office, however, in spite of his dislike of the Bretton Woods institution he was quick to heed its suggestion, and

[33] Government of Sierra Leone and United States Agency for International Development, *Sierra Leone: National Nutrition Survey*, 1978, University of California at Los Angeles, Nutrition Assessment Unit, Division of Population, Family and International Health, School of Public Health.

he began to phase the railway out in the early 1970s. As Abraham and Sesay have suggested, his motive was mainly political, and in the most depraved sense: he wanted to undermine the influence of the SLPP in that party's key strongholds of Kailahun, Pendembu and Bo, and punish residents for their determined loyalty to the party.[34] He made sure that a network of highways, constructed with West German aid money to replace the railway, never got to these areas. Since then the whole of Kailahun district, as Paul Richards has noted, remained 'beyond the state' with residents maintaining more connection with Monrovia in Liberia, which could be reached by taxis in a day, than with Freetown, which was closer but could take days to reach by the unpaved 'bush roads'.[35] The dynamics of state recession in Sierra Leone, therefore, were deliberately enhanced by Stevens' destructive misrule, and it was something that would come to haunt the country in the 1990s.

In Syl Cheney-Coker's novel *The Last Harmattan of Alusine Dunbar*, a powerful satire on Stevens' kleptocratic regime, the President of the banana republic of Malagueta, Sanka Maru, who has been known for 'the arbitrariness of his laws, the profligacy of his mistresses and the shameless nepotism of his government', and who has just sentenced his armed forces chief, General Tamba Masimera, to death for treason, finally succumbs to a mysterious force and dies:

The light of the testicles glowed with a fierce brilliance, and he felt lifted out of the grandiloquent illusion of power, borne into space as if he were a dwarf, by a force too terrible to contemplate but which left him awed by the realization that in the history of creation no one had told him that what had been ordained by Divine Providence could not be altered by man; not even by a presidential decree, as he came crashing down in the middle of the street so that when the dust had been cleared, his countrymen and women would see not the eyes of a dead general, but the paralysed wreck of Sanku Maru.[36]

In reality Stevens' end was not so dramatic: in 1985 he handed over the bankrupt state to his handpicked successor, the lacklustre army

[34] Arthur Abraham and Habid Sesay, 'Regional Politics and Social Services Provisions since Independence' in C. Magbaily Fyle (ed.), *The State and the Provision of Social Services since Independence, 1961–1991*, Dakar: CODESRIA, 1993.
[35] Paul Richards, *Fighting for the Rainforest: War, Youth and Resources in Sierra Leone*, London: International African Institute/James Currey (Oxford) and Heinemann (Portsmouth, NH), 1996, p. 43.
[36] Syl Cheney-Coker (note 2), p. 397.

commander Joseph Momoh, and lived peacefully in Freetown till he died of a stroke at an estimated age of eighty-five.

Momoh assumed office announcing that 'the nation's kitty is empty' and declared a 'new order' aimed at 'constructive nationalism'. 'Our concern,' he said, 'should be directed, henceforth, towards defining the policies and actions that are required to resuscitate the economy and keep it going.'[37] Notice that the new President was concerned only about 'defining policies', not enacting them. The forty-nine-year-old former army chief declared, plaintively, that he was waging war on 'profiteers, hoarders and smugglers'.[38] In fact there was hardly anything new about this 'New Order'. Momoh's cabinet was dominated by leftovers of Stevens' regime, one being Joe Amara Bangalie, who was appointed head of a newly-created office for marketing diamonds and gold, and Minister of Finance, Economic Planning and Development. Bangalie soon announced that the new Government Gold and Diamond Office (GGDO) had received about $25 million from a well-known Lebanese dealer, Jamil, who had been appointed adviser for the running of the office. At the time Jamil already had vital stakes in the fisheries, tourism and manufacturing sectors, paid the salaries of senior military and police officers, and even attended cabinet meetings. He was also allowed to maintain a well-armed 500-strong personal security force, almost all of them Palestinians.[39]

Finally it got to Momoh that such a development was unacceptable to the vast majority of his country's long-suffering citizens, who had naively looked for a better future under him. Now it was widely believed that Stevens was still in control. When he acted Momoh acted as gangsters would do: he announced, in 1987, a foiled coup plot, had some of Stevens' leftover ministers arrested or sacked, and then forced Jamil into exile. It was time to forge his own partnership, but he did not try to build one with his own people, and instead brought in Israeli businessmen to replace his former Lebanese clients. It was replacing one set of predators with another. The whole APC one-party state was rotten to the core; it was a near-kleptocratic outfit serving only a few people, mostly foreigners, although it still maintained the trappings of state bureaucracy.

[37] Koroma (note 22), p. 55.
[38] 'Momoh tightens the screws', *West Africa*, 10 February 1986.
[39] Jimmy Kandeh, 'Sierra Leone and "Soft" State', *Review of African Political Economy*, 1990.

A BBC documentary, *Trade Slaves*, appearing in 1990, showed in depressing detail the extent of the rot and near-criminality, and especially the rot in the extractive mining sector, including diamond fields and the titanium mines (centre of another lucrative racket that benefited a few people, mostly foreigners). Shot by Steve Hewlett, the film showed 'a man-made tragedy brought by government mismanagement, corruption, and the misuse of millions of dollars by companies from the industrialised world'. It showed a potentially wealthy country with life expectancy standing at a dismal forty-two years; where 'one in every four children die before the age of five; where vital operations at the country's best hospital are carried out under a rickety angle-poised lamp and suspended when the hospital generator breaks down; and where teachers are forced to eke a living as labourers because their salaries have not been paid.'[40] It was a memorable indictment of a sordid regime, and an accurate depiction of what came to be known as a failed state.

A memorandum issued by the Sierra Leone Bar Association in July 1990, which called for the scrapping of the one-party state and the reinstitution of multiparty democracy, blamed the one-party system for the abysmal state of the country, and contended that its net effect was to engender 'disunity, mistrust, hatred, tribalism, bitterness, dissatisfaction, poverty, ignorance and diseases among Sierra Leoneans to a level never before experienced in post-independence Sierra Leone.' To the lawyers the one-party state had 'clearly failed to achieve any of the goals it set itself in the constitution of 1978.'

On the contrary, there has been a devastating economic decline; a disastrous deterioration in the value of the national currency, the leone; a permanent shortage of all essential commodities such as rice, fuel, electricity and medicines; a disintegration of the educational system resulting in non-functioning of schools and colleges; rampant bribery and corruption in every aspect of public life; unabated misuse and mismanagement of public funds and property at every level of government; non-accountability of members of government, civil servants and all other persons in positions of trust and responsibility in respect of their dealings with public funds and property while in the discharge of their duties; thinly-veiled nepotism and tribalism in every area of government and public life, and stagnation of political progress, all of which have contributed to reduce the standard of living and life expectancy of every Sierra Leonean.[41]

[40] For a review of the documentary, see Chris Simpson, 'A lost cause?', *West Africa*, 14–20 October 1991.
[41] 'Lawyers turn the tide of history: they vote 100 per cent for multiparty', *New Shaft* (Freetown), 9–15 July 1990.

It was against this state, with all its criminal tendencies, that the RUF took up arms, just at the point when a serious campaign by civil society was forcing Momoh—far less able than Stevens and, perhaps connected with this, less autocratic—to submit to demands for dramatic reforms. A nationwide campaign for a return to multi-party democracy was gaining ground, and although acutely aware of the possible outcome—given the predatory political tradition he represented, Momoh could not have been unaware of Machiavelli's warning that a reformer always risks phasing himself out—the President did not attempt to stamp it out. Indeed, to his credit, he showed extraordinarily tolerance of dissenting views, and even appeared to have enjoyed the debate. Although heading a dictatorial system, Momoh was not the typical autocrat; indeed he was a benign figure, if a thoroughly incompetent one. On the issue of free expression and independent journalism, for example, the President showed extraordinary patience and even insight, making his position clear on those issues in an interview with a foreign-based magazine:

'We believe that the media must be given every amount of freedom. If you muzzle the people for too long, it will get to a point when they'll not be able to absorb it, they will explode and there will be developments similar to what is taking place in eastern Europe. However, the media too should realize this in going about their duties; they must be responsible, they cannot afford to be reckless. We feel very worried when we see people using irresponsibly and recklessly. My argument has always been that the journalist's pen is as lethal as the rifle in the hands of a military marksman. This means the pressman should be extremely cautious about what he commits to paper. This doesn't mean he should not criticize...As long as the criticism is objective, there is nothing wrong with it. We sincerely hope that people in such a noble profession as the media should carry themselves with the decorum expected of them.'[42]

The President's concern over 'irresponsible' and 'reckless' reporting by the press was understandable. At the time he made the statement, there were sixteen newspapers in the country; all but two, the government-owned *Daily Mail* and the APC party mouthpiece *We Yone*, were small-scale independent publications owned and edited by their proprietors, and all of them based in Freetown. Few of the editors—never mind the reporters—were trained journalists. But what they lacked in professionalism they attempted to make up for by enthusiasm. They had correctly gauged the public mood against

---

[42] *West Africa*, 5–11 February 1990.

the decrepit APC system and all that the party stood for, and in favour of a return to pluralist democracy. In order to gain a larger share in the restricted market (restricted by the low level of literacy in the country as a whole, which was about 30 per cent in a small population of about 4 million), almost all the papers maintained a compulsive obsession with corruption and abuse of power, even when they had little or no evidence. Stories featuring sordid details of government ineptitude, corruption and nepotism were a daily diet, and they helped to erode confidence in the state and all those involved in its administration still further.

The most successful in this enterprise was an eight-page tabloid called the *New Shaft*, edited by a mercurial and sensationalist former schoolteacher, Franklyn Bunting-Davies. From January 1989 to April 1991 hardly any edition of the paper appeared without being dominated by a corruption story. The 24 April 1989 edition of the paper, which featured on its front page a picture of the unpopular Minister of Information, Victor Mambu, standing beside a 'palace' he was building for himself, was deemed offensive enough by the authorities for them suspend the paper's license; in effect it was banned.[43] But the paper had become so popular that a public outcry forced Momoh to intervene personally and have the ban lifted. It was a sign that things had become truly desperate for the once ultra-powerful one-party state.

Still, Momoh perhaps thought, like Gorbachev in another country at about the same time, that he could manipulate the outcome of the national debate about reforms to his advantage. But such matters as reforming a failing system, as both leaders found out to their cost, do not always play out in hygienic conditions. And as both Sierra Leone and Russia were to discover painfully, the results do not always conform to a simple morality tale of good triumphing over evil. It is often less clear-cut and more complicated.

[43] Adewale Maja-Pearce, 'The Press in West Africa', *Index on Censorship*, June/July 1990, pp. 55–7.

3

THE MAKING OF THE REVOLUTIONARY UNITED FRONT

'What we are saying is the only way to a democratic future for all Africans in Sierra Leone lies in the abolishment of militarism and dictatorship. And the only force that can defeat militarism and dictatorship is the armed force of the suffering people as expressed in a guerrilla campaign. The guerrilla is the people in arms. It is the guerrilla who removes the fear imposed on society by the uniformed 'men in arms'. These watchdogs of the corrupt and rotten APC regime are still with us....' (RUF/SL, *Footpaths to Democracy*[1])

'Sankoh came to my village at the start of the war ...he handed out a lot of newly printed money, and there was a lot of merriment. But soon afterward his men accused a boy of stealing from them, and they cut his head off and placed it on a stick in the road, saying the perfume was good for us. When people complained that the head had to be buried, his men burned our village down.' (refugee victim of RUF attacks[2])

Foday Saybanah Sankoh was born in the early 1930s in a small village in Tonkolili district. The son of peasant farmers in a district not particularly congenial to large scale commercial agriculture, Sankoh grew up in poverty. His education was limited; he managed to attend only primary school. According to his own accounts, he was a stubborn and troublesome child. He loved fighting with other children, and was known as a bully. As a young man he got a job with the postal services but, bored by it, quit and joined the army in 1956.[3]

---

[1] RUF/SL, *Footpaths to Democracy* (published by RUF).
[2] Testimony of 'starving refugee' in 'Refugees starving in West Africa's latest war', 3 October 1995, *International Herald Tribune*, p. 2.
[3] Ebow Godwin, '"I don't want you to join the Police and become a criminal": Interview with Foday Sankoh', *New African* no. 379, November 1999.

The Sierra Leone army, at the time that Sankoh joined it, attracted only people with little or no education. For many people in the country, and especially those in Freetown, which was fairly literate and had a concentration of state institutions, the army was the place for those who could not make it into the civil service or any other white collar employment. A local newspaper commented on the army at about the time that Sankoh joined in these wonderfully suggestive terms: 'All soldiers are considered to be of the same category, that is they are a menace to education.' It concluded that 'there is no public interest in the Sierra Leone Army' and 'in all respects ex-servicemen and serving soldiers are looked upon as worthless beings.'[4] This negative perception of the army was the result of two factors. The first was that the army's officer corps was almost entirely made up of Europeans, and Africans were kept firmly in the rank and file. It was a policy begun in 1902, the year that the Ordinance establishing the Sierra Leone Battalion came into effect. Before that, there were two Sierra Leonean officers in the Sierra Leone Frontier Force, the forerunner of the Sierra Leone army, but these were retired in December 1902 by Governor Frederick Cardew, a former British soldier with negative views of African capability and a tendency, no doubt developed during his service in South Africa, to see everything in terms of race. It would take over fifty years for an African to be appointed to the officer corps again.

The main problem, however, was more fundamental: the army was seen largely as an instrument of colonial repression, and a particularly brutal one at that. The forerunner of the Sierra Leone army was the much-hated Frontier Police Force, which was instrumental in the brutal suppression of the insurgents in the Hut Tax War in 1898. The war started as a popular revolt against British colonial imposition of tax on households in the newly declared Protectorate. The British-led force employed scorched-earth tactics against defenceless villages, burning down towns and starving or killing the inhabitants. After several months of fighting, the force crushed all resistance and arrested hundreds of people, including chiefs who were deemed to have instigated the revolt. After a show trial ninety-six of them were hanged.[5] The army was essentially a law

[4] *Daily Mail*, 13 April 1956.
[5] See La Ray Denzer, 'Sierra Leone: Bai Bureh' in Michael Crowder (ed.), *West African Resistance*, London: Hutchinson, 1971; also Arthur Abraham, 'Bai Bureh, the British and the Hut Tax War', *International Journal of African Historical Studies*, vol. 7 no. 1, 1974, pp. 99–106.

and order instrument: it was meant to ensure civilian compliance with state authority and operated almost entirely to that end. As Edward Turay and Arthur Abraham have noted in *The Sierra Leone Army: a Century of History*, apart from its participation on a small scale in the First World War and on a larger scale in the Second, the force's 'traditional role' was 'being the answer to any civilian uprising which threatened to upset the status quo; in colonial parlance, the army was always ready "to come to the aid of civil authority."'[6] This was dramatically demonstrated after riots broke out in February 1955 in which workers and looters broke into shops and attacked the homes of politicians. The army was called in to quell the riots and according to the Shaw Commission set up to investigate the riots, acted with extraordinary brutality: 'There was wild, indiscriminate shooting...including the promiscuous use of automatic weapons, a callous disregard for the lives of unarmed and innocent civilians and indifference to the sufferings of the wounded.'[7] In all eighteen people were killed and 121 wounded.

Interestingly, Foday Sankoh joined the army that year, encouraged to do so, he has said, by a British patron. Hence he was brought up in this depraved tradition. Sankoh remained in the army until 1971, managing to attain, even after a vigorous programme to Africanise the army's officer corps, no higher rank than corporal. Sankoh was attached to the signals squadron at the army headquarters, then at Tower Hill in central Freetown. In 1963 he was sent to Nigeria for a six months' training course in radio communications. Three years later, in 1966, he was sent to Hythe in the English county of Kent for another six months' training, again in communications, including radio and television operations. On his return to Sierra Leone, he was attached to the TV section of the Sierra Leone Broadcasting Service (SLBS).

In that year, 1967, the army, under Brigadier David Lansana, staged a military intervention to prevent Siaka Stevens' APC from taking power, thus beginning another tradition that would finally lead to the army's undoing. Sankoh did not play any role in that military intervention, and probably did not support it. In any case his opinion would have counted for very little: the action was strictly controlled by the army commander and NCOs would simply

---

[6] E.D.A. Turay and A. Abraham, *The Sierra Leone Army: a Century of History*, London: Macmillan, 1987, p. 88.

[7] *Report of the Commission of Inquiry into the Strike and Riots in Freetown during February 1955*, Freetown: Government Printer, 1956.

have had to obey. The army as an institution was cohesive and functioning. It was people like Hinga Norman, later to become Sankoh's most formidable opponent and at the time a captain in the army, who played prominent roles: it was he who, on the orders of Lansana, placed Stevens and Governor-General Lightfoot-Boston under arrest. Unfortunately this coherent military command structure did not last. Lansana in his turn was unseated after two days by a trio of majors. However, these majors, like Lansana, were firmly part of the officer corps, and were well-educated and respected. They appointed Colonel Andrew Juxon-Smith head of their junta, which they styled the National Reformation Council (NRC).

A year later, as recorded earlier, the NRC was overthrown, this time by junior rank and file soldiers. Sankoh has claimed that he was a part of the coup, and has justified it in these frankly self-serving terms: 'The economy was not getting better. Our salaries were two to three months behind. Finally, we decided to take power and ousted the NRC.'[8] The new junta was called the Anti-Corruption Revolutionary Council (ARC), and to the surprise of many it handed over power to Stevens' APC in April 1968. Sankoh has explained that he supported this decision, but soon 'Stevens turned the APC into a tribal outfit...many of us soldiers felt betrayed.'[9]

Less than three years later, on 23 March 1971, army chief Brigadier John Bangura attempted a coup. Sankoh was attached to the SLBS TV, and has boasted of enthusiastically rushing to have Bangura's coup broadcast. He was, of course, only a corporal, and had no part in the decision to make the coup. But partly because of his job at the strategic TV station, and partly because he, like Bangura, was from Tonkolili district, Sankoh had advance knowledge of the coup, and supported it. He has explained that he was with Bangura when the Stevens loyalists Major Joseph Momoh (who would soon become army chief and subsequently head of state) and Major Abu Noah (an amiable poet and now the owner of Sierra Leone's largest private security agency) counter-attacked and had Bangura arrested. Sankoh has claimed that he noisily grumbled about the 'betrayal', and was later arrested and charged with 'misprision of treason', that is, failing to report a plot in advance. He was tried, found guilty of the charge and gaoled for seven years at the harsh Pademba Road prison.

Prison has a way of radicalising would-be dissidents, but Sankoh has claimed that he was already yearning for a revolution by the

[8] *New African*, no. 310, July/August 1993.
[9] 'Foday Sankoh breaks his silence', *The Ninja*, 22 April 1999.

time the coup happened. Of the abortive coup itself he has said,
'They [the senior officers] wanted to make coups, while I always
wanted a revolution. But I was still a corporal and nobody listened
to my suggestions because of my rank.'[10] This retrospective bravado
was another attempt at self-mythologising, and if Bangura, a career
soldier, had heard this talk about a 'revolution' from Sankoh, he
would almost certainly have dismissed it, not only because of Sankoh's low rank. Sankoh's idea of revolution would have appeared
to anyone with knowledge of the world as reckless. About his war,
which he started decades after Bangura's ill-fated coup attempt,
Sankoh said, 'We are fighting a holy war and so I have never worried about treason charge. God used to provide many visions to me
at Pademba Road telling me that I will be well. And I always believed
God.'[11] Exactly twenty years after the failed coup, on 23 March
1991, Sankoh announced that he had launched a 'people's armed
struggle' to overthrow the APC government, then headed by his
former army boss and the man who he felt betrayed Bangura,
Joseph Momoh.

Sankoh was released from prison in 1978, the year that the APC
enacted a one-party state. Thus means he was in prison when university students, led by Hindolo Trye, sparked almost nationwide
violent protests against the Stevens regime. The protests, which
became a riot, started after the students attacked the President as
he presided, as Chancellor of the University of Sierra Leone, over
the 150th anniversary ceremony of Fourah Bay College, the oldest
Western-style university institution in West Africa, which is beauti-
fully perched on the Mount Aureol hills over looking the city, in
February 1977. The protests were not well-organised and planned;
there was a spontaneous, desperate quality about them. The students waited until the President got up to sum up the events of the
day, which had lasted about three hours, and drowned out his
speech with jeering and shouted allegations of corruption, theft
and murder. The students accused Stevens of stealing $40 million
for his personal use, along with charges of tyranny and unconstitu-
tional acts. Stevens was hastily driven off the university campus by
his security details.[12]

[10] Howard French, 'African rebel with room service', *New York Times*,
23 June 1996.
[11] *The Ninja* (note 9).
[12] George O. Roberts, *The Anguish of Third World Independence: The Sierra
Leone Experience*, Washington, DC: University Press of America, 1984,
p. 252.

The demonstration quickly spread to Freetown city. Thousands of unemployed youth from the east end of the city joined in, and they directed their anger mainly against shops and businesses owned by Lebanese traders. Shops were looted, government offices broken into, and cars and buses wrecked.

Feeling humiliated, Stevens struck back, arming his youth wing and sending them to counter-attack the students at Fourah Bay College. Among the counter-demonstrators was Stevens' own daughter, who went to the university campus armed with a pistol. Student dormitories were broken into, female students raped and beaten, and university property vandalised. The riot spread to other urban centres, including Bo and Kenema. Things were getting out of hand, and Stevens realised that a gangster-type reaction would not do. In an inspired move he announced on radio and TV that new elections would be held to decide the future of the country. The protests and riots subsided, allowing him to organise elections and a referendum on a proposed one-party state, both of which he rigged, using violence. Truck-loads of armed Internal Security Unit (ISU) personnel, most of them trained in Cuba, were sent across the country to intimidate and brutalise voters. In Bo, the principal southern city and bastion of the opposition SLPP, the ISU engaged in full battle with residents, leading to the loss of many lives and the destruction of property. Locals subsequently dubbed the ISU 'I Shoot You', and many opposition candidates withdrew from the polls. In the event only fifteen of them made it to the eighty-member Parliament. With such a majority Stevens had no problems passing his one-party bill.

The student-inspired protests, in that sense, were a failure: they had precisely the opposite effect of what perhaps the students had envisaged, for they led to the consolidation of Stevens' hold on power and to the considerable worsening of an already debased political climate. But they also exposed the weaknesses of the state, and the potential for small groups of dissidents to shake it to its foundations. Stevens' call for elections was clearly a concession made to the students' leadership (the students had called for 'free and fair elections to be held within nine months and a public announcement to be made to the effect now'). The demonstrations were 'a lesson of student power', as Abdullah and Muana[13] termed it, that was not forgotten by the students and others less idealistic.

[13] Ibrahim Abdullah and Patrick Muana, 'The Revolutionary United Front of Sierra Leone', in C. Clapham (ed.), *African Guerrillas*, Bloomington: Indiana University Press, 1998, p. 175.

Foday Sankoh emerged from prison embittered and determined to strike back at the APC state, which had now become, in the eyes of many in the country, a very palpable instrument of oppression and terror, hardly a social institution. All political opposition had been crushed; the army, with its swiftly promoted commander Brigadier Joseph Momoh now a member of the one-party Parliament, had been politicised and corrupted; so had the police force, the civil service and the judiciary. Sankoh could not go back to the army even if he wanted to. With little education and without money he could only toy with the idea of opening a poultry farm in Freetown, which he abandoned as uninteresting. Then he decided to move to Bo to pursue a career he seemed well equipped for: professional photography.

Why Sankoh chose Bo, where he had never lived before, and not Freetown or Makeni, both of which he knew well, has not been made clear, but two things may have influenced his decision. Bo, though smaller than Freetown, was bigger than Makeni, and nearly as cosmopolitan as the capital. It offered a bigger market than Makeni and far less competition than Freetown. The other point is more relevant politically. Bo was the most important centre of discontent against the APC in the country. It was traditionally a stronghold of the SLPP, and many of the city's residents were still openly defiant of the one-party state. Small dissident group meetings could still be held without much fear of being broken into by APC thugs, as would almost certainly have happened if such meetings had been held in Freetown (outside the Fourah Bay College campus, which remained largely insulated from Stevens' totalitarian endeavour) or Makeni.

Sankoh has claimed, in more than one interview, that it was at Bo, in 1982, that he started 'organising' his 'revolutionary movement'. This claim is clearly an attempt at self-mythologising, for this 'organising' was nothing more than Sankoh's association with a 'study cell' of a radical, but little known and ineffectual, organisation called the Pan African Union (Panafu), which had been founded at Fourah Bay College by young university lecturers (most of whom were part of the 1977 student-led protests) and students in the early 1980s. The group was closely aligned to other radical student groups in the country, and attracted some so-called organic intellectuals in the city and in large urban centres like Bo and Kenema. Sankoh is believed to have been recruited into the group by Ebeyemi Reader,[14] who himself never went to college but was

---

[14] Ibid. p. 177.

from a middle class background in Freetown and was close friends with some of the Panafu founders. Sankoh has repeatedly claimed that the study cell was the beginning of the RUF, which may be true but only in the sense that it marked his exposure to a group of starry-eyed activists who would introduce him to some highly potent contacts that would prove crucial in his launching of the war. But the name 'Revolutionary United Front' did not exist in the 1980s, and members of Panafu have been very quick to disavow any association with it.

Sankoh made this claim to me in 1996 after he emerged from his forest enclaves to engage the then military government of Sierra Leone, the National Provisional Ruling Council (NPRC), in peace talks at Yamoussoukro in Côte d'Ivoire. I met him in his Hotel President suite, surrounded by a group of four beautiful women who I was told were his bodyguards. It was something he had copied from Libya's Muammar Gaddafi, whose personal security details are dominated by women who are said to be virgins. I was slightly taken aback by Sankoh's physical build. He was shorter than I had imagined, rotund and bearded, the face chubby and jovial. He was very well dressed, in a richly embroidered African garment, and was pacing about the suite in an animated manner, like a figure on a Swiss clock. 'I did not start a war,' he said, responding to a question about what he aimed to accomplish by his vicious bush campaign. 'It is a people's struggle. The people rose up against the rotten APC system. Before it all started, everyone was crying for war. Everybody wanted the rotten APC to be overthrown. Now that there is a people's struggle against that system, why should I be blamed for it?' He added, 'You ask me about my war aims. Everyone knows what Sierra Leoneans want: free education, free health care, proper use of our natural resources, provision of basic necessities which the politicians have denied them. That's what the people's struggle is all about.'

It was all rhetoric and rage, I thought. Nothing specific, no grievance that you wouldn't hear from a mid-level civil servant in Freetown earning the equivalent of $100 a month. It all struck me as decidedly creepy coming from this well-fed elderly man surrounded by a group of adoring (and adorable) young women. Then there was the unsettling literalism: 'Everyone has been crying for this war, now they have it!'

Before my meeting with Sankoh, I had interviewed his former neighbour who knew him quite well in Bo, a willowy woman with a shy smile. She remembered him distinctly as 'a strange, funny man' who was very jovial but otherwise secretive. He had few friends, she said, and he was single. 'There were a number of women visitors to his house but I don't think they were very close,' she told me. 'They would come and go, and that was about it.' One of Sankoh's closest associates at the time was one Dr Bangura. Bangura, it turned out, was an intellectual of sorts, trained at the Sorbonne in Paris, and a teacher at the government secondary school in Bo. Bangura was a character who seemed to have been plucked straight from a Dostoevsky novel: brilliant, contradictory, mysterious and full of resentments. He was a playwright, and had written a play called *The Horses of Unzagga*, which seemed to adapt the sullen tone of Samuel Beckett's *Waiting for Godot*: it ends without ending—unresolved and mysterious. Its theme, however, is Orwellian (recalling *Animal Farm*). Everyone in the play is a Horse, except the Masters who are working the Horses. A young 'rebel' among the Horses, uncertain about himself and his cause, is trying to organise the 'comrades' to resist the oppression of the Masters while the Chief Horse is urging every-one to obey the orders of the Masters. The play is a satire on the APC kleptocracy and its opponents, depicting the impatience of the general populace for the liberators who will kick them out, and who appear to be tantalisingly hovering on the horizon but do not appear to have the resolve to strike. It was first staged by Bo School students in 1978.

Bangura's grievance against the APC appeared to have been that his application to teach at Fourah Bay College when he returned from the Sorbonne was rejected because, as he was fond of telling everyone willing to listen, as a student in France he had been active in campaigning against Stevens' tyranny. This was why Sankoh was attracted to him. His political ideas were not particularly well-formed or well-articulated: he appeared more like a nineteenth-century European nihilist, seeming to want only simple rejection. He may not have been exactly like Dostoevsky's Underground Man—a 'spiteful man...unattractive...sufficiently educated not to be superstitious', but superstitious out of spite—but his deliberately dishevelled appearance gave him the look of sustained discontent, something that appealed to a lot of young radicals at the time.

If Sankoh had any serious political education, it may well have been from people like Bangura: in the manner of Bangura's play, he had poured scorn on both the APC and groups like his former patron Panafu, which he dismissed as spineless and noisy. Both Bangura and Sankoh were associated with a few radical Panafu members in Bo—people like Alex Nyandemoh, a 'revolutionary'

enthusiast of sorts, a secondary school student at the time—and
they may have been invited to attend some Panafu functions, but
they were never members of the group. Khalilu Totangie, a former
student activist and founding member of the Bo branch of Panafu,
told me in an interview that he saw Sankoh and Bangura attend one
or two Panafu functions, but they were not members of the 'study
cells'. Totangie claimed that Panafu had a 'loose relationship with
all sorts of people who can chant radical slogans'. Some of these
people, he said, were impatient with Panafu's gradualist approach
('organise the masses and inspire a mass uprising') and the group's
core concern with apartheid South Africa. They wanted immediate
'armed struggle'.[15] According to Sankoh, Panafu was 'a playing field;
they were merely talking about Mandela, they were not addressing
Sierra Leone's problems. I said this was not my place.'[16] This confusion about commitment and strategy inevitably infected Panafu
itself, and this led to the expulsion of some members, a few of
whom would surface in the RUF later.

There was another side of Sankoh that came out in my interviews
with people who had known him when he was a photographer in
Bo. Alhaji Galba, a Nigerian-born photographer who had lived in
Bo for over thirty years, recalled having a quarrel with Sankoh over
a stolen camera. Galba had seen his stolen camera with Sankoh,
and politely asked Sankoh to return it. Sankoh refused, saying that
he had purchased the camera legally. The matter ended at the local
police station. When the police took the camera from Sankoh and
handed it over to Galba, Sankoh denounced them for siding, in his
view, with a foreigner, called the police a corrupt wing of the APC
and promised to deal with them at an appropriate time. 'I was flab-
bergasted,' Galba told me. 'It was my camera all right and Sankoh
knew this. We knew each other and he had certainly seen the camera with me before. I just did not understand his rage but he was
clearly very livid. It was beyond belief.' This adolescent sense of
entitlement, this blind rage, was to be as much a defining feature of
the RUF's campaigns as the mutilation of civilians.

Sankoh's rage and spite, however, would never have threatened
society beyond perhaps the occasional case of anti-social conduct—
which the police, however weakened by inadequate resources and
institutional corruption, were well equipped to handle—had it not
been for the geopolitical adventurism of Libya's Colonel Gaddafi

[15] Interview in Washington, DC, December 2001.
[16] *Newswave* magazine (Freetown), December 1999–January 2000.

and the mix of enthusiasm and opportunism of a few university student 'radicals'. In 1982 Gaddafi, who had come to power in Libya
by staging a coup in 1969 and had since become an outspoken
critic of 'Western imperialism', was scheduled to host the annual
Organisation of African Unity (OAU) meeting in Tripoli. The United States, which regarded Gaddafi as a terrorist and was alarmed at
the prospect of him having such a high-profile platform as host to
so many African leaders, lobbied sedulously to have as many leaders
boycott the Tripoli summit as possible. Already some African leaders were angry with Gaddafi for his policies, including his military
intervention in Chad whose regime was backed by the United
States and France. President Stevens was one of those who were
persuaded, no doubt by bribery rather than principle, to boycott
the summit. This was the root of Gaddafi's hostility to the APC
regime, and henceforth he spared no opportunity to embarrass
and undermine the Sierra Leone government. Through the Libyan
People's Bureaux in Ghana and Guinea, he decided to channel
funds and other forms of support to the only potent opposition
grouping left in the country: university student radicals. Abdullah[17]
has drawn attention to the existence at Fourah Bay, in the 1980s, of
a Green Book Study Group which dedicated itself to propagating
Gaddafi's political ideas, as expressed in the *Green Book*, a document which extols an assortment of ideas of naïve humanism, anti-
capitalist rhetoric and charismatic rule.

In 1984 a virulently pro-Gaddafi student movement, led by a student activist named Alie Kabba, staged a destructive demonstration
at Fourah Bay College (FBC). Kabba had been elected unopposed
as student president while attending the annual *Green Book* celebrations in Libya, and his anti-administration antics and brand of 'student power' were already in issue on campus and perhaps within
APC government circles. As part of his application of the *Green Book*
principles he instituted a People's Tribunal to adjudicate problems
between students, which at one time decreed the public flogging of
a student accused of theft. Some members of this People's Tribunal
wore Halloween-type masks at night and set fire to a car belonging
to the Vice-Principal of FBC, Cyril Patrick Foray, a former Foreign
Minister and a historian of note. Forty-one students were identified

[17] Ibrahim Abdullah, 'Bush Path to destruction: the Origins and Character
of the RUF/SL' in *Between Democracy and Terror* (Dakar: CODESRIA, 2003,
previously published as a special issue of *Africa Development*, vol. XXII nos
3–4, 1997), pp. 41–65.

as having masterminded the arson and were expelled in 1985; five were charged in court and detained for two months. Momoh was then newly installed as President of the country, and Gaddafi had a particular contempt for him, describing him in a statement after he took office as a 'scout'. In his view, a military man should not allow himself to be handpicked as a successor to a civilian leader; he must take power in a coup.

The expulsion of the student leaders triggered more protest and vandalism, and the notorious ISU (now the Special Security Division, SSD) was brought in to crush them, and did so with characteristic brutality. Feeling unjustly treated, Kabba and some of his colleagues initiated something that would have a profound and destructive result much later: the training of would-be revolutionaries in Libya in preparation for an armed assault against the APC state.

According to Abdullah,[18] who has provided a convincing account of the dangerous adventurism of the students, the project began in 1987 after the expelled students, under the leadership of Kabba, flew to Ghana and then to Libya under the patronage of Gaddafi to receive military and 'ideological' training at the so-called al-Mathabh al-Thauriya al-Alamiya World Revolutionary Headquarters somewhere in the Libyan desert. The students subsequently recruited mostly urban drifters ('lumpens', as Abdullah describes them) and secondary school students, some of whom were associated with Panafu, and spirited them to Libya for the same purpose. Foday Sankoh, whose deep-seated grudges against the APC were well known, was among the recruits. The student leaders soon realised, however, that they were confusing their irritation with ideology, and that they had no serious organisational base or realistic means of launching a revolutionary war. There were also internal squabbles about money and about the commitment of some members, including Kabba himself. So the project came to nothing. Some of the student leaders got funding to finish their university education in Ghana, and the rest of the revolutionary enthusiasts returned to Sierra Leone and settled back to whatever they were doing before.

However, at least three of them did not just settle down. Sankoh, Abu Kanu and Rashid Mansaray, feeling let down by the student leaders and still determined to stir up trouble, did some travelling, spending time in the diamond mining district of Kono and in Liberia trying to find support for their revolutionary endeavour. Kanu and Mansaray had been expelled from Panafu for their virulently

[18] Ibid.

radical views: there was even talk after the American bombing of Libya in 1986 that Kabba, Mansaray and Kanu were plotting to bomb the US embassy in Freetown with support from the Libyan People's Bureau in Ghana. However, revolutionary uprisings, even in (or perhaps especially in) impoverished and technologically backward societies, do not happen simply because within those societies a handful of disaffected citizens wish them to happen: they demand a level of organisation and social mobilisation that must be painstakingly built up. This the trio clearly lacked, and so even they decided to give up. Sankoh once again settled in Freetown, destitute and dejected.

Perhaps because of his disappointment over the Libyan project, Sankoh has always tried to play it down. In an interview with the *Newswave* magazine at the height of his triumph—for signing the Lome Peace Accord in 1999 he had just then been awarded the very important post of chairman of the quaintly named Commission for the Management of Strategic Resources, National Reconstruction and Development, which in effect made him the diamond tsar and therefore the most powerful figure in Sierra Leone—Sankoh gave this confusing account of the Libyan training:

Alie Kabba, you may know, I condemn corruption. Nobody will try to corrupt Sankoh. They were in Libya for dollars [laughs], they were for money. They were in Ghana receiving money from other people in the name of the revolution. They pay [*sic*] for their girlfriends in university. You know that, eh? I was in the provinces organizing, they went to meet me for their selfish ends. They say because I have a movement, we were organizing, there was no leadership. I was in the provinces. You know boys in Freetown are trouble makers, they feel that people in the rural areas could be used to their advantage. But I told them, stop making nonsense in exile, let's go to Sierra Leone and fight. But they were for money. How can a man say until I get my degree before I go and fight to liberate my people. But where are they now?[19]

This interview was conducted in English, and the ebullient and talkative Sankoh spoke English with great effort. Two things, however, can be easily deduced from it. First, that contrary to assertions that he had made to other reporters, the RUF did not exist in any form except perhaps as part of his wishful thinking at the time that the Libyan project took place in 1987 and 1988. And second, that those who recruited Sankoh for the project had all but given up on

[19] Abu Talib and Kingsley Lington, 'Interview: Eyes on the Presidency', *Newswave*, December 1999–January 2000.

the idea of 'revolution' by 1988. He disdainfully dismissed them in the same interview in these words, 'Some today have got the degrees, PhDs, Masters. And Foday Sankoh is who today? The chairman.'

In spite of these dismissive statements, however, the Libyan project was crucial in the making of the RUF. In the 1980s, as part of his demented Pan-African policy, Gaddafi actively recruited and trained in his World Revolutionary headquarters many disaffected radicals and dissidents from a number of African countries with whose leaders he was in disagreement. In the dying days of General Idi Amin's murderous regime in Uganda, he had sent 600 troops to defend that tyrant, a fellow Muslim, against the forces of Tanzania and insurgents in the country. The mission was a tragic failure but Gaddafi was not ready to give up. He found a new Ugandan friend, Yoweri Museveni, who was part of the opposition to Amin and who was of a completely different mould from the ousted General. Libyan-trained recruits fought with Museveni in his bush war against Amin's successors, Milton Obote and Tito Okello, until Museveni emerged victorious in 1986.

Other would-be African revolutionaries who trained in the Benghazi camps included Kukoi Samba Sanyang, who led a freakish coup attempt against The Gambia's President Dauda Jawara, a conservative and mild mannered leader disliked by Gaddafi, no doubt for that very reason as well as for boycotting (with US encouragement) the 1982 OAU conference in Libya. Laurent-Désiré Kabila, who was to oust the vigorously pro-American President Mobutu of Zaire, also reportedly visited the 'World Revolutionary headquarters' in Libya in the 1980s. Indeed in the 1980s the Libyan World Revolution headquarters had become, in the words of the historian Stephen Ellis, 'the Harvard and Yale of a whole generation of African revolutionaries'.[20]

Crucially for the RUF, Charles Taylor, a former Liberian government procurement officer who had fallen out with the bloodthirsty American stooge President Samuel Doe over a financial transaction, also trained in the Benghazi camps at the same time as Sankoh, in 1987 and part of 1988.

Sankoh and Taylor first met in Ghana, through Alie Kabba and on his way to Libya, in 1987, and then in 1988 in Libya, but there is no evidence that the urbane and hard-headed Taylor gave much thought to the middle-aged and barely literate Sankoh and his

---

[20] Stephen Ellis, *The Mask of Anarchy: The Destruction of Liberia and the Religious Dimension of an African Civil War*, London: Hurst, 1999, p. 107.

comrades, the dispirited collection of secondary students and college drop-outs from Sierra Leone. Taylor already had an organisation, the National Patriotic Front of Liberia (NPFL), which had been founded by General Thomas Quiwonkpa, a former second in command to Doe, and other prominent Liberian dissident politicians.[21] Quiwonkpa had been brutally murdered, in 1985, after he attempted to make a coup against Doe. Taylor was a protégé of Quiwonkpa. Shortly before the coup, and in the midst of widespread rice riots and rumours of coup plots, Taylor returned to Liberia. He had earned an economics degree at Bentley College in Massachusetts and before his return to Liberia was working, like most immigrants, in a lowly-paid job—as a petrol station assistant in Boston—during which time he was active in the exiled opposition to Doe's predecessor, William Tolbert. A bloody coup in 1980 ended the life of Tolbert and his government, and Doe, then a master-sergeant, became President with Quiwonkpa as his Vice President. In 1983, shortly after Quiwonkpa fell out with the increasingly despotic and corrupt Doe, Taylor left once again for the United States, having been accused of stealing $900,000 from state funds in Liberia.

In the United States, where the government was fêting Doe for his anti-Gaddafi and anti-Communist rhetoric, Taylor was arrested and detained pending extradition to Liberia, but he escaped after allegedly bribing the prison authorities.[22] He travelled first to Mexico and then to Ghana (where he was later briefly detained) before going on to Burkina Faso where Blaise Compaore, a friend of Gaddafi, introduced him to the eccentric Libyan leader. Compaore was at the time second in command, with Thomas Sankara as leader of Burkina Faso. The country was host to a small concentration of Liberian exiles, including former army officers like Prince Johnson and Samuel Varney. Compaore approached the Liberians and asked them for help in overthrowing Sankara, and on 15 October 1987, supported by these Liberians, Compaore led rogue elements of the Burkinabe army and overthrew and killed Sankara.[23] Compaore, Taylor's friend, now became President of Burkina Faso. 'For the first time', writes Ellis, who has provided the most compelling account of the Liberian civil war, 'Taylor now had access to a foreign government which had the wherewithal to finance and arm an insurrection on a large scale. Gaddafi took an interest in these West

---

[21] Ibid., p. 71.
[22] Ibid., p. 67.
[23] Ibid., p. 68.

African intrigues in pursuit of his own vast revolutionary ambitions, which extended to the whole of Africa, the Middle East and other parts of the world, from Northern Ireland to Colombia and the Philippines.'[24]

With his forces which had received Libyan training now based in Burkina Faso, all that Taylor needed was a base from which to launch his war in Liberia. In 1989 he flew to Sierra Leone using a Burkinabe diplomatic passport to seek President Momoh's endorsement for the use of Sierra Leone as a base to launch his armed insurgency, as his former mentor Quiwonkpa had done in 1985. Momoh's Foreign Minister at the time, Abdul Karim Koroma,[25] has informed us that Momoh, thinking of the strained relations with Liberia that resulted from the failed Quiwonkpa adventure, summarily turned down Taylor's request and had the Liberian dissident arrested and detained at Pademba Road prison. While in prison Taylor may have bribed the compulsively corrupt Momoh administration, since he was quietly released and allowed extraordinary laxity in Freetown, where he stayed for a few weeks and was able to link up with Sankoh—living then in eastern Freetown, sometimes sleeping in a garage for want of better accommodation—and recruit Sierra Leonean young men in Freetown and in the illicit diamond mines in Kono. Sankoh, Abu Kanu and Rashid Mansaray later joined him in Burkina Faso, and they were among the first set of National Patriotic Front of Liberia fighters to enter Liberia from Côte d'Ivoire in 1989, triggering Liberia's civil war.

The force of about 150 fighters led by Charles Taylor advanced over the border from Côte d'Ivoire and attacked the town of Butou in Liberia's Nimba County on Christmas Eve in 1989. Taylor announced that his aim was to overthrow Doe's depraved regime, but it was widely suspected that he harboured aims far beyond that: that the core of his NPFL fighters were what Ellis has called 'internationalist revolutionaries'[26] from other parts of West Africa, including Sierra Leone and The Gambia, and that the real aim was to spread destabilisation in the region for the purpose of broader hegemonic control, in which Gaddafi would emerge as the new, shadowy master of West Africa. A secret diplomatic despatch from Lagos confirmed

[24] Ibid., p. 69.
[25] Abdul Karim Koroma, *Sierra Leone: the Agony of a Nation*, Freetown: Afromedia Publications, 1996, p. 141.
[26] Stephen Ellis, 'Liberia 1989–1994: a Study in Ethnic and Spiritual Violence', *African Affairs*, vol. 94 no. 375, April 1995, pp. 165–97.

this fear to the Sierra Leonean authorities in November 1990. A Nigerian businessman who escaped capture by the NPFL reported seeing Sierra Leonean and Gambian dissidents, as well as Burkinabe mercenaries, fighting alongside Taylor and seeming to be recruiting Sierra Leonean migrant workers in Liberia for the purpose of starting a 'rebellion' in Sierra Leone after Taylor's capture of state power in Liberia.[27] Taylor's closest aide was the veteran Gambian dissident and revolutionary fantasist Kukoi Samba Samyang, known in Liberia as 'Dr Manning'.

For Liberians, however, Taylor astutely used the BBC World Service for Africa as a means both to bolster his support in the country and to appeal to ethnic support in a sordid propaganda war that would eventual plunge the country into horrific pogroms and destruction. Here he made no Pan-Africanist pretentions. Over the BBC he declared his war as a 'continuation' of the failed Quiwonkpa coup, a message aimed to appeal to the ethnic Gio and Mano who dominated Nimba County and who were massacred by Doe for allegedly supporting Quiwonkpa's abortive coup in 1985.[28] Doe's demented troops, led by an officer named Charles Julu, launched a massive scorched earth campaign in Nimba County. Julu, of Doe's Krahn ethnic group, had been sent by Doe in 1985 to pacify Nimba after Quiwonkpa's coup attempt, and he did so killing thousands of defenceless peasants and raping women. After Taylor's forces struck, it was Julu again whom Doe called upon to deal with the situation in Nimba.

Julu's forces could easily have crushed Taylor's lightly armed guerrillas, but this was not the aim of his 'counter-insurgency'. He wanted to teach Nimba residents a hard lesson once and for all. It was a repeat of the 1985 massacres, only this was more intense. Julu's almost entirely Krahn soldiers killed and raped with abandon, rounded up opposition figures and had them beheaded, their remains left unburied. The result, as the incisive *New York Times* writer Bill Berkeley has informed us, 'was exactly what Taylor might have hoped for. Gios and Manos by the thousands rushed to join up with Taylor's forces'. And he welcomed them. 'As the NPFL came in', Taylor told me, 'we didn't even have to act. People came to us

---

[27] Secret diplomatic dispatch from the Sierra Leone High Commission in Lagos to the Ministry of Foreign Affairs in Freetown, 14 November 1990. Copy in author's possession. See also Koroma (note 25).

[28] Bill Berkeley, *The Graves are not yet Full: Race, Tribe and Power in the Heart of Africa*, New York: Basic Books, 2001, p. 48.

and said, "Give me a gun. How can I kill the man who killed my mother?"[29]

The war easily took on an ethnic character, with the Gio and Mano peoples rallying to Taylor's NPFL (even though Taylor himself was a member of the Americo-Liberian elite), and the Krahn and Mandingo peoples rallying to Doe. Ethnic violence and massacres became a commonplace, and by the mid-1990s, the war had killed tens of thousands of Liberians, almost all of them civilians targeted largely because of their ethnicity. By mid-1990 Doe's regime was on the verge of collapse, and the NPFL forces were investing the capital, Monrovia. By this time Taylor's NPFL had split in two, with the breakaway, and better trained, faction led by his former forces commander Prince Yormie Johnson, who called his group the Independent National Patriotic Front of Liberia (INPFL).

Inevitably the war unleashed a massive humanitarian catastrophe. In its first year as many as 700,000 Liberians fled the country, many of them to Ivory Coast, Guinea and Sierra Leone. By August 1990 there were officially 80,000 Liberian refugees in Sierra Leone, who included the country's most politically active leaders, like Doe's Vice President Harry Moniba. The government of Sierra Leone announced that month that it was spending 80 million leones (about $1 million) a month to maintain the refugees and fund peace talks that were being held in Freetown.[30] That same month the Economic Community of West African States (ECOWAS), led by the regional giant Nigeria, hastily put together an intervention force, known as Ecomog (the ECOWAS Monitoring Group), to stem the carnage in Monrovia and re-establish normative order. At the time the remnants of Doe's defeated but heavily equipped Armed Forces of Liberia were trapped in the enclave around the Executive Mansion (the presidential palace), where Doe and his remaining officials were holed up. A sustained and deadly battle for control was going on between these forces and Taylor's forces on the one hand and between Taylor's forces and Johnson's on the other.

Of the 3,455 troops who were dispatched to Monrovia from their rear base in Freetown, under the command of the Ghanaian General Arnold Quainoo, Sierra Leone contributed 300. Significantly, only Guinea of all the French-speaking members of ECOWAS contributed troops to the venture. The main rebel leader, Taylor,

---

[29] Ibid., p. 49.
[30] 'Le. 80 million spent on war', *New Citizen* (Freetown), 11 August 1990.

opposed the intervention and vowed to fight it; but President Momoh defended the action as a disinterested and necessary humanitarian intervention:

We view such an initiative as both timely and appropriate and we hope that all the warring factions in Liberia will see reason and agree with us...Sierra Leone being one of the next door neighbours of Liberia is in a position to appreciate the seriousness of the Liberian situation as we are directly feeling the heat. The massive influx of refugees into our country with its attendant economic and social consequences is just one of the many grave responsibilities we are now called upon to shoulder...it is our duty as leaders to re-affirm to the world and all those involved in the Liberian conflict that the ECOWAS is a genuine effort aimed at bringing peace and happiness to war torn Liberia.[31]

However, many in Sierra Leone were not so enthusiastic about the initiative or convinced of its sincerity. *Vision*, a leading opposition newspaper, seemed to speak for many when it characterised the Ecomog intervention as an attempt to frustrate a popular uprising against a soldier-turned-politician by regimes of which almost all, with the exception of the tiny Gambia, were headed by soldier-politicians. The paper then nominated Taylor 'Man of the Year'.[32]

President Doe was captured on 9 September 1990 by Prince Johnson's faction when he ventured, unannounced, to Ecomog's headquarters in Monrovia, in an area that had been secured by Johnson's INPFL which, unlike Taylor's faction, welcomed the West African peacekeepers. According to Ellis, 'Ecomog's peacekeepers looked on as Johnson's men pushed Doe downstairs, bound him and drove off to Prince Johnson's Caldwell base, a few minutes' drive away... There he was stripped of his five-star general's uniform and shown to a crowd of bystanders.' He was then tortured in the most brutal fashion; his ears were first sliced off, and Doe was then beaten to pulp and finally murdered. The torture and murder were filmed by a Palestinian correspondent of a Middle Eastern news agency who was only too eager to capture the graphic details of the humiliation and end of a President who had been an outspoken supporter of Israel against the Arab world.[33] The event severely undermined the credibility of Ecomog, because there were strong suspicions that the peacekeepers 'sold' Doe to Johnson. Quainoo was promptly recalled and replaced by a Nigerian general, Moses

[31] 'Sierra Leone's position on Liberia', *New Citizen*, 11 August 1990.
[32] *Vision*, 10 January 1990.
[33] Ellis (note 20), p. 9.

Dongonyaro, an effective and highly competent leader. Contrary to initial expectations, Doe's removal did not bring the factions closer to an agreement. In fact it compounded the crisis as the most powerful factional leader, Taylor, felt robbed of the symbolic price of victory—capture of the sitting President—in his view through the machinations of Ecomog, and became even more bellicose and determined to fight to the finish.

On 1 November 1990 Taylor broadcast on the BBC African Service a threat to attack and destroy Freetown's international airport, arguing that by allowing its territory to be used as an operational base for Ecomog Sierra Leone had made itself a legitimate target.[34] President Momoh responded by naively describing Taylor as 'ungrateful'. 'Of all people', he said, 'Charles Taylor should appreciate the problems he has created for us here with his war in Liberia. We are overstretching our resources to care for his people, our social amenities have been over-tasked and even our economy dislodged. A man like that should not think of making such a statement.'[35] An 'army spokesman' then added his, more bellicose, voice to his Commander-in-Chief's desperately uninspiring one: 'Sierra Leone has a trained army, with World War II experience and success. We need not remind Charles Taylor of our performance at the Somalia Drive in Monrovia to make our point.'[36]

In fact, Sierra Leone's performance in Ecomog was hardly laudable. Barely three weeks after the force landed in Monrovia, the new no-nonsense Nigerian commander, General Dongonyaro, asked for the withdrawal of the commander of the Sierra Leonean contingent, Lt.-Col. Modu Hanciles, for cowardice and neglect of duty.[37] Elsewhere in the country, reactions to the threat of war were also less than heroic. In Bo, when two Nigerian F-14 fighters flew low over the city shortly after Taylor's broadcast, 'some personnel of the Special Security Division (SSD), on hearing the sound of the planes, hid their red berets in their pockets for fear of being easily identified by Charles Taylor. Five police constables fled from the barracks to Messima village, about half a mile away.' The confusion was such that a middle-aged man died of a heart attack.[38] Since Tay-

---

[34] Koroma (note 25), p. 140.
[35] 'Taylor ungrateful—Momoh', *New Citizen*, 8 November 1990.
[36] *The New Citizen*, 8 November 1990.
[37] 'Liberian crisis takes its toll: Modu Hanciles sacked', *New Citizen*, 8 December 1990.
[38] 'Plane scare claims a life', *New Citizen*, 24 November 1990.

lor's forces did not possess fighter planes, the incident demonstrated the effectiveness of rebel propaganda.

In early March 1991 Foday Sankoh announced, also via the BBC World Service for Africa, that President Momoh should quit office within ninety days or face an armed rebellion which he himself would lead to oust him. There had been a number of cross-border attacks by the NPFL rebels into Sierra Leone before Sankoh's threats. On 18 December 1990 about 100 NPFL rebels crossed into eastern Sierra Leone and attacked and looted the village of Kissy-Tongay. That same month another Liberian rebel attack was reported in Kailahun district, and again it was loot-related. The RUF war, however, began officially on 23 March 1991 when the rebels, numbering about 100 (and mainly NPFL commandos and Burkinabe mercenaries leading Sierra Leoneans recruited in Liberia), carried out a surprise attack on Bomaru and Sienga, two obscure border towns in Kailahun district. The rebels killed one Sierra Leone army major, one lieutenant and eleven civilians, looted the towns and withdrew into Liberia after troops from the neighbouring Daru Barracks counter-attacked.

Speculation in Freetown that the attacks were an NPFL revenge mission against Sierra Leonean border guards who had cheated them (a brisk business in looted goods was then going on between the soldiers and the Liberian rebels) was cut short soon afterwards as Foday Sankoh, speaking from Taylor's base in Liberia, announced via the BBC that the attacks were the beginning of his 'people's struggle' against Momoh's venal regime, and that his group, the Revolutionary United Front of Sierra Leone (RUF/SL), was spearheading that 'struggle'.

It took nineteen instead of ninety days between Sankoh's first broadcast and the attacks. Still, some observers, like Chris Squire,[39] have seen some significance in the timing of the attacks: 23 March 1991, as we have seen, was exactly twenty years after the failed coup attempt for which Sankoh was gaoled and then expelled from the army. This is a tantalising observation—revolutionaries are nothing if not also romantic—but in the case of the RUF war this was almost certainly a tidy coincidence. When he was pointedly asked by a fawning reporter from a pro-RUF publication about this timing and its coinciding with the twentieth anniversary of his first imprisonment, Sankoh (referring to his period of imprisonment in Freetown in 1998) gave a somewhat confusing answer: 'I am a man of

---

[39] Chris Squire, *Agony in Sierra Leone,* Freetown, 1997.

God. God chose me to lead the revolution that will save Sierra Leone…The number 23 has always been a sign to me. On 23rd October 1998 I was sentenced to death. On 23rd December 1998 I was moved from my prison cell…'[40] Confusing perhaps; but clearly Sankoh did not seem to think the timing of the 23 March 1991 attacks specially significant: they were significant only because Momoh's government decided to take them as the official beginning of hostilities with the forces from Liberia, and almost certainly because also, unlike the previous incursions, they led to the death of an army major and a number of other soldiers.

After the attacks Momoh summoned an emergency cabinet meeting and issued a statement completely ignoring Sankoh and blaming the attacks on Charles Taylor.[41] A few days later the rebels struck at other towns in the Kailahun district. On 27 March Buedu was attacked again and occupied by a rebel force of 300 heavily armed fighters; two days later the main commercial centre in the district, Koindu, was attacked and extensively looted by the rebels. That same week, however, Sierra Leone government troops counter-attacked, recaptured the town and killed sixteen rebel soldiers. Three rebel commanders were captured, all of them Liberians: Fallah Stallon Koluba, Harrison George and Max Noah Wossandon. The three men were shown at a press conference in Freetown by the Sierra Leonean military authorities to demonstrate that the attacks on Sierra Leone were the work of Charles Taylor, not of any Sierra Leonean rebel group. However, rebel counter-attacks led to the recapture of the town shortly afterwards, and almost the whole of Kailahun district fell to the rebels in less than a month of fighting. The rebels quickly opened another front in the Pujehun district in the south of the country. The 3,000-man Sierra Leone army faced a challenge well beyond the capacity of its already severely limited resources.

A video clip captured by government forces much later illuminates the nature of the RUF 'rebellion' at the very early stages of the war. It shows a bearded middle-aged Sankoh, in combat fatigues and carrying a rifle, surrounded by dozens of mainly ragtag teenage fighters in the town of Koidu. Sankoh and his men had just captured the town, and there are visible signs of destruction and looting, walls riddled with bullet holes, houses burnt down, a crowd of mystified civilians looking hopeless and terrified. Constantly at the

---

[40] 'Foday Sankoh breaks his silence', *The Ninja*, 22 April 1999.
[41] *New Citizen*, 10 April 1991.

side of Sankoh is Sam Bockarie, thin and mean-looking, pointing his rifle menacingly at the crowd who have been gathered in front of a derelict courtyard (so it appears) to be addressed by the new master of the place, Foday Sankoh. Sankoh's tone is hectoring and threatening. He is in town to liberate 'you people,' he says, and this is a fight everyone has been asking for. The APC is rotten and oppressive, and it is time to oust them and institute 'people's power'. Everyone must be a part of this effort. Someone in the crowd asks to speak. She is a demure-looking woman who seems to summon up all her courage. We welcome every chance to improve our lot, she says. We are quiet hardworking citizens, but in the past few days there have been incidents of strange people attacking homes and looting them, there have been some killings. 'We don't know who is doing these things,' she appeals, 'and will there be protection for us now?' Sankoh eyes the woman coldly, and says curtly that everything will be all right now that he is in town. Then his teenage fighters, most of them speaking with distinctly Liberian accents, burst into a song with the refrain 'Anyone who does not support Sankoh will be killed like a dog'. This was the end of one instance of Sankoh's effort at canvassing political support or mobilising his fellow citizens to participate in the 'struggle': it was the performance of the conqueror. The video clip was being sold, in 2001, by vendors in Freetown as a kind of tourist curiosity, and is called, inventively 'The History of the RUF'.

No one knows what happened to the brave woman who raised those misgivings, but we have the testimony of a former RUF fighter from which to infer her fate. According to his own testimony, Mohamed Keita was forcefully conscripted into the RUF as a very young man after the rebels, led by Sam Bockarie, tied his father and mother up and had them shot in his presence as 'an example of what would happen to any of us who attempt to escape'. He was then 'stripped naked together with other young men captured from the surrounding villages' and made to carry looted goods on their heads to the rebel base several miles away in the Kailahun district. At the base a 'parade' of the captives was organised by Bockarie, and Sankoh appeared to talk to them:

He said he was fighting against the APC because the APC had destroyed the country. He said education facilities were poor and so was health. He added that we had a lot of minerals which were being exploited and sold without any benefit to the country. He urged us to join him to purge the system. At the parade one of the captives pointed [to Sankoh and said] that he was quite willing to join him but he could not understand why his men

62   *A Dirty War in West Africa*

were killing (and) maiming innocent civilians and looting their property. [Sankoh] asked the young man to come up. He ordered that the young man be shot. He was shot. After that no one in the parade uttered a word again...[42]

Keita, who had surrendered to Nigerian troops in 1997, was then living at the New England Prison Camp, and he was giving this testimony in the presence of Sankoh at the trial of the RUF leader for treason in 1998. Sankoh, who represented himself at the trial, called Keita 'Brother Keita', asked him a few questions relating to other statements he had made, but never challenged this testimony.

All the ex-RUF fighters who testified at the trial described how they were abducted and then inducted into the rebel forces through violence and utter fear and a sense of helplessness. Some who were abducted earlier told of how the RUF was dominated in 1991 by Liberians. Among these were Martin Moinina, who was forced into the rebel movement in 1991 after the rebels destroyed his village and captured him, and who later became a personal bodyguard of Sankoh (and radio operator) until Sankoh's arrest in Nigeria in 1997, and Timothy Serry, who also became a RUF member in 1991. They also spoke of the great awe in which Sankoh was held by all the fighters. 'From my personal knowledge,' Serry said, 'it is not possible for anybody to disobey his command. He is endowed with a commanding voice and he is held in awe by us all.' These recruits, as we have noted, were extremely young, many of them teenagers and even pre-teenagers, and the elderly Sankoh was an unmistakable father-figure to them; this was made more compelling by the traumatic nature of their conscription into the RUF. They called Sankoh 'Papay', a Liberian expression for 'father' or 'Papa'.[43]

---

[42] *In the Court of Appeal for Sierra Leone—Documents relating to the trial of Corporal Foday Sankoh, 23rd of October 1998*, Freetown.

[43] I am aware of the argument, most convincingly made by Paul Richards, that the RUF attracted a significant number of 'willing recruits' among the 'borderline' youths of far-eastern Sierra Leone—people already living effectively beyond the withered Sierra Leonean state, and mainly in the illicit diamond fields—and that these were recruits among whom could be 'detected significant signs of voluntary adhesion'. I will address this point in due course, but it is safe to say at this point that although this is largely true, one must be careful not to misunderstand the context of their 'willingness', and not to exaggerate their role in the RUF. See Paul Richards, *Fighting for the Rainforest: War, Youth and Resources in Sierra Leone*, London: International African Institute in association with James Currey (Oxford) and Heinemann (Portsmouth, NH), 1996.

The testimonies and court documents also revealed the extent to which Libyan support for the RUF, knowledge of which had always been based on anecdotal evidence, was so crucial. The trial focused mainly on Sankoh's activities in 1996–7, so the prosecutors did not bother to marshal evidence of Libyan support, which was assumed to be a given anyway, before that period. But two letters that Sankoh wrote to Mohamed Talibi of the Libyan People's Bureau in Accra revealed that his forces had received a constant flow of cash from the Libyans for the purchase of arms and other forms of logistical support. In one letter, dated 26 June 1996, Sankoh thanked Talibi and 'the other brothers back home [i.e. in Libya] again very much for the half million United States dollars which I received through you for the purchase of needed material [*sic*] to pursue the military mission.' The letter requested another 'one and a half million United States dollars ($1,500,000) in order to purchase twice the listed materials for effective and smooth operation.' Another letter dated 4 December 1996—i.e. after the first peace accord had been signed between the Sierra Leone government and the RUF at Abidjan in Ivory Coast, and when the accord was officially still in place—thanked Talibi for sending Sankoh $29,000, and requested Talibi and 'your brothers to urgently provide...USD 700,000' in order for more arms to be purchased. Sankoh stated that he signed the accord for tactical reasons, in his words 'just so as to relieve our movement of the enormous pressure from the international community while I will use this opportunity to transact my business in getting our fighting materials freely and easily'. At the time the RUF had lost the important diamond mining district of Kono but was still holding on to other, but less significant, such areas in the east and south of the country. Hence Sankoh could report to Talibi that he had 'last week' been able to 'organize mining operations in precious minerals which I believe will help us generate the needed foreign exchange for our mission'.

One would like to note, at this point, the dangerous nature of Sankoh's duplicity, but that would not be necessary. For the moment, the pertinent observation is this: it could be reasonably inferred from these letters that Libyan financial support for the RUF, which flowed directly from its support for the NPFL, was a very important factor in the making of the RUF, and especially in the early stages of the war.[44]

---

[44] President Kabbah told this writer that when he confronted Gaddafi with this allegation, the Libyan leader readily accepted that he had provided

The RUF seemed to have had little trouble at first in defeating Momoh's dispirited troops sent to combat them, but it is not clear whether there was any serious military engagement between the two forces. The RUF mainly targeted civilian settlements. Often they used model guns to scare peasants away, loot their villages and then move on to other targets. Government forces would then arrive, plunder what the RUF couldn't take away (as a highly mobile bush guerrilla force, the RUF necessarily avoided stealing heavy household goods and other equipment) and then cart them to cities like Bo and Kenema where they were sold in the open market. Observers began to suspect, as early as the late 1991, a form of informal collaboration between the two apparently opposing forces, and among people in eastern Sierra Leone the war became known as '*humagoi*' (a Mende word meaning theft as warfare).

Towards the end of 1991, however, with troops from Guinea (which had a defence pact with Sierra Leone) arriving to boost the government's defence, the Sierra Leone army went on the offensive. A small contingent of Nigerian troops was also deployed in parts of the country as part of the Ecomog arrangement, but they took a defensive posture, more or less avoiding combat with the rebels. Momoh also expanded the army to about 6,000 by recruiting, as it turned out, mostly vagrants in Freetown, 'rural...unemployed, a fair number of hooligans, drug addicts and thieves'.[45] These underwent a crash training programme that produced little more than a uniformed rabble which acted and looked much like the ragtag rebels they were sent to fight. Maada Bio, an army lieutenant fighting on the eastern front at the time, recalled that indiscipline and cowardice were such a problem with these new recruits that in many cases battlefront commanders would discover that half of the men assigned to their units were not available at crucial moments.[46] But they were not the only problem. Most of the officers themselves were recruited and promoted in the force by a patronage system designed by the APC to make sure that party loyalists or their relatives dominated the army. Their incompetence

---

money and other forms of logistical support for Taylor and the RUF, and that he did so because both Samuel Doe and Joseph Momoh were 'fascist leaders'. He claimed to have cut down the support since the election of Kabbah as President (interview in Freetown, April 2002). The evidence suggests that in fact this support continued throughout the war.

[45] Koroma (note 25), p. 144.

[46] Telephone interview, January 2002.

and lack of professionalism were glaringly obvious at a very early stage in the war. In June Momoh dismissed five officers—Colonel L.M.S. Durey, Major Demby, Major S.O. Wellington, Captain Banya and Captain Tengbe—for 'activities incompatible with their military status.' These officers were alleged to have given up strategic positions to the rebels without a fight, and in circumstances that suggested they were 'giving aid to the enemy'.[47] Fortunately for the country, these ineffective forces came to be boosted by a new element that was to change the dynamics of the fighting in Sierra Leone and Liberia significantly: Ulimo.

The United Liberation Movement of Liberia, Ulimo, was forged in Sierra Leone out of the remnants of Doe's disintegrated army, as well as Krahn and Mandingo refugees from Liberia. They were trained and armed in Kenema, in eastern Sierra Leone, under the command of General Karpeh, a Doe loyalist, with political control exerted by Alhaji Kromah, a Mandingo and former Doe official, and Roosevelt Johnson, also a former Doe official. They were extremely brave and highly motivated fighters, determined both to seek revenge on Taylor's ethnocidal forces and to return to their homes in Liberia. This force launched an offensive against the RUF in the Pujehun district and succeeded in pushing it back into Liberia within two months. I visited Pujehun town in October 1991 shortly after its capture from the RUF. The town was almost entirely derelict, and the few residents remaining there appeared in a brooding, shocked state. Many houses had been destroyed in the fighting and in gratuitous acts of violence by the RUF. I was told that radio and record players were banned during the RUF occupation, and that nearly half a dozen people were publicly executed when caught, often under their beds, listening to the radio. The RUF was determined that no news from the outside world got to local residents, but only what it told them itself. The Front's propaganda was blatant. At one point, an old man who survived the occupation told me, its representatives summoned all the residents to the town centre and announced that Bo had fallen to them, and that in a few weeks' time, they would capture Freetown. Boys and girls at St Paul's secondary school were conscripted into the force en masse, with many made to commit atrocities against family members and neighbours as part of the 'initiation' process.

Many signs of the brutality of the Ulimo fighters were visible. On the road leading to the town, I saw freshly severed human heads

[47] 'Taylor's war in Sierra Leone,' *New African* no. 286, July 1991.

impaled on wooden posts, apparently as a warning to would-be mis-
chief makers. This was a familiar RUF tactic, but clearly the heads
were too fresh to have been severed by the RUF, who had been
driven from the town a week or so before. Indeed a Ulimo soldier I
spoke to later told me that the heads were those of 'captured
rebels'. But thinking of the freshly severed heads, some of the faces
calm, seemingly meditative, and some with lines suggesting a life of
peasant hardship, I could only recall the reaction of Joseph Conrad's Marlow (in *Heart of Darkness*), on being told that the human
heads displayed before Mr Kurtz's house were those of 'rebels': 'Rebels! What would be the next definition I was to hear? There had
been enemies, criminals, workers—and these were rebels. Those
rebellious heads looked very subdued to me on their sticks.' Stories
of family or local political feuds compounding the RUF carnage
were also heard. Such age-old disputes were brutally settled as
aggrieved but once powerless parties quickly joined the rebels and
denounced their enemies as APC sympathisers—the result in many
cases being summary execution.

Pujehun, a small craggy town in the fertile rainforest province
bordering Liberia, had a long history of defiance towards the APC
regime, and there can be little doubt that the RUF was quickly able
to tap the deep-seated hatred for Momoh's decrepit regime to win
some willing recruits. Quite a few number of people were linked to
the Ndorgborwusui crisis of 1982—a local armed uprising that
erupted after a senior APC politician rigged elections in the district
and threatened to punish the people of Sorogbema, who cried foul
at the electoral fraud—may have joined the RUF enthusiastically,
beguiled by the rebels' anti-APC rhetoric. One such figure, and one
who was to become notorious in the RUF, was Momoh Konneh. He
was said to have enthusiastically joined the RUF when the rebels
entered Sorogbema, and then gone about attacking 'all those he
believed were against his Ndorgborwusui group'.[48] The notoriety of
Konneh in the Pujehun area led many people to conclude,
wrongly, that the rebel activities were a continuation of the earlier
Ndorgborwusui campaigns.[49]

[48] 'Pujehun: Who is Momoh Konneh?', *Vision*, 4 February 1992.
[49] This view was even expressed by the Chief of Staff of the Sierra Leone
    Army, Brigadier Jusu Gottor, who pointedly declared in 1993 that the
    rebel warfare in Pujehun district was solely an Ndorgborwusui affair. For
    this he was rightly berated by the editor of *Vision* newspaper and a native
    of Pujehun district, Siaka Massaquoi, for making a 'cynical statement...a

Unconcerned with any consideration other than to take the war to Taylor's doorstep, Ulimo moved on and entered Liberia in late 1991/early 1992, opening a new front in the almost stalemated Liberian conflict. On the eastern front in Sierra Leone, Guinean and Sierra Leonean troops fought the rebels to a stalemate. Both sides were under-equipped and poorly trained, or were not motivated enough for decisive battle. Outright military victory did not appear even to have been an option. We have an interesting, if bizarre, account of one of the more memorable battles fought during the period, in eastern Sierra Leone:

On May 1 [1991]…we had to confront the rebels at the Mano bridge. They attacked Daru town, they recaptured Daru town and they were attempting to recapture the barracks. They wanted to cross the Mano bridge; and our defences were on the other side of the bridge. Mortar shells flew all over the place…. We saw the rebels themselves take position on the other side of the bridge… We told our boys to put their heads down. We got down, we thought that probably if he fires it would just come and go over our defence. Well, we miscalculated. The fellow was a good shot…and he aimed at the centre. It came right into our midst. I was blasted with fragments which opened up my legs.[50]

This account was provided by Captain Valentine Strasser, a soldier who went on to make a coup, and it describes how he got slightly disabled in the leg during a major battle with the RUF. On a closer look, however, the description reveals something far less inspiring and more prosaic: Strasser's unit seems to have been decimated by just one rebel with an RPG. Such was the nature of the stalemated war.

This stalemate, in remote eastern Sierra Leone, was enough to shift national attention from the war to politics. A referendum was conducted on the one-party state, and when over 90 per cent voted to scrap it Momoh signed into law a new multiparty constitution, recommendations for which had been made by a commission he had earlier appointed, headed by Peter Tucker. In the atmosphere of bitter campaigning that followed the launching of new political parties, there were even claims that the war was a phony business

---

terrible example of what psychologists describe as blaming the victim… This rebel war is Charles Taylor's and Foday Sankoh's war, and both of them are not natives of Pujehun district.' See *Vision*, 3–10 June 1993.

[50] Hilton Fyle, '"We need urgent help": Interview with Captain Valentine Strasser', *West Africa*, 15–21 June 1992.

contrived by the APC to ensure that nationwide elections planned for June 1992 would be indefinitely suspended. One opposition party newspaper even published a sensational story reporting a 'meeting' at which the plot was hatched by the APC.[51] More level-headed people thought this was going too far. The editors of the *New Citizen*, a pro-APC but remarkably fair and serious-minded newspaper, warned against allowing 'the euphoria of multiparty politics to blind [our] eyes to a possible catastrophe' and called for 'all other activities to be shelved so as to allow government to put in all its resources to bring this horrible war to a close.'[52] It was an echo of an earlier admonition by another paper with a very serious editorial commitment, the *Vision*. The editors had warned about the 'danger in not heeding the warning [that politics might complicate the war] because if we don't…we might well get the rude and brutal shock just when we are in the middle of the fun. Guerrillas are an unpredictable element.'[53]

When the 'fun' was interrupted it was not the guerrillas who were the spoilers; it was the nation's own army. Momoh claimed he was spending 250 million leones monthly on the army in the form of pay, rations and other support, but much of this, it turned out, was not getting to the frontline troops. Apparently, funds were being embezzled by the senior officers.[54] By April 1991 frontline troops had gone for three months without pay. One group of soldiers led by twenty-six-year-old Lieutenant Solomon Musa abandoned their positions at the eastern front and descended on the capital on 29 April 1992. They were heavily armed and quickly took State House, the head of state's official residence in Freetown. By midday the mutiny had escalated into a coup and Momoh fled to neighbouring Guinea. The soldiers announced that they had formed a junta, the National Provisional Ruling Council (NPRC), to replace Momoh's APC regime. The country's leader, whose heavily abbreviated and lugubrious voice announced the coup, was now a twenty-seven-year-old former paymaster named Captain Valentine Strasser, chosen by the group of lieutenants who staged the coup because of his higher

---

[51] 'APC secret meeting to prolong rebel war', *New Breed*, 19 December 1991. The paper was forced to apologise later when it was established that a number of the people it named as having attended the 'meeting' were not even in the country at the time.

[52] Editorial, *New Citizen*, 9 December 1991.

[53] 'Politics and war', *Vision*, 17–24 1991.

[54] Koroma (note 25), p. 149.

rank and conciliatory personality.[55] Strasser announced the junta's aim to be a quick end to the war, rehabilitation of the battered country, and a return to civil rule. In fact, his regime would see the war escalate beyond everyone's comprehension, and the RUF grow from a marginal band of bush guerrillas dismissed by almost everybody as common bandits into a very destructive and indeed decisive force in the country.

---

[55] Interview with Brigadier Maada Bio, one of the coup makers and a lieutenant in the Sierra Leone army at the time, Washington, DC, December 2001.

4

WAR AND STATE COLLAPSE

'…but already the walls are closing around me the rain has stopped
and once again I am alone waiting for them, the politicians of my
country to come for me to silence my right to shouting poetry loud in
the parks, but who can shut up the rage the melodrama of being
Sierra Leone? The farce of seeing their pictures daily in the papers
The knowledge of how though blindfolded and muzzled
Something is growing, bloating, voluptuous and not Despairing…'
(Syl Cheney-Coker[1])

'A soldier (in power) without political education is a criminal with a
gun.' (Thomas Sankara)

Captain Valentine Esegrabo Melvin Strasser grew up in the east-end
slums of Freetown. He joined the army as a cadet officer under the
patronage system which had been devised by the APC to keep the
army compliant. His patron was Thaimu Bangura, a former APC
minister. Strasser, however, like many young men from a poor background who joined the army as the most attractive paid employment option, detested the APC and its closed, elitist and corrupt
leadership. Shortly after becoming head of the NPRC junta, Strasser
let slip to a foreign correspondent that he joined the army, at the
age of twenty-one, primarily to overthrow the APC.[2] The new master of Sierra Leone and many of his colleagues were dashing and
brash, and for a time their presence in the capital was a much-
needed antidote to the ageing and effete APC leadership that was
such a blight on the country's landscape. Almost immediately after

[1] Syl Cheney-Coker, 'Letter to a Tormented Playwright' in Adewale Maja-
Pearce (ed.), *The Heineman Book of African Poetry in English*, London: Heinemann, 1990, p. 60.
[2] Ann Busby, 'The quiet coup of Captain Valentine', *Observer*, 9 August
1992.

the coup, the long queues for petrol and rice, the country's staple—both routinely hoarded by business cronies of the APC to create artificial scarcity and thereby price increases—disappeared. The NPRC was instantly popular. Strasser quickly became an almost cult figure, and was described by the press as a 'redeemer' and his junta as the 'Glorious Revolution'.[3] In fact the long-suffering Sierra Leonean state, hopelessly weakened by the corrupt and inept APC, would now be thoroughly downgraded and finally battered beyond recognition.

Part of the NPRC's popularity had to do with the credible promise the junta leaders offered to end the increasingly destructive and demoralising war. By the time the NPRC took over State House in April 1992, the war had been raging for just over one year and the destruction was already immense. Whole towns in the Southern and Eastern Provinces had been razed to the ground, and the number of refugees fleeing from Sierra Leone to Guinea alone had reached 120,000. As the war-affected areas were the most productive in agriculture (the Eastern Province is traditionally Sierra Leone's breadbasket), the food situation in much of the country was becoming desperate. The brutalities associated with the war—hacking off hands and limbs, rape, all forms of torture, and the destruction of schools and the violent recruitment of schoolchildren into the rebel fighting force, all frequently reported in the country's lively tabloids—were causing deep demoralisation in the nation's population. The war had seemingly settled into a self-destructive stalemate out of which no breakthrough was possible.

About four months before the coup the respected editor of the *New Citizen* newspaper, Ibrahim Ben Kargbo, wrote a 'commentary' in his paper focusing on the tragedy of a nation being torn apart by 'the machinations of the heartless armed bandits from a foreign country'. His language was dark. He spoke about a nation being bled to death, of whole families being torn apart, of gruesome savagery, barbarism and terror. But actually Kargbo was not writing about the war as such. He used it merely to make a point. The editor was bemoaning the crucial absence of 'that extra something [in the Sierra Leonean] which makes the man decide to fight and die for his fatherland'. Kargbo wrote:

One could easily conclude that if some of our people were motivated and convinced enough that Sierra-Leone is worth fighting for, the rebels would

---

[3] Siaka Massaquoi, *The Glorious Revolution*, Freetown: Vision Publications, 1992.

not have penetrated the heartland of our country with the rapidity with which they did. In some areas, whole villages were occupied by a mere handful of rebels for no other purpose than the fact that nobody was prepared to fight back.[4]

It was all rhetoric, of course, but it aptly captured the mood of a nation battered and traumatised, feeling helpless and impotent under a hopelessly uninspiring leadership. The problem was made more intolerable by the fact that many Sierra Leoneans were contemptuous of the rebels, whom they regarded as mercenary bands of ruffians who should be hunted down and exterminated as a threat to the very notion of society. The fact that this was not happening quickly enough was itself a source of demoralisation. The soldiers, young but astute, made an easily understandable and even inspired appeal.

The first post-coup broadcast by Strasser spoke about 'the patriotic officers and men of the Sierra Leone Armed Forces' coming together to rid the nation of 'an oppressive, corrupt, exploitative and tribalistic bunch of crooks and traitors under the umbrella of the APC government'. In halting but striking sentences, Strasser declared that the Momoh administration had 'failed the nation woefully' because of the 'permanent poverty' it had inflicted on Sierra Leoneans and its inability to rid the country of the marauding rebels.[5]

As justifications for coups go, this one was beyond dispute. However, in a more reflective mood Strasser revealed that his motivation was much more self-serving; he accused Momoh of neglecting him and his men at the front and thus helping to prolong the war. He spoke about Momoh's failure 'to give us the necessary support,' saying that 'there was no communications (*sic*), we were forced to use 1962 mortars, almost all of the missiles couldn't fire.' Speaking about his own painful experiences after he was wounded at the front, he continued:

We thought that it was unfair for our soldiers to be out there at the front and when he [*sic*] is wounded or becomes a casualty, he cannot receive the kind of treatment he deserves. And so I said to myself, this cannot be allowed to go on, besides, when we look around we see those who are responsible for the situation live big, riding flashy cars, going around on

---

[4] 'Sierra Leone should come first', *New Citizen* (Freetown), 16 December 1991.
[5] *West Africa*, 11–17 May 1992.

spending sprees, expensive travels abroad and allowing us to live like second class citizens. We felt very terrible about this.[6]

There was an element of self-mythologising about this understandable if quite pedestrian complaint. For Strasser did not plan the coup; in spite of his views about the Momoh regime and his own ambitions, he was literally co-opted into it. But this pithy rhetoric helps to explain why he was favoured by his colleagues to lead a junta he played little role in creating.

The poor logistical capability of Sierra Leone's army had become common knowledge long before the NPRC seized power. A foreign newspaper correspondent who stopped by briefly in Freetown in January 1992 reported that because the army lacked even rudimentary communications equipment, orders and messages were exchanged between frontline commanders by the use of runners 'as they did during Trojan War'.[7] But from his new base in Guinea, Momoh indignantly challenged Strasser's charges:

...my government made available to the Army the huge sum of 250 million leones each month for rations, medicaments, petroleum products and spare parts for the prosecution of the war. Further, because of their unceasing demands for ammunition [*sic*], my government spent large sums of money, in foreign exchange, to purchase ammunition for the Army. Sadly, it has now turned out that instead of using this ammunition for the purpose for which it was intended, it was being stockpiled by these officers to be used for the illegal purpose of seizing power.[8]

No doubt most of the supplies sent to the front were routinely embezzled by senior military officers, and Momoh—mired in politics and fighting desperately to keep his party together in the face of massive defections following the lifting of the ban on political activities—was not sufficiently attentive to take action. But the force of about 100 mutinous soldiers which took Freetown on 29 April displaying rocket launchers, heavy machine guns and even anti-aircraft guns could hardly be described as ill-equipped. Whatever concern the young soldiers had for the plight of their country under the lacklustre leadership of Momoh, self-interest seems to have been a large motivation indeed.

The coup was marked by widespread looting of homes of politicians and businessmen, and the NPRC later claimed that they were

[6] 'We need urgent help', *West Africa*, 15–21 June 1992.
[7] See 'Wake up and it's still there', *The New Shaft* (Freetown), 29 January 1992.
[8] 'Momoh answers Strasser', *West Africa*, 29 June–5 July 1992.

able to retrieve Le41 billion in local and foreign currencies hidden
in the homes of ex-ministers and senior APC functionaries. In the
home of one minister the NPRC claimed to have discovered over
$1 million and several hundreds of millions of leones in suitcases,[9]
and in spite of assurances from the junta's spokesman, Lieutenant Karefa Kargbo, these sums were never accounted for to the
public. Instead Sierra Leoneans were treated to flamboyant dis-
plays of wealth by members of the junta in the form of newly
imported four-wheel-drive vehicles, Mercedes Benz cars and other
marks of a lavish lifestyle. One NPRC officer was reported to have
incurred bills at a local hotel amounting to 786,000 leones (equivalent to more than $10,000 at the time) in a week soon after
the coup.[10] Newspapers reporting such excesses had their editors
harassed. It was evident that the 'revolution' was straying far from
its conception.

    Still, the coup seemed to offer prospects for an end to the war. In
the first week of the coup at least two RUF spokesmen broadcast
messages through the BBC announcing a ceasefire and readiness
to work with the junta in the interests of peace and reconstruction.
A ceasefire at the front reportedly held for well over a week after
the coup. But the NPRC appeared to have little regard for the rebels who were dismissed by Strasser as 'bandits sent by Charles Taylor' to wreak havoc on the country.[11] Many of the leading NPRC
figures, including its powerful Secretary General John Benjamin,
hailed from the southern and eastern parts of the country, areas
that had suffered heavily at the hands of the rebels, and revenge
may have been the motive behind this hardline stance. The NPRC
also seems to have believed that the rebels, confined to small swathes
of territories in the Kailahun district, could be hunted down and
crushed if the fighting forces were given adequate support. This
they set about doing by importing sophisticated weaponry and
communications equipment from Belgium and Romania, largely
in exchange for diamonds.[12] In response to the RUF's call for dialogue Strasser offered an amnesty in return for unconditional surrender, a virtual non-starter since the rebels considered the NPRC
coup a by-product of their 'struggle' and therefore argued that
their participation in the junta was imperative. As Richards noted,

[9] *Africa Analysis*, 29 May 1992.
[10] *For Di People*, 27 November 1992.
[11] Massaquoi (note 3), p. 4.
[12] 'Revolution in Crisis', *West Africa*, 7 December 1992.

the RUF seemed to have totally underestimated the impact of its 'unopposed mercenary terror on civilian attitudes in the war zone' and indeed in the country as a whole.[13]

The NPRC coup was widely popular with the country's youth. Most of the coup leaders themselves grew up in Freetown's slums, a fact which helped them to understand early enough the value of youth mobilisation and anti-corruption campaigns against the country's elites, the so-called 'system men'. A highly successful clean-up campaign organised every Saturday in Freetown and other cities and towns across the country was the beginning of this process of youth mobilisation. It later crystallised into a creative youth movement for the 'beautification' of the capital and other cities by the painting of colourful murals, mainly showing the NPRC leaders and other symbols of 'youth power', and regular volunteer work in cleaning and repairing some public spaces. An American anthropologist and longtime Sierra Leone observer, Joseph Opala, who spent years in the country and was active in its politics, has called this creative moment 'Ecstatic Renovation', borrowing the title of one of such street paintings.[14]

What was hardly commented on at the time was that without any political doctrine, and armed with enthusiasm and resentment only, the NPRC would squander this immense goodwill. The regime seemed more interested in appearances than the substantive work of political and social mobilisation. Soon the 'beautification' campaign began to go badly wrong. An NPRC minister severely beat up a clergyman in Bo and insulted an archbishop because the unfortunate churchmen did not show enough enthusiasm for the mass cleaning campaign. The NPRC officer then told Bishop Keilli, 'Go tell your God that I did it.'[15] In another, far more gruesome incident the NPRC picked up dozens of mentally handicapped mendicants from the streets of Freetown—no doubt to make the city of a largely impoverished people look more trim—and had them detained in a tight, faraway prison at Mafanta in the north of the country. All of them died in the gaol. Confinement of mad peo-

---

[13] Paul Richards, *Fighting for the Rainforest: War, Youth and Resources in Sierra Leone*, London: International African Institute/James Currey (Oxford) and Heinemann (Portsmouth, NH), 1996, p. 12.

[14] Joseph Opala, '"Ecstatic Renovation": Street Art Celebrating Sierra Leone's 1992 Revolution', *African Affairs*, vol. 93 no. 371, April 1994, pp. 195–218.

[15] Interview with the late Bishop Keilli and eyewitnesses, Bo, 1993.

ple as an act of ritual cleansing is something that has always been part of the cruelties and terrors of societies in transition, as Foucault has shown in *Madness and Civilization*.[16] But unlike the societies and regimes that Foucault studied, the NPRC was not even systematic about it: after random acts of terror the regime turned its attention to other 'pressing national issues'. Dostoevsky's pithy comment, in his *Diary of a Writer*, seems particularly pertinent in this regard: 'It is not by confining one's neighbour that one is convinced of one's own sanity.'[17]

Vigilante justice was also common. NPRC soldiers in Bo forced a man caught stealing a hen to eat it raw, with the feathers. The man died a few days later. This all happened in the first year of the 'revolution'. At the war front the NPRC's desperate machismo took on more creative forms. There was the mass mobilisation of 'Youth Volunteers' or 'irregulars' in the war-affected areas. These unemployed young people received a week or two of training before being asked to fight the rebels. The hope was that knowledge of the local terrain and strong motivation to liberate their villages and seek revenge would compensate for lack of training.

The tactic of using such volunteers to fight the rebels predated the NPRC. Many of the Liberian irregulars who formed themselves into the factional army, Ulimo, including particularly their feared teenage commandos, were volunteers motivated by a desire for revenge against the NPFL which had killed their relatives and destroyed their homes. The exploits of one such thirteen-year-old commando, simply called Junior, its became legendary in Sierra Leone. An indigenous Sierra Leonean experiment was begun shortly after the war reached a stalemate in the Eastern Province in 1991 when a young officer, Captain Prince Benjamin-Hirsch, recruited most of the unemployed young men and diamond miners in the area around Segbwema into a strong force known as the 'Airborne Division'. In this way he was able to deny the RUF its potential support from the youth of the diamond fields, alienated from the state and virtually in permanent rebellion against it. The area remained relatively free of rebel attacks until Benjamin-Hirsch himself was murdered by his own enemies in the army in October

---

[16] Michel Foucault, *Madness and Civilization: a History of Insanity in the Age of Reason*, New York: Vintage Books, 1965.

[17] The NPRC head, Valentine Strasser, suffered a mental disorder not long after he was overthrown by his own deputy. In 2002 he was leading a secluded, almost confined, life in Freetown.

1991. He is believed to have been a principal source of inspiration for the NPRC coup makers.[18]

The NPRC's new youth volunteer force contained many children, who were orphaned when the RUF rebels murdered their parents. By early 1993, over 1,000 boys under fifteen years of age, some as young as seven, were reported to have been enlisted in the force[19], and only after persistent protest from human rights monitoring groups like the London-based Amnesty International did the NPRC announce in June 1993 that these children were to be demobilised. The decision took over a year to implement.

But the fighting that broke out not long after the NPRC takeover saw major reverses for the junta. In June 1992 the RUF captured Gandorhun, a diamond mining town from where forays could be made against Koidu, the regional centre and Sierra Leone's main diamond centre, a city with an estimated population of 200,000. Soldiers in Koidu appear to have been busy mining diamonds when the rebels struck there in October 1992. The attack seemed to have been well-planned. Some of the rebels had infiltrated the town to reconnoitre and take strategic positions at least a month earlier. Survivors reported seeing their former workmates, friends and seemingly innocent residents firing AK-48 rifles and directing rebel movements in the town on the fateful day of the attack. Panic broke out as a result in the heavily populated town, with the soldiers stationed there taking the lead in running away.

It became a humanitarian crisis of massive proportions. The mass exodus of people, young and old, jammed the main exit road from the town to safer areas like Makeni, in the Northern Province. Exhausted mothers abandoned their babies along the way. Hardly any fled with possessions of any value, and when the great movement of people was over, hundreds lay dead. The town came under the control of the RUF.[20]

The capture of the principal town in Sierra Leone's premier mining district was seen as a national tragedy and it helped to make every home in the country aware of the reality of the national carnage. Kono district accounted for over 60 per cent of the country's export earnings. Henceforth the war ceased to be seen as a purely

---

[18] Richards (note 13), p. 9.

[19] Amnesty International, *Sierra Leone: Prisoners of War? Children Detained in Barracks and Prison*, London, August 1993, p. 12.

[20] For details of the Koidu attack, see Abdul Karim Koroma, *Sierra Leone: The Agony of a Nation*, Freetown: Afromedia Publications, 1996, pp. 180–2.

'south-eastern affair'. The image of the NPRC as 'gallant soldiers' was badly seared too. Freetown's vocal press speculated that these setbacks came about because most of the 'gallant soldiers' were now away from the front, having taken positions in government, and therefore the morale of the army was affected.[21] As a result most of the NPRC officers announced that they were now leading the troops at the front in an operation they code-named 'Genesis'. A detachment of troops led by the Deputy Defence Minister, Komba Mondeh, recaptured Gandorhun before the end of October. Koidu town itself was retaken after a fierce battle in which many civilians were killed.

The soldiers then began punitive actions against prominent Kono residents who were held to have collaborated with the rebels. The paramount Chief, S.G. Fania, and other officials were arrested and detained at Pademba Road prison. Another Paramount Chief, Songo-Mbriwa, died after he was severely tortured. Most of these chiefs were former key supporters of the APC, and probably they were specifically targeted by the vengeful NPRC because of this. Equally plausible is the possibility that the chiefs cooperated with the RUF to wipe out the NPRC soldiers who, before the attack, were frenetically engaged in lawless mining, including mining plots belonging to the chiefs, whose main source of income and patrimony was from diamond mining.[22]

Abdul Karim Koroma, a former APC Foreign Minister, has criticised the NPRC for what he feels was unjust persecution of 'prominent Kono citizens'.[23] But the evidence suggests that quite a number of these 'prominent citizens', disaffected by the NPRC's own cavalier behaviour in the district, may well have cooperated with the rebels for personal benefit. One of them, Chief Konomanyi, left with the rebels to become their 'Vice President' and defected only in 1995.

'Operation Genesis' successfully pushed back the rebels from all

[21] See *Vision* (Freetown), 6–13 November 1992.
[22] The case of Chief Tamba Gborie created immediate controversy. Gborie was reported to have shot dead an NPRC officer, Major Sankoh, when he found the officer raping his wife. The story was reported in the *Daily Mail*, for which reason its editor, the courageous George Khoryama, was promptly arrested, detained and then fired. He was charged with sedition and libel, but the case was later quietly dropped. See *Daily Mail*, 14 November 1992.
[23] Koroma (note 20), p. 181.

of Kono district into Kailahun district in the far east of the country, their original base. But Koidu town was to be retaken later, in 1993. This time again, NPRC soldiers were busy mining diamonds when the rebels struck at the town and took it. By a cruel twist of fate for the government, the recapture of the town almost coincided with thoroughly damning allegations against Strasser, which first appeared in a Swedish tabloid and were reported in a radical Freetown paper, *The New Breed*.[24]

The war had become a see-saw conflict with towns changing hands with dizzying rapidity. Popular euphoria for the 'revolution' was waning rapidly. The junta compounded its public relations difficulty when, in a sordid moment of frenzy, it summarily executed twenty-nine people, including a pregnant woman, a palm wine tapper, several newly-recruited police constables, a popular Freetown socialite, and several soldiers—among them Major Yayah Kanu— who were then in detention at Pademba Road prison, for allegedly plotting a coup in December 1992. The executions drew international outrage, in reaction to which the junta's spokesman, Karefa-Kargbo, announced in an interview with the BBC that among the many important and convincing pieces of evidence they had of the coup plot was 'a written contract' between the coup plotters and 'an illiterate herbalist'. Few appeared convinced, and Britain, the country's most important foreign supporter, quickly suspended bilateral aid to the junta. The junta grew only more churlish and paranoid after this. In an utterly reckless move the NPRC soon afterwards declared the charismatic German ambassador Karl Prinz, an outspoken critic of the junta's appalling human rights record and the most popular Western diplomat in Freetown, *persona non grata*. Germany, also an important bilateral donor, responded by simply scaling down its mission in Sierra Leone and refusing to appoint a successor to Prinz.

Martin van Creveld has postulated that low-intensity conflicts— internal wars of the nature of the RUF rebellion—will cause the obliteration of 'social entities'. He suggests that to the extent that states are social entities with distinctions between civilians and soldiers, combatants and non-combatants, then states engaged in such wars will self-destruct because such distinctions will be impossible to maintain in the course of such wars. Combatants on both sides, the insurgents and 'government soldiers', are pretty likely to

---

[24] 'Redeemers or Villains?', *The New Breed*, 13–19 October 1993.

behave in the same way, targeting civilians rather than armed opponents, and engaging in banditry. 'War being among the most imitative of all human activities', Creveld wrote, 'the very process of
combating low-intensity conflicts will cause both sides to look alike,
unless it can be brought to a quick end.'[25]

Creveld's fears appeared to have been realised in Sierra Leone by
the end of 1993, but in a more sinister way than even he, with his
brutally realistic notion of war, could have imagined. NPRC soldiers,
with the aid of irregulars, had recaptured Kailahun, Koidu and
even Pendembu, the rebels' 'headquarters' which Strasser visited in
June 1993. Strasser flew to the town by helicopter. Pendembu was
empty at the time, with residents who had been held in virtual cap-
tivity by the foraging and thuggish RUF having fled to the bush, no
doubt to avoid persecution at the hands of the NPRC's brutal
troops, for whom anyone in 'rebel territory' was perforce a 'rebel'.
Sankoh himself was rumoured to have been shot and wounded during the attack on Pendembu, and eye-witnesses reported seeing a
small, battered convoy of vehicles leaving Kailahun, loaded with
RUF leaders and their effects and heading towards Liberia. The
RUF itself has admitted that at this stage 'frankly, we were beaten
and on the run', so 'we dispersed into the comforting bosom of
mother earth—the forest.'[26] In December 1993 Strasser announced
a ceasefire and called on the remaining rebels to surrender.

Barely a month later, however, the war escalated to a point never
before imagined. The rebels recaptured Koidu in the Kailahun district, moved on to take Kono district and threatened Bo, the second
most important city in the country. There were two reasons for the
renewal of the war at this stage. The first was that the ceasefire coincided with the annual Zone Two soccer festival, a hugely popular
event which brings together soccer teams from West African countries, and which was held in Freetown that year. Many of Strasser's
troops, convinced that the war was over, abandoned their positions
at the front to watch the matches, and thus provided an opportunity for the rebels to regroup and launch deadly offensives.[27] The

[25] Martin van Creveld, *The Transformation of War*, New York: The Free Press,
1991, p. 225.
[26] RUF/SL, *Footpaths to Democracy*, 1995.
[27] See *Lorda Mercy*, February 1994. This paper was published underground
by opponents of the junta and distributed by post freely to selected targets, including registered newspapers, government officials, foreign diplomats and NGOs. It was highly informative, if vigorously anti-NPRC.

other was that Strasser's forces, particularly the irregulars who were not receiving salaries and stood no chance of being co-opted into the army, felt betrayed by their superiors as a rearmed RUF overwhelmed previously liberated areas where they were beginning to resettle. They may have resorted to banditry or even joined the RUF in frustration. Also, in February 1994, over 400 disgruntled soldiers believed to be loyal to Major Yayah Kanu, executed in 1992 for the alleged plot, absconded from the Teko barracks in the north of the country and were reportedly absorbed in to the RUF.[28] Military disloyalty may also have been helped by the NPRC's summary retirement of the army's 12 most senior officers, including the Chief of Staff, Major General Jusu Gottor, and their replacement by far junior officers. Major Kellie Conteh, an articulate but untested young officer and a friend of Strasser, was made Chief of Staff and quickly promoted brigadier. There then followed a spate of promotions which saw NPRC officers rising from captain to colonel, and one, Captain Julius Maada Bio, even to brigadier.

The RUF, no doubt aided by these disloyal soldiers, soon began to raid and set up ambushes along the major highways in the country, indiscriminately burning down villages and towns, and taking hostages. They thereby created the impression of great power which was vastly disproportionate to their actual strength. There also appeared little doubt that in the atmosphere of general insecurity and even chaos in the war-affected areas, groups of bandits (civilians) imitated rebel tactics, carrying out their own attacks on the highway for loot. During this period (1994) there was a sharp drop in armed robbery and other forms of thievery in Bo, the 'pro-

---

Former APC ministers like Abdulai Conteh were credibly believed to be associated with it.

[28] The government denied this when the defections became public, but relatives and friends of the missing soldiers, when interviewed by this writer in April 1994, could not account for their whereabouts. Major Kanu was a hugely popular officer under whose command most of the NPRC leaders served. A professional and dedicated soldier, Kanu was invited by the NPRC leaders on the day of their mutiny-turned-coup to be head of their junta. Kanu vacillated, saying that he would rather remain a soldier. In an interview with the BBC that same day he dissociated himself from the coup, and was promptly arrested and detained at Pademba Road prison by the NPRC. He was still there when the NPRC announced that it had foiled a coup in December 1992 and had him executed as part of the plot.

fessionals' perhaps having found richer pickings in the more unstable areas of eastern Sierra Leone.[29]

The involvement of soldiers in this new wave of attacks gave rise to a new phenomenon called '*sobels*'—soldiers by day and rebels by night. They became perhaps the most important element in the war. In October 1994, one Freetown newspaper described the war as characterised by 'naked banditry, the principal characters being undisciplined soldiers and unpatriotic Sierra Leoneans'.[30] It was against this background that another set of volunteers emerged, or at any rate grew in importance: the Tamaboros and the Kamajoisia.

The Tamaboro 'battalion' was organised towards the end of 1992 under the patronage of a senior NPRC officer, Lieutenant Komba Kambo. They were a group of traditional hunters from the mountainous Koinadugu district, an area known for occultism. Kambo, himself from the district, is believed to have had his body 'washed' (to make it bullet-proof) by a powerful medicine man and ex-politician in the area, Daembaso Samura. The operation was believed to have been so successful that Kambo was convinced of Samura's supernatural powers, which he decided to use in the war effort by pleading with the old man to form a group made up of people like him to help track down the rebels and counteract their perceived special powers. This was how the Tamaboro 'battalion' came to be set up.[31]

In both Mandingo and Koranko, the languages of the two linked ethnic groups from which the Tamaboros sprang, '*tama*' means 'to lead' and '*boro*' 'bag'. Put together, it could mean literally 'bag that leads', implying the use of occult powers. In fact the Tamaboros, whose duties were essentially those of scouts although they participated in combat, were a witchcraft 'battalion'. Samura put together the group, but the actual battlefield leader appears to have been Marie Keita, a fearsome-looking woman who always held a mirror as a guide to the rebels' positions. Another powerful woman among the group was 'Lieutenant' Willimina Bintu Fofana, who was said to have been a formidable specialist in the use of the rocket propelled grenade (RPG). The prominence of women in Tamaboro fascinated the country's press, which clearly exaggerated the impact of the group on the conduct of the war.[32] When in March 1993 the army's

[29] Interview with police in Bo, December 1995.
[30] Editorial, *The Unity Now*, 24 October 1994.
[31] Interview with the Tamaboro militia leader Marie Keita, February 1993.
[32] See, for example, 'The war: women take the lead', *Vision*, 4 February 1993.

Sixth Battalion, led by Kambo and another powerful NPRC figure, Lieutenant Tom Nyuma, recaptured Woama, a strategic town several miles from Koidu and a rebel training base, this victory was held to have been achieved because of the lead provided by the Tamaboros.[33]

The instant popularity of the Tamaboros became a cause of friction between them and members of the regular army. In June 1993 thirty soldiers were arrested at Masingbi, in the Tonkolili district in the rebel-free Northern Province, for deserting the front and engaging in banditry in the area posing as RUF members. The operation was spearheaded by the Tamaboros.[34] So successful had operations against the rebels at this time been that Nyuma boasted: 'The rebels are now in complete disarray with no clear command structure.'[35] 'This claim was to prove disastrously misleading. The Tamaboro 'battalion' was disbanded in October 1993 when the rebels, believed to have been aided by regular army units, surprisingly took Kabala where they were based, and brutally murdered Samura and Keita, who were said to have been stabbed and clubbed to death because bullets could not penetrate their bodies.

However, by then another irregular volunteer group that was to have a more lasting impact on the war against the rebels had emerged. This was the Kamajoisia 'battalion' which was initially set up by the Eastern Region Defence Committee (Eredcom) formed by Alpha Lavalie, a former university history lecturer, on 7 December 1992. Dr Lavalie, a longtime political activist, was Deputy Secretary General of the SLPP, and worked closely with Dr Albert Joe Demby, a medical doctor based at Kenema in eastern Sierra Leone. Demby was also a prominent figure in the SLPP, and in the east, where the SLPP is most popular, this was important to ensure local support and loyalty. The group had to rely only on these for their survival at least till 1996, when the SLPP gained power after elections and took over from the military junta.

A Sierra Leonean anthropologist, Patrick Muana, has provided an interesting account of the origin and character of the Kamajoisia in a paper entitled 'Civil War, Internal Displacement and the Politics of Counter-insurgency: the Kamajoi Militia in Sierra Leone'.[36] This account reveals a combination of esoteric influences and the stark choice faced by displaced and dispossessed villagers

---

[33] *Vision*, 4 February 1993.
[34] '30 soldiers arrested', *Vision*, 22 June–1 July 1993.
[35] *The New Breed*, 19–25 May 1993.
[36] Patrick Muana, 'Civil War, Internal Displacement, and the Politics of

between taking up arms to reclaim their land, in a world where they found they were on their own with the nation's army perceived to be either incompetent or in collusion with the enemy, and remaining in horrible displaced persons' camps for ever.

'*Kamajoi*' is a Mende word meaning 'hunter', and the hunter in traditional Mende society carried with him the traditions of a warrior cult in which he was the guardian of his society. Founders of pre-colonial Mende towns were often famous warriors and hunters, and masters of esoteric skills. Their fame rested on driving out the natural 'lords of the forest', the elephants, and so securing space for the building of settlements which it was their duty to protect. It is an exclusively male preserve.[37] According to Muana's sources, the Kamajoisia as a fighting force against the RUF and the *sobels* emerged in this fascinating way:

Following an RUF attack on a village in the Jong [Jenge] chiefdom, the rebels are reported to have massacred people in the village including a great [kamajoi] and medicine man called Kposowai. His brother Kundor-wai, is said to have been captured by the rebels, forced to carry looted goods and tied [tabay] securely for the night whilst the rebels pitched camp. As he drifted to sleep in spite of his pains, Kundorwai is said to have had a vision of his brother who had been killed the day before. The rope fell loose and the elder brother invested him with the authority to take the message to all able-bodied Mende men that the defence of their own lives, homes, wives and children was a sacred duty. To assist them in that task Kposowai is said to have shown Kundorwai a secret concoction of herbs and instructed that a strident initiation process should precede the 'washing' of the warriors in the herbs. The concoction would make them invincible in battle, impervious to bullets, endow with powers of clairvoyance if all taboos are kept. Kundorwai is said to have then slaughtered the RUF rebels, freed the other captives, and trekked several miles to a secret hiding place where he initiated the first set of men.[38]

This mystical origin may have been ascribed to the Kamajoisia by its leaders in order to achieve the requisite psychological clout effec-

Counter-Insurgency: The Kamajoi Militia in Sierra Leone', *Africa Development* (Dakar: CODESRIA), vol. XXII, nos 3/4, 1997.

[37] See Mary Leach, *Rainforest Relations: Gender and Resource use among the Mende of Gola, Sierra Leone*, Washington, DC: Smithsonian Institution Press, 1994, pp. 161–7. Also Paul Richards *et al.*, 'Reintegration of War-Affected Youths and Ex-Combatants: a Study of Social and Economic Opportunity Structure in Sierra Leone' (Report to Ministry of National Reconstruction, Sierra Leone), 6 December 1996, unpublished paper in author's possession.

[38] Muana (note 36).

tively to confront the RUF rebels, who were themselves claiming invincibility. The significance of this initiation should therefore not be exaggerated. The Kamajoisia has a well organised command structure and its members are trained in the use of modern weaponry, but they still draw on the ancestral spirit and knowledge of a hunters' guild.[39]

The Kamajoisia clashed with NPRC soldiers on a number of occasions in Kenema, and in early 1993 the Kamajoi leader Alpha Lavalie himself was killed when his car hit a landmine believed to have been planted by hostile soldiers who objected to his high-profile involvement in the war. Lavalie's men had apprehended a number of soldiers found looting a village in eastern Sierra Leone, a few weeks before his murder. His death demonstrated the extent to which the corrupt NPRC army was prepared to go to maintain its foraging activities, and it was a setback for the budding militia. However, members of Eredcom—prominent among whom was Demby, later to become the nation's Vice President—continued to garner support for the Kamajoisia. In March 1994 over 500 Kamajoisia fighters were deployed on the war front in Kenema and Kailahun districts.[40]

A similar experiment was begun shortly after Lavalie's death by a retired army officer, Captain Hinga Norman, who had been appointed regent chief of Jaiama Bongor chiefdom in Bo district. Norman, a bearded former army captain who was involved in Brigadier Lansana's military move against the APC in the late 1960s and went into self-exile after the notoriously vengeful Siaka Stevens took power, was a charming, charismatic and highly courageous man. He lived in Liberia for many years during the 1970s and 80s, and there is little doubt that he had a level of contact with Foday Sankoh and other would-be Sierra Leonean dissidents just before the war was launched. But as a Sandhurst-trained professional soldier Norman was never impressed by the activities of the NPFL with which Sankoh was associated at the time, and he was never wooed over to the RUF project.[41] When the NPRC coup happened Norman, now back in Sierra Leone, was selected as regent chief of Jaiama-Bongor, undoubtedly because of his army background and opposition to the deposed APC (he was from Bo, in Kakua chiefdom, which is adjacent to Jaiama-Bongor).

[39] Paul Richards *et al.* (note 37).
[40] *Vision*, 31 March–7 April 1994.
[41] Interview with Hinga Norman, Freetown, September 2002.

Rebel activities had suddenly increased in 1994 in Bo district, and especially in the diamond mining chiefdoms, including Jaiama-Bongor, even though a large Sierra Leone Army brigade was based at Koribondo, less than 20 kilometres away from Telu-Bongor, the headquarters town of Jaiama-Bongor. Norman, a passionate and activist leader, quickly organised young men in the town and started training them in local self-defence. The recruits were not armed, and on 30 June 1994 a large force of rebels and renegade soldiers from the Army Brigade in Koribondo descended on the Jaiama-Bongor chiefdom headquarters town Telu, slaughtered all the Kamajoi recruits and set the town ablaze. Over 100 people were killed in the attack. Norman, who was then in town, miraculously escaped. Telu is about 16 kilometres from Bo, Sierra Leone's second largest city, where a senior NPRC minister, Captain Idrissa Kamara, was based; it is also 7 kilometres from Koribundu, which maintained a large detachment of NPRC troops. Kamara was heavily involved in illicit diamond mining in the area, using mainly soldiers, an activity believed to be aided by the continuing instability in the area: rival civilian groups of miners needed to be kept away. The attack on Telu, which was beginning to develop a civil defence force, was believed to have been largely orchestrated by the soldiers.[42]

Various local defence activities appeared through 1994 and 1995 but it was not until 1996, after Hinga Norman became Deputy Minister of Defence in the elected civilian government, that a more co-ordinated effort to recruit, train and arm the Kamajoisia all over the Southern and Eastern Provinces developed. The aim was to create a civil defence capability for every war-affected Mende chiefdom.[43] The Kamajoisia launched an offensive against the rebels in September 1996, capturing Zogoda, which was the RUF's last remaining stronghold, and helped force the movement to sign a Peace Agreement in 1996.

On 12 March 1994 a pattern for a new wave of senseless killings was established when a rebel group apparently based in the Panguma logging concession area attacked Panguma town and killed at least eleven Sierra Leoneans, the Irish priest Father Felim McAllister, the Dutch doctor Dr Eelco Krijn, his wife Karen van Goucdoever, and their three-year-old daughter Zita during a raid near the hospital.[44] The attack was believed to have been facilitated by NPRC

---

[42] Interview with Hinga Norman, August 1994.

[43] Richards *et al.* (note 37).

[44] Amnesty International, *Sierra Leone: Human Rights Abuses in War against Civilians*, London, 13 September 1995.

soldiers under the command of Lieutenant James Forbie who feared that Father McAllister, who had lived in the area for a long time, knew too much about the atrocities committed by soldiers. Forbie and another soldier, Sergeant Mohammed Jawara, were arrested on the recommendation of a commission set up to investigate the killings and chaired by a prominent lawyer, Solomon Berewa (who subsequently became Attorney-General, Minister of Justice and later still Vice President).[45] Both men were later released and deployed at the NPRC Ministry of Defence on grounds of insufficient evidence, which did nothing to extricate the NPRC's image.

In April 1994 the first rebel attack in the Northern Province occurred when a group of insurgents struck at Masingbi and then moved on to sack Makalie, less than 20 miles from the main northern city, Makeni. The attack created a stir in the country with Abass Bundu, a prominent northern leader then the NPRC's Foreign Minister, declaring that the war 'has now reached where it should not', a comment interpreted as overly tribalistic by people from the south and east of the country that had already been ravaged by the war.[46] Shortly after this Makeni exploded into violent confrontation between soldiers guarding the NPRC Resident Minister in the city, Major Fallah Sewa (from the Eastern Province), and residents of the town, leading to some civilian casualties. Shortly afterwards prominent inhabitants of the city announced the setting up of their own local militia with the patronage of Bundu and another prominent politician, Thaimu Bangura.[47]

On 5 August 1994 a civilian convoy of vehicles with a military escort was attacked by men in government army uniforms. At least three civilians were killed, and the assailants stripped and raped the women passengers. Another convoy was attacked on 25 August 1994 between Matotoka and Makalie, Captain Nasiru Barrie and several civilians being killed.[48] A group of about 100 lightly armed rebels attacked Bo in December 1994 but were repulsed by civilians with heavy losses. I happened to be in Bo when this attack took place. Young men in the city spontaneously mobilised to fight the rebels using sticks, machetes and shotguns. A number of the rebels were captured and lynched. The overwhelming view in the town at the time was that the military was complicit in the attack, and ordi-

---

[45] The Commission's findings were never made public.
[46] See editorial, *Vision*, 5–12 May 1994.
[47] See 'Makeni tragedy: Why and how it happened', *Vision*, 5–12 May 1994.
[48] Amnesty International (note 44).

nary citizens imposed a night time curfew and executed at least two soldiers who violated it—probably the first time in the history of warfare when ordinary civilians, not the government, imposed control over the movement of those who were supposed to be their own soldiers.[49]

The NPRC reacted to the reports of army complicity in acts of banditry, which was making the junta extremely unpopular, by arresting and executing twelve soldiers, all non-commissioned officers, in November 1994. A senior military officer, Lieutenant-Colonel Chernor Deen, was later sentenced to death for collaborating with the rebels, a sentence never carried out, probably because Sankoh threatened to execute all the hostages he had captured if that should happen.

Terrorist attacks spread throughout the country. On 25 December 1994 government soldiers, acting as rebels, shot and killed a prominent lawyer in Kenema, Patrick P.B. Kebbie. Kebbie had just been appointed Director of Public Prosecutions by the NPRC and his murder was believed to be connected to this. No official inquiry was conducted into the killings in spite of calls for one by rights monitoring groups.[50] The month before, the RUF abducted two British nationals, Robert d'Cruz and Calum Murray, both volunteers with Voluntary Service Overseas (VSO), who were working on rural development projects in Kabala. Foday Sankoh then made radio contact with the British High Commission in Freetown demanding arms and recognition of his movement by the British government, a demand summarily turned down.[51] Then in January 1995 the country's last remaining economic strongholds, the bauxite mines at Sieromco and the titanium mines at Sierra Rutile, were closed down after the rebels attacked, looted and destroyed the mines, allegedly with the active collaboration of the soldiers deployed there under the command of Major Johnny Paul Koroma.[52] Goods looted at the mines were later seen in the possession of soldiers, which led to confrontations between them and the civilian

---

[49] See Richards (note 15).
[50] Amnesty International (note 44).
[51] Tim Rayment, 'Foreign Office turns down ransom demand', *Sunday Times*, 20 November 1994.
[52] Koroma denied this in an interview I had with him in April 2001, but the allegations were confirmed by several of his former colleagues in the NPRC army. The junta had refused to allow the companies to bring in their own armed private security forces, and one of the officials of Sierra Rutile, in an interview with the BBC in February 1995, claimed that the attack was led by the NPRC soldiers deployed around the mines.

owners. Seven Europeans, including James Westwood and Ross
Milne from Sieromco and Peter White and Andrew Young from
Sierra Rutile, were abducted by the rebels. Several Sierra Leoneans,
including Dr Mohammed Barrie who later became a public relations officer for the RUF, were also abducted at the two mines. On
25 January, after a vicious attack on Kambia, the RUF abducted
seven Catholic nuns, six Italians and a Brazilian, along with more
than thirty schoolchildren.

No doubt these hostage takings, of foreigners in particular, were
aimed at publicising the RUF's political aims and gaining recognition for the movement, as well as emphasising the impression of the
NPRC's total lack of control in the country. The tactic was successful. Pressure began to mount on the NPRC from all quarters to begin negotiations with the rebels, something that had never before
been hinted at. The call for dialogue was first made in November
1994 by the Catholic Archbishop of Freetown and Bo, Joseph
Ganda, who implored Strasser to 'explore the possibility of engaging in dialogue with the rebels in order to end the untold sufferings
of helpless people, particularly women and children and the
destruction of property throughout the country'.[53] Various 'independent' peace initiatives were also started, including one by an
old SLPP politician from rebel-held Pujehun district, Mana Kpaka,
and another by Omrie Golley, a lawyer and former NPRC special
envoy. Kpaka's mission ended when a RUF commander, Momoh
Konneh, abducted his mother from the group of 'peace delegates'
(the poor woman had been taken along, from her home in a displaced persons' camp, to help lure her son from the bush and facilitate the talks). Golley's initiative went badly wrong after he was
accused by the NPRC of being a 'rebel collaborator' and scheming
to hire mercenaries for the RUF. Yet another group, this time of
women activists, ventured into rebel-held Kailahun district as 'mothers, sisters and wives' to induce the rebels to accept a ceasefire; the
RUF had them all executed. Alarmed by these developments, the
Organisation of African Unity (OAU) Secretary General, Salim
Ahmed Salim, described the proliferation of such peace initiatives
as 'an anarchy of good intentions', and called for a more coordinated, high-level diplomatic effort.[54]

The NPRC responded by setting up a National Security Council
(NSC) comprising representatives of the government, the army,

---

[53] *Concord Times*, 15 November 1994.
[54] *OAU Secretary General's Report*, Addis Ababa, 1995.

the police, the Bar Association, the Sierra Leone Association of Journalists (SLAJ), the Labour Congress and the University of Sierra
Leone. The NSC issued a statement on 25 November calling on the
RUF leadership to accept a ceasefire, release all hostages and
organise itself into a political party in order to be able to participate
in the transition to civil rule process then under way. Sankoh
promptly declared that these demands were unacceptable on the
ground that they failed to recognise the intrinsic legitimacy of his
'struggle'.[55]

The foreign hostages were released later in 1995 after the intervention through Addai Sebo, the Ghanaian publicist for Charles
Taylor mentioned earlier—of a London-based conflict resolution
group, International Alert (IA). Sebo made a documentary of the
event, which was broadcast on British television's Channel 4 News,
showing Sankoh in charge of an organised bush insurgency. The
NPRC alleged that Sebo took diamonds from the rebels to arrange
new supplies of arms.[56]

In December 1994 Strasser sent a letter to the United Nations
Secretary General imploring him to 'use your good offices to assist
in bringing about a peaceful settlement to the rebel war'.[57] The
Tanzanian ambassador to the UN, Felix Mosha, was then despatched
from New York to Freetown to make preliminary contact with all
parties involved in the war and report his findings. Mosha was soon
replaced by Berkhanu Dinka, an Ethiopian, who continued to
make exploratory contacts with the RUF from Freetown. The Commonwealth Secretariat also sent a representative, Moses Anafu, to
help facilitate the process of dialogue. In the mean time, however,
with the RUF remaining intransigent, and with the writ of the
NPRC seemingly limited to the capital, the junta decided to bring
in new forces to assert some control and perhaps force the rebels to
the negotiating table.

[55] See 'Peace moves—Sankoh says NO!', *Concord Times*, 29 November 1994.
[56] Sebo denied the allegation to me in an interview in Ivory Coast at the
time of the peace talks in 1996, during which he was an unofficial and
influential adviser to Foday Sankoh. Certainly Sebo's role went beyond
that of a disinterested peace activist. The RUF's first public relations officer, Alimamy Sankoh, resigned from the group, accusing Sebo of
'treacherous meddling in the Sierra Leone conflict' and of using the war
as a 'money generating source not for the good of deprived Sierra
Leoneans caught in the conflict...but for [the RUF's] own coffers.' (Letter in author's possession)
[57] *Uniweek*, 22 December 1994.

Creveld has argued that most modern-day wars, in situations where states no longer enjoy legal 'monopoly over armed violence', will be conducted not by governments but by 'war-making entities', organisations which unite military and economic functions. In such a situation what is at stake is not 'national defence' but 'security'. This would have to be provided by private mercenary bands or commercial organisations such as the old British East India Company which helped to bring a whole sub-continent under British rule. Creveld writes:

Much of the day-to-day burden of defending society against the threat of low-intensity conflict will be transferred to the booming security business; and indeed the time may come when the organizations that comprise that business will, like the condottieri of old, take over the state.[58]

By early 1995, Sierra Leone appeared to have reached this stage of incipient anarchy and dissolution. Anti-government rebels had besieged the capital, preventing any viable contact with the provinces. Renegade soldiers had run amok, carrying out their own attacks on civilians, mainly for loot. The government itself admitted in late 1994 that at least 20 per cent of its soldiers were disloyal. Strasser characterised the situation as 'nothing short of banditry, looting, maiming and raping' and warned the public against 'harbouring a soldier who does not possess his authentic document... Strident action will be taken against all civilians found in possession of military uniforms and equipment.'[59] The 'real' war, it was proclaimed, was over. What remained was banditry.

The NPRC's response to the problem was to bring in foreign hired guns to do the job of 'flushing out the bandits', as the newspapers were fond of putting it. In February 1995 the junta contacted the British-based Gurkha Security Guards (GSG), made up of demobilised units of Britain's famed Gurkha troops, apparently for the more general task of training the Sierra Leone army in counter-insurgency. The cost of the project was never disclosed but it was believed to be several million dollars. The GSG's Sierra Leone commander was Robert Mackenzie, an American who had served in the Rhodesian Special Forces that battled black nationalist guerrillas in the Zimbabwean war of independence during the 1970s and was also involved in the South African military and private fund-raising efforts for the murderous Renamo rebels in Mozambique.

---

[58] Creveld (note 25), p. 60.
[59] 'The rebel war: Strasser warns civilians', *Vision*, 22–29 September 1994.

The Gurkhas went into combat soon after their arrival, in addition to establishing a training base for selected units of the regular army. They quickly helped to reduce rebel activities around Mile 91, a strategic outpost on the highway leading to the two most important cities in the Southern and Eastern Provinces, Bo and Kenema, and a main operational base for the rebels. But in spite of all his experience of such 'dirty wars', Mackenzie made the mistake of working directly with a contingent of the Sierra Leone army which was apparently not sufficiently screened.[60] He was killed in an ambush in late February, along with Strasser's aide-de-camp, Captain Abu Tarawallie. The ambush appeared to have benefited from inside information regarding Mackenzie's movements.[61] The Gurkhas had their contract terminated and withdrew from the country.

In March 1995 the rebels took Mile 38, another strategic post on the main highway connecting the capital to the rest of the country. It was also uncomfortably close to the capital, and the rebel take-over triggered a mass movement of people from the town to Freetown. The NPRC's forces responded with desperation. Ukrainian-manned helicopter gunships and heavy artillery deployed by the Sierra Leone Army, fighting alongside Nigerian army units, pounded the town to rubble. Many of the rebels survived the attack and fled to the bush. But the extent of the NPRC's firepower was evidently not lost on them. Henceforth, they made no attempt to occupy any town along the highway for more than a few days. The tactic was now to hit, destroy and run. The carnage was unrelenting.

The magnitude of the unfolding chaos seemed beyond the capability of internal forces to handle, even with the support of the Nigerians and Guineans. In May 1995 Strasser's search for help led

---

[60] I am indebted to William Reno for information on Mackenzie and his role in the Gurkha force.

[61] A soldier who survived the attack told me (Freetown, March 1995) that the ambush was well-organised, with more than 200 rebels taking part— an unusual development in itself, since the amorphous RUF hardly had such a large concentration at any one time outside the main bases in Kailahun district and other parts of the eastern and southern Sierra Leone—and it is probable that they were tipped off at least two days before. Needless to say, the junta made all efforts to keep the Gurkha operations secret from all but its most trusted military advisers. *Sobel* activities were becoming blatant. A Ukrainian pilot, hired in April 1995 to fly a Russian-made helicopter gunship bought by the junta, was found shot dead in his room at the Murray Town Military barracks in Freetown. The NPRC claimed that he had committed suicide, but of course no one believed that.

him to Executive Outcomes (EO), a South African mercenary firm.
EO employed black Angolans and Namibians from apartheid
South Africa's old 32nd Battalion, with an officer corps of white
South Africans and a white Rhodesian (Zimbabwean) brigadier.
Harper's Magazine described the controversial outfit as 'a collection
of former spies, assassins, and crack bush guerillas, most of whom
had served for fifteen to twenty years in South Africa's most notorious counter insurgency units'.[62] Colourful though their past may
have been, the EO combatants were phenomenally successful as
hired guns. The mercenary outfit first made its mark in Angola
where it initially served with the UNITA rebels and later, after the
elections which Jonas Savimbi lost, switched sides to the Angolan
government when Savimbi plunged the country into the war again
as a result of his failed electoral bid. EO helped to turn the tide
of the war crucially against UNITA, forcing the intransigent rebel
movement to return the negotiating table. 'It was the best fifty or
sixty million dollars the Angolan government ever spent,' a US
defence expert is quoted as saying, speculating that EO is 'the small
wave of the future in terms of defence and security, because the
international community has abdicated that role.'[63]

Strasser was encouraged to hire EO by the British directors of
Heritage Oil and Gas, an oil firm that had taken EO into Angola,
and Branch Energy, a mining firm with interests in Sierra Leone's
diamond deposits. The contract was signed by Strasser on behalf of
the Sierra Leone government and Anthony Buckingham, the foun-
der of Heritage Oil and Branch Energy. EO's mission was to search
and destroy the 'terrorist enemies of state', restore internal security, and help build and maintain an economic climate where new
investment could be attracted. The price was US$15 million, but
since Strasser could not pay immediately, Buckingham agreed to
bankroll the operation in exchange for future mining concessions.[64]

In May 1995, 150 EO fighters, commanded by Colonel Roelf, a
Namibian-born Afrikaner, were deployed. Once in the country, they
set about training selected units of the army in counter-insurgency,
and incorporated large units of the more reliable Kamajoisia militia into a formidable fighting machine. The EO fighters came
equipped with two M 117 helicopters and an M 124 Hind-Russian
helicopter gunship, a radio intercept system, two Boeing 727s to

[62] Elizabeth Rubin, 'An army of one's own', *Harper's Magazine*, February
1997.
[63] Ibid.
[64] Ibid.

transport troops and supplies, and an Andover casualty-evacuation aircraft. They were supplied in Freetown with Sierra Leonean army uniforms, three armoured personnel carriers equipped with 30-mm. cannons and six Landrovers mounting anti-aircraft guns and other automatic weapons.[65]

EO was also aided by the Nigerians and Guineans, who carried out simultaneous raids against rebel positions in the Northern Province. Within a few months the chaos had abated somewhat. The Kamajoisia then led EO units in the Eastern and Southern Provinces on a 'search and destroy' mission. Rebel activity was brought under control to a considerable extent towards the end of 1995.

Local opposition to the deployment of the mercenaries was ruthlessly crushed by the desperate junta. On 12 July Mban Kabu, a spokesman for the National Coordinating Committee for Peace (NCCP), a coalition of some sixty organisations formed in April 1995 to facilitate a negotiated settlement to the war, was arrested and detained for two weeks without charge for describing EO as 'hard core apartheid attack dogs' at a public meeting of his organisation. The editor of the *Standard Times*, Ibrahim Karim Sei, who reported the comments, was detained for the same period. Both men were released without charge. EO itself mounted a public relations campaign, flying reporters to its 'liberated' zones and showing how people in the areas appreciated their presence.[66] The *Standard Times* was made to carry a few paid advertisers' supplement for the mercenaries, and it soon became a mouthpiece for the outfit in Freetown.

EO was to be portrayed as a Pan-African force formed to help African countries overcome their instabilities, an image which Colonel Roelf insisted was the correct representation. Few took this propaganda seriously, but the mercenary force was immensely popular in areas, like Kono district, over which it helped establish some order where previously there had been only bloody chaos.

With the chaos at least brought under control, the junta moved on to conduct elections aimed at establishing civil rule, under the direction of a former senior UN official, James Jonah. Strasser's clumsy attempts to manipulate the process by having himself metamorphosed into a civilian candidate led to his overthrow by his own deputy, Brigadier Julius Maada Bio, in January 1996.[67] Rebel attempts

---

[65] Interview with Major John Milton, the NPRC army Public Relations Officer, Freetown, August 1995.

[66] 'We are not mercenaries—Col. RUFF', *For Di People*, 21 July 1995.

[67] The NPRC had sponsored the establishment of a political party, the National Unity Party (NUP), and made its Finance Minister, John

to disrupt the polls included the amputation of the limbs of at least fifty-two people around the country, in a campaign in which renegade soldiers objecting to the polls were also believed to have participated. But apart from such outrages, the elections in most parts of the country went ahead smoothly, an indication of the diminishing power of both forces, rebels and *sobels*. The polls were conducted in March 1996, and Ahmed Tejan Kabbah, a former senior UN bureaucrat, emerged as President at the head of the revived Sierra Leone Peoples Party (SLPP).

Peace talks which had begun between the RUF leadership and Maada Bio's junta climaxed on 30 November 1996 with the signing of a Peace Accord by Foday Sankoh and President Kabbah at Abidjan in Ivory Coast. Both sides to the conflict agreed to end the war 'with immediate effect', to ensure that a 'total cessation of hostilities is observed forthwith' and to give priority to 'the establishment and consolidation of a just peace'. Kabbah declared that the 'common enemy' was now hunger, disease and poverty.

But this well-choreographed statement was soon to prove as meaningless as the Accord after Executive Outcomes withdrew from the country, at the insistence of the RUF, leaving the security of the state in the hands of the army. The experiment in democracy lasted until May 1997 when armed soldiers blasted open Pademba Road prison, releasing more than 600 convicts and arming many of them. The force then attacked State House, overcoming a detachment of Nigerian troops stationed there under a defence pact signed with the elected government by Nigeria. President Kabbah was ferried out of the country to neighbouring Guinea, and the rebellious soldiers named Major Johnny Paul Koroma, who had been freed in the break-out from Pademba Road—where he had

---

Karimu, leader. But as elections drew to a close, Strasser began to show increasing signs of wanting to hijack the NUP leadership and declare himself presidential candidate. His brother, Reginald, and other henchmen like the Information Minister, Hindolo Trye, organised a demonstration of youths outside a meeting of the NUP shouting 'No Strasser, No NUP'. Strasser was overthrown a few weeks later and flown out of the country—to Guinea, where the man he overthrew, Joseph Momoh, was also a refugee. The Maada Bio junta explained that Strasser had wanted to tamper with the Constitution by lowering the mandatory age limit from 45 years (he was only 30) for presidential candidates in order to be able to contest, 'a development that would plunge our country into chaos again'.

been kept since August 1996 after a plot for a coup against the elected government was foiled—to be leader of an Armed Forces Ruling Council (AFRC). Koroma's first move in office was to announce
that the RUF was part of his movement; he invited the rebels to join
him in Freetown. Koroma's forces and the RUF were now described
as 'the People's Army'. The RUF leader, Foday Sankoh, was appointed Vice Chairman of the AFRC, but the Nigerian government
placed him under house arrest in Nigeria, preventing his triumphal
entry into Freetown.

It is significant that Koroma, who was in prison at the time of the
coup, was chosen as leader of the junta. This was a coup by the *sobel*
element in the army, and Koroma's own record as a *sobel* officer was
beyond dispute. In a sense the AFRC, of which more in the next
chapter, marked the final stage in the collapse of the long-suffering
Sierra Leonean state, a collapse accelerated by the ravages of the
NPRC's army from which the *sobel* phenomenon emerged. It was
now clear that the war itself was not about politics but organised
theft, and the capture of the state was simply a formal indication of
the absolute criminalisation of the Sierra Leonean state. Bureaucratic order was no longer contemplated; it had been rejected.
That rejection had been shown in the NPRC's sidelining of its own
army in favour of foreign mercenaries. It was then convenient to
talk about the 'privatisation of the state'; but what actually happened was the collapse of formal state institutions and emergence
of criminal gangsterism to replace them. This was the by-product of
the RUF war.

5

NOT JUST A COUP
THE AFRC TAKEOVER OF 1997

'...we may decide to substitute tragic dilettantism for action, and in this case human lives become counters in a game... Then the world will no longer be divided into the just and the unjust, but into masters and slaves. Thus, whichever way we turn, in our abyss of negation and nihilism, murder has its privileged position.' (Albert Camus, *The Rebel*[1])

'A coup? What coup? This is just chaos! The barbarians have arrived.' (Siaka Massaquoi, newspaper editor)

Military coups in postcolonial sub-Saharan Africa have happened with such regularity that they were said to constitute, before the 1990s brought with them a special brand of anarchic civil wars and complete state collapse, the principal bane of the region—and its dominant political reality. So much so that already by 1971 the British humorous magazine *Punch* could conceive this unfunny 'advertisement': 'Want to get ahead faster?. Why, then, enlist in an African army and soon enough you will control part of the world: Yakubu Gowon joined the...army to see the world, and now owns 357,000 square miles [the size of his country, Nigeria] of it.' By 1974 the continent, self-governing for less than two decades, had experienced, by the calculation of one observer, seventy-five to 100 successful and attempted coups, as well as coup plots.[2]

Still, such coups happened in a clear political context: the military leaders had a stake in maintaining the bureaucratic trappings of the state, and some of them at least saw their actions as necessary

[1] Albert Camus, *The Rebel*, New York: Vintage Books, 1956, p. 5.
[2] Thomas Cox, *Civil-Military Relations in Sierra Leone: a Case Study of African Soldiers in Politics*, Cambridge, MA: Harvard University Press, 1976, p. 4.

97

to prevent their countries' slide into greater economic and political rot through the excesses of the bungling political leaders; they saw their actions, in other words, as an extension of their basic duty to 'defend and protect' the state. The argument was that authoritarian regimes which had crushed the political opposition and were busy rifling the state had in effect made the army the *de facto* opposition. 'A coup d'état is the last resort in the range of means whereby an unpopular government may be overthrown,' was how Ghana's Colonel A.A. Afrifa began his tedious rationalisation of the overthrow of Kwame Nkrumah. 'But in our case where there was no constitutional means offering a political opposition to the one-party government the Armed Forces were automatically made to become the official opposition of the government.'

Such an argument can of course be easily parodied, as indeed it has been by the Nigerian writer Chinua Achebe, who has despaired of such a development as 'a new cloud... a new estrangement': 'The party boss was chased out by the bright military boys, new idols of the people. But the party boss knows how to wait...One hears that the party boss is already conducting a whispering campaign: "You don see us chop," he says, "now you see them chop. Which one you like pass?" And the people are truly confused.' Coups, counter-coups and restoration of civilian leaders looked like a game of musical chairs, with each new occupant apparently worse than his predecessor. But Afrifa's argument, for many military officers as well as their civilian supporters (usually frustrated by the gimmicks of the political leadership), was no less compelling for this fact. The NPRC coup, in spite of its confusions and amateurism, could be analysed as falling within the above tangent. However, the coup by the Armed Forces Ruling Council (AFRC) in 1997 represented a new, more profound and entirely destructive form of praetorianism, one that led to normative collapse of the long-suffering Sierra Leone state. This chapter examines the coup, its dynamics and significance, in the context of state disintegration.

In an earlier evaluation,[3] I characterised the coup as the ultimate triumph of a lumpen-proletarian culture: it was street power taking over the state. The coup was peculiarly anti-state, driven by criminal impulses, wholly self-serving and predatory, and carried out by people who had no conception of governance, let alone aiming at it.

[3] Lansana Gberie, 'The May 1997 Coup: a Militariat Revolt' in Ibrahim Abdullah (ed.), *Between Democracy and Terror* (Dakar: CODESRIA, 2003, published earlier as special issue of *Africa Development*, vol. XXII, nos 3–4, 1997), pp. 144–63.

My paper was a critique of the late Steve Riley's 'briefing' in the *Review of African Political Economy* (1997)[4] in which the AFRC was analysed as a 'militariat' revolt, a characterisation that I found inadequate. In Riley's truculent view, the mayhem that accompanied the coup was a result of the AFRC being led by the 'militariat', which he defined as 'a social group' within the army of relatively junior officers and 'other ranks' 'who lack the clientelist ties of more senior officers and who are therefore prone to institutional instability and some orchestrated violence'. This approach no doubt flowed from the belief at the time of the coup that there was an institutional army, reasonably well integrated, and that the 'revolt' would stabilise into governance. This analysis, I argued, failed to understand the basic character of the coup: that it was less the formal military acting than its rogue, decidedly criminal elements who had been, at least since the period of NPRC rule, in active collaboration with the RUF forces. The coup, in other words, was the product of the *sobel* phenomenon. I wrote then:

Certainly the takeover was led by junior officers...who then initially proceeded to arrest the senior officers. But the ruling council was dominated by brigadiers, colonels and other officers, although the real power brokers seemed to have been army rank and file individuals...A large number of junior rank soldiers were given posts in the Supreme Military Council. If the unnamed positions for civilian participation in the council are excluded, the lower rank sergeants, staff sergeants, privates, corporals and lance corporals accounted for 17 of the 22 positions occupied by the military—an unprecedented development in the history of military and probably in Africa and the world.[5]

In retrospect this is obviously a little confusing. Senior officers held apparently prominent positions in the junta, but they did not dominate it. In fact, from all accounts, they seemed to have been held hostage to the whims and depredations of the junior rank and file soldiers, and more especially, of the RUF members who joined the ruling council. The army, if it was an institution of command and control, was clearly not in charge.

I was spending a pleasant weekend with a friend in Cambridge when I watched, in horror, a CNN news broadcast that there had been a coup in the 'small West African state of Sierra Leone'. I thought it was a mistake, but then a map of Sierra Leone was displayed, quickly dispelling my doubts. It subsequently emerged that

[4] Steven Riley, 'The Militariat Strikes Again', *Review of African Political Economy*, July 1997.
[5] Gberie (note 3).

CNN had picked up the news from an announcement on Sierra Leone's state radio by a breathless and unknown soldier, Corporal Tamba Gborie, early on Sunday 25 May 1997, telling the world that the elected leadership of President Kabbah (in office for barely a year) had been overthrown and a 'dusk to dawn curfew' (his words) imposed on the capital of Sierra Leone, Freetown. There had been no apparent signs of trouble in the capital at that time, and I was therefore stunned by the news. President Kabbah had registered significant successes with the country's shattered economy and international image. He had moved the economy from a negative growth rate of minus 6.4 per cent to a positive rate of 6 per cent in just one year. Soon after taking office in March 1996 the president had vigorously pursued peace negotiations with the leadership of the RUF, and in November 1996 they signed an accord announcing the ending of the war. Investors and indigenous business people who had fled the country amid the RUF's terror campaigns were returning, and many in the country concluded that good times were not far away. International donors generally expressed satisfaction, and the International Monetary Fund (IMF), the World Bank and bilateral donors allocated over a half a billion dollars for infrastructural reconstruction and rehabilitation.

True, there had been widespread and persistent reports of clashes between the discredited army and members of the Kamajoisia militia, upon which the new civilian regime was increasingly relying. On 1 May serious clashes occurred between that group and the regular army in Kenema. Soldiers had attempted to block the wedding procession of a major Kamajor leader from entering the town for no apparent reason. Heavy fighting followed in which over 100 combatants on both sides were killed. Shops were looted. Clashes between the two groups were also reported in the Kambia and Pujehun districts. It would appear that the high profile which the Mende-dominated Civil Defence Force (CDF) had earned through its effective combat with the RUF had triggered the ire of the army which, since the late 1960s, has been dominated by northerners in orientation and sympathy. It was even reported in one of the local newspapers, not always reliable, that the Army Chief of Staff—Brigadier Hassan Conteh, a northerner—issued 'shoot-and-kill' orders to soldiers encountering the CDF in certain contested areas.[6] Alarmed by such a development, President Kabbah appointed a commission, headed by the respected Anglican Bishop Keillie, to look into the

[6] *Expo Times* (Freetown), 14 March 1997.

relations between the two groups and make recommendations. Meetings were arranged between the CDF and the army leaders, and by mid-May things appeared to have calmed down. The flying in of 900 Nigerian soldiers as part of a bilateral military agreement signed by Kabbah and the Nigerian government helped further to calm nerves in the country.

Corporal Gborie's announcement was therefore wholly unexpected and shocking, and much of what preceded the announcement became clear only later. That Sunday morning he and about two dozen heavily armed soldiers unusually attired in civilian clothing had driven to the main penal centre, Pademba Road prison, blasted the gates open with grenades and released 600 convicts, some of them the country's worst criminals. Major Johnny Paul Koroma, gaoled since August 1996 for plotting a coup, was among those sprung from the prison. The soldiers armed many of the convicts with guns stolen from a military depot and led them to attack State House, the country's seat of power, where they fought a small detachment of Nigerian soldiers and loyal army units and overwhelmed them. The next target was the state radio, and by the afternoon President Kabbah was ferried out of the country to Guinea. The rebellious soldiers declared him overthrown, and named Major Koroma leader of their Armed Forces Ruling Council.

This was followed by twelve hours of shelling in Freetown, and nearly a week of looting, murder and rape in which as many as 200 civilians were killed.[7] Property, both public and private, was vandalised, and parts of the Central Bank and the whole of the colonial Treasury Building were destroyed. The coup was bizarre even by the appalling standards of West African soldiery; but in itself it could hardly have been remarkable given the country's recent history of coups and terror. However, the real importance of the events of 25 May 1997 did not lie in the overthrow of President Kabbah.

Accusing Kabbah of failure to consolidate the peace with the RUF, the AFRC immediately invited the dreaded rebel group to the capital and announced that it was a part of the junta. Apparently without hesitation, the ragtag RUF fighters, many of them very young, poured into the seaside capital and took up strategic positions. They were led by Sam Bockarie (alias Maskita), a blood-

---

[7] Ian Douglas, 'Fighting for Diamonds—Private Military Companies in Sierra Leone' in Jakkie Cilliers and Peggy Mason (eds), *Peace, Profit or Plunder? The Privatization of Security in War-Torn African Societies* (Pretoria: ISS, 1999), pp. 175–200.

thirsty—not to say unstable—former hairdresser and illicit diamond miner. The two forces, now described as the 'People's Army', declared the war over, and Koroma called on Sierra Leoneans to rally to his junta because he had brought peace by the only way possible: aligning with the 'enemy', the RUF. He declared that the RUF leader, Foday Sankoh, who was in detention in Nigeria at the time for weapons-related offences (he had been arrested at the airport in Lagos for entering the country with four pistols), was the Vice Chairman of the AFRC—and Vice President of Sierra Leone. Koroma then dissolved the elected parliament, suspended the Constitution and banned political activities. Governance became little more than a chaotic orgy of rapine and terror and systematic intimidation; the beleaguered state effectively ceased to function in any meaningful sense. And this was hardly praetorian terror: there was nothing of the discipline, precision, sense of purpose and cold-bloodedness of military rule. The whole thing had an exuberant, disorganised and millenarian quality.

It subsequently emerged that the coup was planned and executed by very low-ranking soldiers, who had first discussed their plot on a football field and tapped into their a long-time collusion with elements in the RUF. This collaboration, which gave rise to the phenomenon of *sobels*, was the result of shared interest and background. This is an important point, to which we return. After over six years of unsuccessful but highly destructive warfare to wrest control of the state and loot its resources more comprehensively, the RUF rebels simply 'marched proudly and jubilantly' into the capital, as Koroma himself put it. The RUF quickly established itself as the force behind the AFRC power, taking what amounted to full control over everything in the capital, including the lives and bodies of residents. This development triggered a mass exodus to neighbouring states, Guinea, Liberia and The Gambia. About 400,000 people fled Sierra Leone in the first three months after the coup, more than during the entire six-year war period.

Why did the army, which had fought the RUF for six years, invite the rebel group to join them in a struggle against the lawfully constituted government? In a 'Position Paper' issued on 17 July 1997, Koroma declared that the RUF and the Sierra Leone army shared 'a combination of experience, talent and patriotism that cannot be questioned'. It was a devastating statement, but for many Sierra Leoneans it was not entirely surprising: it was common knowledge that a significant component of the army was colluding in the acts of banditry and terror of which the RUF's campaigns largely consisted. As we have seen, Captain Valentine Strasser of the National Provisional Ruling Council (NPRC) had admitted this in 1994 when he declared that at least 20 per cent of the army was disloyal, and he then characterised the war as 'nothing short of banditry, looting, maiming and raping'.[8] The army, which at the start of the war in 1991 was 3,000 strong, had become a bloated, ill-trained, badly coordinated collection of armed men existing, outside Freetown, very much like the RUF in a foraging mode, with many of the soldiers engaged in illicit diamond mining or armed banditry.

But what exactly was the basis of this profoundly disturbing collaboration? This is not simply a question of motive. The RUF, after all, had begun its war in March 1991 by targeting both the army and civilians, and in six short years had destroyed much of the country's infrastructure and by 1997 killed at least 20,000 Sierra Leoneans, mainly civilians. It was made up of young men, already with criminal tendencies, mostly recruited in Liberia and in the illicit diamond mining forests of eastern and southern Sierra Leone. The regular army, on the other hand, was a nearly century-old institution which in 1987 was described, if somewhat exaggeratedly, by two distinguished Sierra Leonean scholars as 'trustworthy, dependable and an efficient instrument of national security'.[9] This was the pre-war army, made up largely of nominees of the All Peoples Congress (APC) in a patronage system designed by Stevens to ensure that the army remained loyal to him and his one-party state. It certainly did, and Stevens chose Major-General Momoh to succeed him as President in 1985; there is no reason to doubt Momoh's statement that he 'never dreamed' of such a position.

However, this force proved wholly inadequate to meet the challenge posed by the RUF incursions in 1991, and Momoh was forced to double its strength. The new recruits, unlike those recruited within the well-regulated patronage system, were never properly screened, and Momoh's expanded army came to be dominated mostly by drifters and thieves. Strasser, who succeeded Momoh, further expanded the army by recruiting from much the same source as Momoh and it is hardly surprising that this uniformed rabble, once sent to the frontline, found with the RUF a natural affinity which easily translated into active collaboration. Without this collusion the war would surely have ended long before, and certainly the 25 May 1997 coup would never have happened. To understand why

---

[8] *Vision*, 29 September 1994.
[9] Arthur Abraham and E.D.A. Turay, *The Sierra Leone Army*, Freetown, 1987.

it did, its one needs only to examine the nature of the army, its concerns, its worldview and perspectives on its place in society.

A report entitled *Socio-Economic Profile of the Armed Forces of the Republic of Sierra Leone* by Bob Kandeh and John Pemagbi, published in 1997, provides a fascinating and highly illuminating glimpse into the Sierra Leone army at the time of the coup. The report was commissioned by President Kabbah as a basis for a blueprint for a 'demobilisation and reintegration programme as part of its transition process from a state of war to a state of peace'. It was just after the Abidjan Peace Accord, and it was thought necessary to cut down the size of the bloated and criminally inefficient army. The report was to be used in 'planning assistance to the characteristics, needs and aspirations of the beneficiaries,' that is, those who would be demobilised.

The report found that the overwhelmingly male (98.1 per cent) and young (nearly 60 per cent were under thirty years old) army consisted mainly of secondary school drop-outs; but nearly 30 per cent were totally illiterate and had never been to school. Less than 2 per cent were university graduates or medical doctors, lawyers or engineers. Over 60 per cent had served for less than six years, which means that they were recruited into the force after the war started. Only 2.9 per cent, mainly the old and disabled, indicated that they wanted to be demobilised. The rest were hostile to the idea of demobilisation mainly because, according to the report, they 'fear that they would lose the facilities they now enjoy', which included free accommodation, water, electricity, uniform, medical services and (subsidised) rice. The real problem was that with limited skills and education the soldiers felt that they would not be able to adjust to normal, wage-earning civilian life. Although many of the soldiers predictably claimed that they joined the army 'because they [the RUF] were killing my people', some of them were more frank. One participant claimed to have joined the army 'because of the respect and fear people had for members of the army. This I wanted to be reflected in me.'

Bob Kandeh, one of the authors of the report, has shown how difficult it was even to carry out the survey for the report since the army insisted, suspiciously, that only soldiers should be part of the entire survey team, and that 'every step had to be approved by Defence HQ'.

In co-ordinating the survey I always found it quite delicate...as the [army] was really an unwilling partner in the exercise... The survey team reported that selected interviewees openly wept as they interpreted their selection into the sample as the first step to their demobilisation. Some even professed that they would not go alone. One such participant was put in the guard-room for insubordination...both officers and privates voiced out their bitterness about the demobilisation exercise and even hinted that armed robberies etc would be on the increase if such a large number of personnel suddenly lost the benefits they were used to, however meagre.

There can be little doubt that fear of demobilisation was a strong factor leading to the coup, a fear made more acute after President Kabbah, in an incredibly impolitic move, announced that his government would be cutting down on the subsidised rice for the army in the wave of general economic adjustment. Indeed, Kandeh reports that there was an increase in overt insubordination after the demobilisation process was announced—one such incident being a group of soldiers 'leaving for the war-front to engage the RUF, only to disembark at some point with comments that Kabbah should select those he was going to retain in his restructured army to go and fight'. But such insubordination, which was widespread and involved attacks on loyal units and the CDF, was only possible because the basic element of command and cohesion had long ceased to exist within the army. Indeed, no later than 1994 officers operating outside Freetown were basically held hostage to the caprices of the rank and file. The problem appeared to have intensified after Strasser summarily retired the army's twelve most senior professional officers, including the Chief of Staff, Major-General Jusu Gottor, in 1993, and replaced them with young and untested junior officers. There was a spate of unprecedented promotions of the junta's members and closest friends. Such a development was no recipe for institutional coherence. Respect for authority within the ranks was undermined, and the process of disintegration, already evident after the coup, was given a further push.

But it was only a push. Even before the NPRC takeover, military indiscipline and especially army collusion in 'rebel' activities were already evident, if somewhat muted. The problem certainly began to be noticed after Momoh's new recruits were sent to the front. Even the NPRC coup was significantly aided by these recruits; they certainly played a major role in the looting of Freetown after the coup. But the NPRC leadership, all of them belonging to the old APC army, were quickly able to bring them under relative control and stabilise their regime. This did not happen after the AFRC coup, for the simple and sufficient reason that the people who made this coup were the drifters and thieves who were so hastily brought into the army after the war started. They now dominated the military structure, and for all practical purposes the army as an institution had collapsed.

As a junta (a word that has now taken a profoundly sinister connotation in Sierra Leone) the AFRC acted in a completely anarchic manner. Now free from the control of civil society and government, the so-called People's Army conveniently jettisoned the conventions and restraints and even the symbols of military life. At the junta's HQ in Freetown, AFRC members moved around without their uniforms. Indeed, unlike all other coups in history, this one was made by soldiers wearing civilian clothes and was crucially aided by common criminals serving gaol sentences. That certainly goes beyond what can be reasonably considered tactical considerations, as does Major Koroma's appearance in public and before the international press clad in denim jeans and trade mark T-shirts. He even drove through the capital once in a stolen UN vehicle, wearing a University of Maryland T-shirt. Koroma, a disarmingly taciturn and apparently naïve man with a well-shaven, anodyne face, acted throughout the junta's period of chaotic rule with extraordinary recklessness and brutality. By inviting the RUF to join his junta in Freetown, and having the rebels take command of the junta's security, he virtually made himself hostage to the demented tactics of the RUF. RUF members in the AFRC at one meeting reportedly tore the insignia off the uniforms of Sierra Leone army personnel who attended a meeting of the council in May as a way of showing who really was now in command. Actions like these went beyond evidence of institutional instability: there was no longer any military institution to speak of.

I had heard about Koroma before, and in no less villainous circumstances. It was in 1995 after the rebel attack on and destruction of the Sierra Rutile titanium mines, a rich venture run mainly by British and Australian officials which Koroma had been assigned by the NPRC to protect. Officials at the mines were unimpressed by the conduct of his troops in the area, and asked that they be allowed to bring in armed security personnel. Their request, however, was turned down by the junta. Pride was mainly responsible for this: the NPRC junta's soldiers were unwilling just yet to concede that they had lost control of their own troops or how bad the security situation had become. When the RUF rebels struck at the mines, there was no resistance from the junta's troops. Soon after that, property from the mines, including VCRs, computers and furniture, began to surface in the underground markets in Freetown, and there were strong rumours that Koroma had 'sold out' the mines to the RUF so that he and his troops would share in the loot.[10]

The next news about Koroma came in 1996, shortly after the new, elected government of President Kabbah took office: Koroma was arrested, along with a few other soldiers, on an allegation that he was plotting a coup, and was detained at Pademba Road prison to await trial. In the prison he became a born-again Christian. Shortly afterwards a most un-Christian event occurred, and Koroma was at the centre of it: the AFRC coup.

In his first public statement after the coup Koroma declared that the military had to overthrow the Kabbah government because the President's brand of ethnic politics had polarised the country into regional and ethnic factions, and his democracy was flawed. Quite how the democracy was flawed was not made clear; but the AFRC's insistence that Kabbah had given greater attention and support to the Mende-dominated CDF at the expense of the army, and that this had caused ethnic tensions, reflected resentment not just among the decidedly northern-dominated army but increasingly among the country's opposition politicians, most of them from the Northern Province. Perhaps the most vocal in this respect were Abass Bundu and John Karefa-Smart,[11] who frequently appeared in the local press, and whose rhetoric was inflammatory and clearly subversive. Predictably both of these politicians rallied to the sup-

---

[10] Koroma persistently denied this interpretation to me. Needless to say, he never convinced me.

[11] In *Democracy by Force?* (Boca Raton, FL: Universal Publishers, 2000), a stinging attack on President Kabbah and the Nigerian-led intervention that reinstated him after the 1997–8 rule of the AFRC, Abass Bundu argues that he and Karefa-Smart were never supporters of the junta but merely wanted a peaceful resolution of the crisis. He writes that the depiction of their role as collaborators of the junta was Kabbah-led propaganda: 'Democratic opponents were dressed up in the garb of rebel collaborators. By engaging in such vitriol, cloaked with officialese, the government's calculation must have been that its propaganda would take root and multiply until it became commonplace, until it became parody and until it became popular jargon...' (p. xiii) This obviously confusing and tortuous defence only raises the obvious question: would the government, then in exile, have attempted this kind of propaganda if, by their pronouncements and actions, Bundu and Karefa-Smart had not made their closeness to the junta obvious? In fact, even Sierra Leoneans who had little time for Kabbah and his SLPP government—including journalists who had had brushes with that government—found Bundu's anti-Kabbah rhetoric during the junta's rule in very bad taste.

port of the AFRC. But most of the charges against the CDF, and particularly the fear that Kabbah intended to have them replace the army as the national defence force, were false, and few took them seriously.

Still, Koroma, pointing to the number of bloody clashes, most of them provoked by the national army's *sobel* elements, between the militia group and the army before the coup, claimed that the AFRC by taking over had rescued the nation 'from a brink of a calamity that is too horrendous to contemplate'. The coup, therefore, was 'not actuated by lust for power, nor motivated by malice or a desire to bring untold suffering on the people and Sierra Leone'. This is an interesting defence—whose charges he was responding to no one could tell at the time, for the statement was made shortly after the coup—and it certainly spoke volumes about the true intentions of the coup leaders. Not surprisingly, Koroma also attacked the demobilisation process, accusing Kabbah of the 'arbitrary discharge of soldiers and retirement of officers from the army, without availing them of earned entitlements.' At the time of the coup the government had pressured the army to retire 200 of their oldest personnel, some of them nearly eighty years old. Before this there had been no retirement from the army apart from political dismissals and voluntary withdrawal. The government had proposed halving the army within six months, but the army insisted that the demobilisation process should be spread over a three-year period. The retirement of the 200 soldiers amounted to a compromise step taken by the army, and it was bitterly resented by many soldiers because the action was seen as a prelude to more comprehensive demobilisation.

All of these things were well known, at least in Freetown. As a result, the AFRC coup was condemned by many as self-serving and a disaster, and a massive nationwide effort was almost spontaneously launched to overturn it. The Kamajors were the first to vow resistance to the junta, but the vast majority of Sierra Leoneans showed their opposition to the coup by simply staying at home and refusing to go to work even after repeated threats of dismissal by the junta. Out of this nationwide resistance sprang the Movement for the Restoration of Democracy (MRD), which incorporated almost all the pressure groups and civil organisations plus the Kamajors and the northern-based Kapras, a very anti-RUF group. The latter two groups came together to form a stronger, more diversified CDF force to oppose the AFRC. President Kabbah, in exile in Guinea, was supreme head of this new CDF, with his Vice

President, Joe Demby, as deputy head. Hinga Norman was third in command, but because of his great popularity among the grass-roots and the Kamajors, and his demonstrated courage (he was the only cabinet member who stayed in the country, in hiding, after the coup), he effectively became the coordinator of the CDF.

But this nationwide resistance at first appeared to be undermined by the apparent fragmentation of the country along political party/ethnic lines, with the United National Peoples Party (UNPP) led by Karefa-Smart, the All Peoples Congress (APC) led by Eddie Turay, and the Peoples Progressive Party (PPP) led by Abass Bundu, all of them drawing their support largely from the Northern Province, increasingly tending to support the AFRC. Of course Kabbah's Sierra Leone Peoples Party (SLPP) quickly condemned the coup and became a vocal part of the MRD; and so did the Peoples Democratic Party (PDP) of Thaimu Bangura (a cabinet minister in Kabbah's government), although the PDP itself drew its support largely from the north. It soon became clear, however, that the pro-AFRC politicians, many of whom had bad reputations anyway, were actuated not by principle but by sheer opportunism. The UNPP itself had split into two factions a few months before the coup: 14 out of 17 members of the parliamentary wing had been expelled from the party by Karefa-Smart, who was later suspended from Parliament for one year. Some members of the parliamentary wing did not follow Karefa-Smart's pro-AFRC position, but joined other parliamentarians in passing a resolution which called for the reinstatement of the country's legitimate government. In contrast Karefa-Smart became an envoy of the AFRC in its diplomatic efforts to frustrate the Nigerian-led force in Sierra Leone, which vowed to oust the AFRC. Soon afterwards, his diplomatic endeavours having been repudiated by the UN and Western governments, Karefa-Smart's relationship with the junta became strained, and he put out a 'Position Paper' calling for a 'national conference' of representative of all political parties, ethnic groups and civic organisations, and the release of Foday Sankoh to take part in this conference. That too was ignored, and the octogenarian politician retired to the United States once again in self-exile. Abass Bundu's case was a different one altogether; unlike Karefa-Smart, Bundu did not have support or standing to begin with: his party could muster only 3 per cent of the vote in the 1996 elections, and therefore had no seats in Parliament.

So the initial impression that the AFRC's coup was a northern one was a myth; it quickly dissolved in the face of hard reality.

The junta attracted mainly opportunistic politicians no longer in office such as Joe Amara Bangalie (a southerner), Pallo Bangura (a northerner, sacked by Kabbah as ambassador to the UN), and ex-President Momoh, who became an unofficial adviser to the junta. It also appointed Solomon Musa, the former deputy leader of the NPRC who had been sacked and sent into exile in Britain. A flamboyant and irresponsible figure, Musa was later killed during the rebel attack on Freetown in January 1999. The presence of all these figures in the AFRC and the persistent terror and instability of the regime only fuelled popular resentment and resistance; six months after the coup, the AFRC leadership was still complaining of general acts of lawlessness and anarchy perpetrated by its own members and supporters, which, it claimed, were 'inconsistent with state stability'.

On 25 June, the AFRC announced that it had foiled a coup plot and proceeded to arrest and detain a number of senior officers, including Colonel Tom Carew, a northerner. Politicians linked to the SLPP, including Sama Banya, Elizabeth Lavalie (the country's most prominent female parliamentarian) and Abu Aiah Koroma, Kabbah's Minister of Presidential Affairs, were also arrested and detained but all released without charge a month later. The junta thereafter launched a vicious offensive against towns and villages they believed to be harbouring the CDF. Moyamba, a large town in the south of the country, was attacked in June and sacked. About 100 people were massacred by the AFRC's People's Army. On 28 June junta troops struck at various parts of Bo district, killing twenty-five people and razing to the ground Telu, HQ town of Jaiama Bongor chiefdom, where Hinga Norman was regent chief. The AFRC also cold-bloodedly murdered the octogenarian Paramount Chief Sami Demby, uncle of Vice President Joe Demby. Needless to say, the press was also not spared in these attacks. Newspapers perceived to be opposed to the AFRC, which meant all but a few of the existing papers, were raided, journalists beaten up and tortured, and in some cases their offices ransacked and equipment and vehicles stolen. More than half of the journalists in the country fled into exile. But the pressure on the junta remained unrelenting.

Sierra Leoneans abroad condemned and agitated against the coup. About a week after the takeover 1,500 demonstrated in Washington against the AFRC and called for US military intervention to overturn it. Through the Sierra Leone e-mail discussion group Leonenet, some formed Citizens for the Restoration of Democracy and sent a letter to the UN Secretary General supporting the efforts of the Nigerian-led intervention force in its determination to overturn the coup. Many of these agitations were launched in North America, and were largely inspired by John Leigh, Sierra Leone's outspoken Ambassador in the United States and High Commissioner in Canada, and James Jonah, the country's urbane Permanent Representative at the UN.

Opposition to the coup took a dramatic turn in August after university students announced a massive nationwide demonstration against the junta. The National Union of Sierra Leone Students (NUSS) soon received the support of the Labour Congress, the Sierra Leone Association of Journalists (SLAJ), the Women's Movement for Peace (led by Zainab Bangura) and other civil society organisations. But the demonstration was ruthlessly crushed by the junta on Monday 18 August. The People's Army attacked the peaceful demonstrators with machetes and live bullets. At least two students were killed as they tried to take cover at the Nursing Home, and another was murdered by the soldiers in his room at Fourah Bay College. In Bo demonstrators were dispersed by the junta's soldiers who fired live bullets over their heads. At Lungi, the location of the only international airport—which was occupied by Nigerian troops shortly after the coup—the demonstration went ahead without incident, with hundreds turning up to condemn the junta and demand the restoration of the elected government.

Overall the demonstration was bloodily crushed, but the verdict of the lively Freetown daily, the *Standard Times*, in an editorial (22 August 1997), was: 'The brutal action of the [AFRC] in killing, wounding and maiming pro-democrats is an affront not only to the people of this country but to the whole world. The nation, particularly the students, had nonetheless succeeded in letting their voices be heard: that they have not and will not tolerate the leadership of the junta no matter what resistance they face.' The AFRC was soon to face other opponents, this time ones who could not be scared away by its tactics.

Ecomog and Sandline

Although the Nigerian-led force that finally ousted the AFRC in February 1998 was called the ECOWAS Monitoring Group, or Ecomog, the initial Nigerian intervention to restore President Kabbah to power after the coup was a bilateral one. It flowed from the Status of Forces Agreement (SOFA) signed as part of the bilateral military pact. The agreement provided for the deployment of Nigerian troops in Sierra Leone to protect the elected government, help retrain the disintegrated Sierra Leone army and oversee implementation of the Abidjan Accord in the absence of UN troops (the United States vetoed a UN suggestion to deploy 700 troops for that purpose). But the SOFA had one serious defect: the Nigerian troops would only go into action after direct orders from the Nigerian government or in self-defence. In the event, even though plans for the AFRC coup were leaked to the Nigerians at least three days in advance, they could not attempt to pre-empt it. The few dozen armed soldiers and their convict allies who led the coup easily overwhelmed the Nigerian unit based at State House and the main government radio station, and forced President Kabbah to flee to Guinea. It was then that the Nigerian leader General Sani Abacha vowed to overturn the coup and reinstate his friend Kabbah.

But the first Nigerian attempts to do so were clumsy and ended in failure. On 31 May, after its 900-strong contingent had been reinforced by a further 700, the Nigerians moved to take over strategic positions in the capital. The attempt was botched, and the People's Army quickly rounded up 300 Nigerian soldiers and detained them. The Nigerians responded by using their gunboats to attack the junta's HQ and other targets. Most of the shells missed their targets and struck civilians. In the ensuing confusion the AFRC also attacked civilian areas to give the impression that the Nigerians were doing so. Over sixty civilians—some say 300—were killed as a result. The Nigerians withdrew their warships in June but they proceeded slowly to reinforce their troops. The AFRC unexpectedly freed the 300 Nigerian soldiers it was holding after a week, but there were other issues to tackle. Nigeria itself was ruled by a brutal and obdurate military regime, so it was necessary to build up an alliance of West African states to ensure that the campaign against the AFRC would not appear as a stand-off between General Abacha and the Freetown junta. Ecomog came in handy.

A four-nation committee comprising the foreign ministers of Nigeria, Ghana, Côte d'Ivoire and Guinea met in July 1997 and agreed to pursue 'any method that would restore the legitimate government of Sierra Leone'. But the agreement did not extend to a specific and concrete method. The problem was not merely a matter of awkward detail. Two committee members, Ghana and Côte d'Ivoire, said they favoured peaceful negotiations, including the use of sanctions. The West African states imposed a 'general and total embargo on all supplies of petroleum products, arms and military equipment' to Sierra Leone, and travel bans on members of the Freetown junta. All members of ECOWAS were called upon to 'abstain from transacting any business' with Sierra Leone. This was followed by a British-sponsored UN resolution which imposed a comprehensive set of sanctions on the junta, thus making the campaign against the AFRC a global one.

However, enforcement of the sanctions, which was left in the hands of the Nigerians, created controversy. Nigerian troops, which had been significantly reinforced since the May fiasco (there were only 3,000 in the country at the time), controlled land access to Freetown and its main airport at Lungi. Its navy prevented ships from unloading not just fuel (which was covered by the sanctions regime) but also rice (which was not), thus virtually 'besieging' Freetown, in the words of the influential French daily *Le Monde*.[12] Voices of outrage were raised when the Nigerians bombed selected targets in Freetown, including the main military barracks at Cockerill. There was no doubt that the Nigerians were at war with the AFRC.

The AFRC's response, while perhaps predictable, was horrific nonetheless. Their most effective resistance was to attempt to portray the Nigerians as killing civilians in Freetown in their heavy-handed effort to enforce the sanctions, and thereby trigger international outrage against the Nigerians. Their weapons of choice were mortars and grenade launchers, weapons whose projectiles exploded on hitting the ground. In October 1997, a flypast by some Nigerian jets over Freetown left thirty-five civilians dead, victims of projectiles fired by the junta's forces.[13] This was the famous Mabayla incident. The BBC, reporting the incident, announced that the Nigerians were responsible for the killings. Events such as these underlined the urgency of unseating the junta.

The AFRC announced its intention to stay in power until 2001, but sustained military, civil society and diplomatic pressures forced it to sign a 'peace plan' on 23 October 1997, which committed it to hand over power in 1998. This was the Conakry Peace Plan. Shortly before the meetings in the Guinean capital that led to the accord, Kabbah, who was still recognised by all governments and international organisations as Sierra Leone's legitimate head of state, made an impressive presentation of the country's woes at the UN General Assembly. He appealed eloquently for the restoration of his legiti-

[12] *Le Monde*, 28 January 1998.
[13] Ibid.

mate government. Kabbah was to follow this with a one-day work-shop on his government's plans for its projected ninety days in office after restoration to power. The workshop was sponsored by the British Department for International Development, which was effectively bankrolling the exiled government. At the time of the workshop, Kabbah also had the opportunity to make his case at the Commonwealth Heads of Government meeting in Edinburgh, to which he was invited by the Blair government and the Common-wealth Secretariat. It was during this same period that the Security Council passed its unanimous resolution on the immediate rein-statement of Kabbah and support for the ECOWAS-initiated sanc-tion regime.

The Conakry Peace Plan was brokered by the ECOWAS Commit-tee, and it called for the immediate cessation of hostilities in Sierra Leone, the restoration of Kabbah, the demobilisation of all combat-ants by Ecomog (to start on 1 December), the commencement of humanitarian assistance (on 15 November), the return of refugees from neighbouring countries, the granting of immunity to mem-bers of the AFRC, and the release of Foday Sankoh from detention in Nigeria. Sankoh 'could continue to play an active role and partic-ipate in the peace process', the Accord stated, without specifying what that role might be. The Plan also called for the formation of a broad-based government after Kabbah's restoration, and for an eth-nic balance in top-level appointments to the public service.[14]

Both the exiled Kabbah government and the AFRC accepted the Plan in principle, but its implementation was soon undermined by the incoherence and unpredictability of the junta. A few preliminary meetings were held between the AFRC and Ecomog to establish the groundwork for the deployment of Ecomog troops throughout the country. But the junta began to raise objections in a number of vital areas. It first called for the reduction and then the removal of Nige-rian troops in Ecomog, as well as the immediate release of Sankoh, as conditions to move forward. It claimed that Nigerian troops were effectively part of the problem, their main enemy. The junta also opposed plans to disband the army on grounds that it was a 'national institution' protected by the Constitution. The Ecomog comman-der, Victor Malu, countered that the AFRC was illegal and therefore had no authority to question the composition of Ecomog.

[14] ECOWAS Six Month Peace Plan for Sierra Leone, 23 October 1997–22 April 1998, Conakry (Sierra Leone Web, Documents Section).

Internal problems within the AFRC probably posed graver threats to the implementation of the Conakry Plan. In November the junta announced that it had foiled a coup plot organised by some of its own members and staunch supporters who were opposed to the Conakry Plan. The coup plot was said to have been led by Steven Bio, a wealthy businessman who had allegedly sponsored an earlier coup plot against Kabbah in August 1996. Bio, elder brother of the former NPRC leader Brigadier Julius Maada Bio, was arrested by the AFRC and detained at Pademba Road prison along with many soldiers and civilians.[15] Koroma also arrested a number of his aides, including Tamba Gborie (who originally announced the coup), because of their involvement in 'some dubious activities' aimed at 'undermining the revenue-generating capacity' of the Ministry of Mines and Mineral Resouces. The soldiers, who had allegedly 'set in place a reign of anarchy inconsistent with state stability' in the diamond mining areas, were put under arrest.

The junta's inconsistencies and instability forced its opponents to consider other options. Kabbah became busy on another, far less diplomatic front. Through the energetic and amiable British High Commissioner to Sierra Leone, Peter Penfold—who, like the entire diplomatic corps in the country (except for a downsized staff at the Guinean embassy), had gone to Guinea and helped set up the Sierra Leonean government in exile (in a disused Chinese restaurant)—Kabbah made contacts with a British mercenary firm, Sandline International, and the Vancouver-based diamond mining company, DiamondWorks, to provide military expertise and arms for the CDF to oust the AFRC. DiamondWorks' main shareholder, a Canadian-based Thai businessman named Rakesh Saxena, agreed to underwrite the military assistance in exchange for diamond mining concessions.[16] The Sandline-Sierra Leone story is still obscure, even though the British government carried out extensive investigations into allegations of UN sanctions-busting by the mercenary outfit in collaboration with the British Foreign and Commonwealth Office in mid-1998. But it appears that apart from logistical and intelligence support to the Nigerians, the mercenary firm played only a small role in the eventual ousting of the AFRC. The 28 tons of small arms for the CDF it bought in Bulgaria arrived in Sierra Leone on 23 February 1998, after the AFRC had been expelled by the Nigerians, and were impounded by Ecomog.

[15] Steven Bio was still in detention when Kabbah was reinstated, and was killed during the rebel attack on Freetown in January 1999.
[16] *The Globe and Mail* (Toronto), 27 November 1997.

By January 1998 the Nigerians had amassed 10,000 troops around Freetown. But the assault against the junta's forces was not an entirely Nigerian action. Operation Sandstorm was coordinated between the Nigerians and the CDF, and Hinga Norman played a key role in it. The CDF began the operation by carrying out strikes against the junta's forces in strategic parts of the country, including the diamond regions of Kono and Tongo Field. This strategy was intended to keep the bulk of the People's Army away from the capital, and it worked. In the event, when the Nigerians struck in early February, most of the junta's best commanders, like Sam Bockarie, were away in the provinces battling against the CDF. The Nigerians struck at the junta's forces around Freetown at the end of January and secured the capital on 12 February 1998. Koroma and most of the leading junta figures fled to the interior of the country. President Kabbah triumphantly returned to Freetown on 10 March, and by April, 90 per cent of Sierra Leonean territory, including the diamond mining districts, had been secured by the Nigerians and the CDF. The intervention was a success, and the Nigerian commander, General Maxwell Khobe, won praise both in Sierra Leone and abroad as a remarkable and courageous military leader. He was later made Chief of Staff of the Sierra Leone army.

Shortly after Kabbah was reinstated, the government charged sixty people, members of the junta who were arrested as well as 'junta collaborators', with treason in four courts. The accused included Foday Sankoh, who was flown in by the Nigerians to face the charges, and prominent journalists like Hilton Fyle (a former presenter on the BBC World Service's popular early morning show 'Network Africa'), who allegedly used his private radio station during the junta's rule to incite soldiers against Kabbah's supporters and Nigerian interests in the country. The first trial of eighteen people, all civilians, ended on 25 August 1998. Sixteen were found guilty of treason and sentenced to death by hanging; they included a female broadcaster and Fyle. The other two were acquitted. A second trial, of twenty accused, convicted sixteen of treason and acquitted five. A third trial, which lasted till 4 November 1998, led to the conviction of sixteen civilians for treason and the acquittal of five. Among those acquitted of the treason charges was former President Momoh. The ex-President, however, was convicted on the lesser charge of conspiracy and sentenced to five years in prison. The fourth trial involved only Foday Sankoh, who was convicted of treason and condemned to be hanged. All those convicted appealed against their sentences.

Soldiers arrested in connection with the coup were tried separately, by court martial. On 12 October a court martial, presided over by a Nigerian officer, handed down its judgment on thirty-eight soldiers who were accused of treason. The court found thirty-four guilty and condemned them to death by firing squad. Unlike the civilian accused, the soldiers did not have the privilege of appeal, and on 19 October, twenty-four soldiers convicted of treason, including a woman officer who was a minister in the AFRC government, were executed by firing squad on the beaches of Freetown. The execution was open to public view. They were the unlucky ones. The convicted civilians, including Sankoh, were still awaiting the hearing of their appeals when the rebels, who had withdrawn to the countryside after their ousting by the Nigerians, struck at Freetown and freed almost all of them. Sankoh was not among those freed; Fyle was, and he subsequently fled to the United States and wrote a confused and highly coloured account of his exploits and tribulations, entitled *A Fighter From Death Row.*[17]

The January 1999 attack, the climax of the rebels' campaigns, finally brought more concentrated international attention to the crisis. To that we now turn.

---

[17] Hilton Ebenezer Fyle, *Sierra Leone: a Fighter from Death Row: Testimony of Survival by a Christian Journalist* (USA: Universal Publishers, 2000).

6

'OPERATION NO LIVING THING' AND TERROR AS WARFARE[1]

'I saw stiffened, blood-caked corpses littering sidewalks like macabre manikins placed there to haunt the living. The stink of death—dried blood, stale urine, and monkey-house fear—hung all over Freetown. Black smoke billowed from dozens of arson fires that still smoldered from combat several days earlier.' (Ian Stewart, AP correspondent shot in the head in Freetown during the rebel attack in January 1999[2])

'Immediately rebellion, forgetful of its generous origins, allows itself to be contaminated by resentment, it denies life, dashes toward destruction, and raises the grimacing cohorts of petty rebels...who end up offering themselves for sale...It is no longer either revolution or rebellion but rancor, malice, and tyranny.' (Albert Camus[3])

The east end of Freetown was a sprawling shantytown extending several miles from near the city centre, past the old colonial settlements of Kossoh Town, Kissy and Wellington to the newer, more isolated and bucolic Calabar Town, on the fringes of a charming but decaying city. Its wooden buildings, which had mostly become shiny with grime, told of an orderly, more hopeful colonial past. The settlements were built by liberated slaves—liberated by the British Anti-Slavery Squadron in the nineteenth century—who were reset-

---

[1] This account is mainly reconstructed from interviews the author conducted in Sierra Leone in July and August 1999, and again between February and May 2001. News reports on the Sierra Leone Web (www.sierra-leone.org, run by my good friend Peter Andersen in Minnesota) and *Ninja*, a clandestine publication run by pro-RUF activists with direct access to the rebel group's leadership, are also extensively used.

[2] Ian Stewart, *Freetown Ambush: A Reporter's Year in Africa*, Toronto: Penguin, 2002, p. xvi.

[3] Albert Camus, *The Rebel*, New York: Vintage Books, 1956, pp. 304–5.

tled in Freetown as part of Britain's anti-slavery effort. These ex-slaves, soon to emerge as enthusiastic (if sometimes caricature) Victorians, would become something of a vanguard of a British West African empire that was soon to extend from the small coastal settlement named Sierra Leone to places as far to the east as Nigeria, Ghana and Cameroon. The small wooden buildings were—with small touches of austere African style—in the style of North American colonial houses, particularly those found in Nova Scotia and the American South, from where the earlier settlers, all of them freed slaves, mostly originated. Newer, more extravagant modern brick buildings with wide verandas and open stores selling everything from groceries to textiles and wrist-watches had sprouted up—mainly the work of Fula, Temne and Lebanese traders, and mainly along Kissy Road, Kissy Street and Fourah Bay Road—since at least the 1950s, but these, especially in the Foulah Town, Fourah Bay and Kossoh Town areas, looked like exotic intrusions into an otherwise uniformly drab landscape.

This settlement, with its thousands of unemployed youth, rough streets and the miseries of poor or working-class life, including drugs, gambling, prostitution, petty theft and armed robbery, had been a hotbed of violent agitation since the days of British colonial rule. As early as 1919 unemployed youths in the area rioted because of rice scarcity, non-payment of war bonuses and what they saw as the unscrupulous trading practices of Syrian/Lebanese merchants. Many houses were set ablaze and shops looted. The colonial government used the army to crush the riots. Again in 1955 and 1956 riots broke out in the east end, with youths attacking and looting shops and the homes of local politicians. The riots were ostensibly sparked by allegations of corruption against local politicians and business people. Again the army was called in to quell the riots.

The youth of Freetown's seedy east end held a special fascination for the English novelist Graham Greene, who spent time in the country as a secret service agent during the Second World War to investigate suspicions that diamonds from the old British colony were being smuggled to Germany to be used in armaments factories, particularly those making rockets. He called them 'wharf rats', because they were mostly found about the area of the bustling Government Wharf (the country's main port) in the east end. In his famous novel *The Heart of the Matter*,[4] he described them as 'cowards but dangerous, boys of sixteen or so, armed with razors or bits of

[4] Graham Greene, *The Heart of the Matter*, New York: Viking Press, 1948, p. 34.

broken bottle. They swarmed in groups around the warehouses, pilfering if they found an easily opened case, settling like flies around any drunken sailor who stumbled their way, occasionally slashing a policeman who had made himself unpopular.'

It was little wonder that unscrupulous local politicians exploited this Dickensian environment for political purposes. Sierra Leone's longtime plunderer Siaka Stevens, who governed and looted the country for over two decades, recruited most of his party thugs and the notoriously brutal Special Security Division (SSD) forces from there. Others, less scrupulous about form and protocol, learned from Stevens' tactics. When the soldiers who formed the National Provisional Ruling Council (NPRC) junta in April 1992 stormed Freetown from the war front to unseat President Joseph Momoh, they struck first in the east end, quickly mobilising a large mass of unemployed youths who overwhelmed the city in an orgy of looting that convinced everyone that Momoh was finally gone. Shortly after this, the soldiers stormed State House, forcing the President to flee.

But nothing seemed to have prepared the east end's volatile residents for the events from early January 1999 to the end of the month. That was when the whole area became 'ground zero'. It was when, as one writer noted, 'the killers arrived in town':[5] the 6 January 1999 invasion of the city by rogue elements of the Sierra Leone Army, who had forged a marriage-of-convenience with the RUF after the coup by junior officers in 1997, to be joined by the rebels in an orgy of killing and destruction. The invasion even had a name: it was called 'Operation No Living Thing'.

'Operation No Living Thing' was declared in 1998 by the RUF's forces commander Sam Bockarie (alias Maskita or Mosquito) in a statement which was recklessly (perhaps criminally) broadcast on the BBC African Service, in which he declared that he was going to kill everyone in the country 'to the last chicken'.[6] It was his way of

[5] Omoru E. A. David, *The Coming of the Killers: Operation Burn Freetown*, Freetown, 1999.

[6] Throughout much of the conflict, the BBC World Service for Africa—with the exception of insightful reporters like Mark Doyle and Lansana Fofana—was a willing dupe, unprofessionally broadcasting highly inflammatory statements issued by the rebels, of which this broadcast was simply their most destructive. The rebel leadership, whose internal communications infrastructure was mostly poor, adeptly used the BBC to communicate orders to their fighters in the bush. According to several ex-RUF combatants I spoke to in Freetown in April 2002, a broadcast from Bockarie threatening, for example, to attack Freetown in a week would be inter-

avenging the ousting of the rebels from Freetown by Nigerian-led troops. Bockarie had taken over command of the RUF forces after the arrest of Foday Sankoh by the Nigerian government in 1997. A homicidal thug with little education, Bockarie was fiercely loyal to Sankoh. His brutality verged on the psychotic. Heeding Sankoh's encouragement, while in detention in Nigeria, of the RUF to join the bloody coup by renegade soldiers in 1997, Maskita soon became the principal muscle of the AFRC junta, carrying out several mass executions in its name in Freetown.

The overriding motivation for 'Operation No Living Thing' seems to have been Bockarie's determination to free Sankoh, who was then gaoled at Pademba Road prison, having been charged and found guilty of treason for his role in the 1997 coup. In the forests of Kailahun, where he had assembled his defeated forces, Bockarie had become their chief spokesman.

Bockarie's threats, however, were summarily dismissed by both the Kabbah government and Ecomog, which was effectively the government's only defence. The Sierra Leone Army (SLA) had largely self-destructed after the ousting of the AFRC, with many of its members fleeing to the bush with the RUF. The few thousand remaining, organised under the command of the Nigerian Brigadier-General Maxwell Khobe, proved treacherous in key engagements, joining the rebels and turning their guns against Nigerian Ecomog soldiers. The Civil Defence Force (CDF), principally the Kamajors, was kept largely unarmed by the Kabbah government, which did not entirely trust them. However, the Nigerians appeared on top of the situation. They were a 15,000-strong army, appearing to be professional, equipped with tanks and heavy artillery and backed by a sizeable air force. Surely the ragtag army of teenage hoodlums and dispirited SLA gangsters they had so easily thrown out of Freetown early in 1998 and swept out of most of the country would be no match for them?

In spite of gallant proclamations by the Ecomog commanders and spokesmen, however, observers were troubled by a string of stunning reverses that the Nigerian-dominated Ecomog forces were fac-

---

preted as an order to the scattered RUF fighters to move towards the city. The former British High Commissioner to Freetown, Peter Penfold, who was there at the time, told me (London, August 2002) that he protested to the BBC management about the 'Operation No Living Thing' broadcast, 'a form of murderous incitement which, if issued against British citizens, would certainly never have been broadcast by the BBC.'

ing in many parts of the country. By mid-December, the rebels had captured Koidu Town, the main city in Sierra Leone's premier diamond mining district. The Nigerian soldiers were busy mining diamonds when the rebels struck, after a mock attack on New Lebanon, a small diamond mining town once dominated by Lebanese traders. Several hundred Nigerian soldiers were killed in the Koidu Town attack and the rest fled to Makeni, dispirited and in disorder. Dozens more were killed in ambushes along the way. The rebel army captured a huge stockpile of arms and ammunition from the Nigerians, a loss which would badly reduce the military capacity of the Ecomog force. Koidu Town had been a major base, and a huge quantity—some reports say nearly 50 per cent—of Ecomog arms had been stockpiled there.

Next came the dramatic fall of Makeni to the rebel forces just about Christmas time. The strategically important northern city had been controlled by Ecomog since it ousted the AFRC. Again, hundreds of Nigerian soldiers were killed in the fighting. That same week the rebels attacked and overran Waterloo, only 20 miles from Freetown. This was followed by a rebel attack on Benguema, a major military barracks just a few miles from the capital. The rebel forces, led by Major Eddie Kanneh, a former Sierra Leone Army (SLA) officer, executed nine Ecomog soldiers they captured in their uniquely inventive style: they had their heads cut off, working from the back with near-blunt machetes.

This spectacular resurgence in rebel activities caused much bewilderment. How was it that a group that had been routed from power without much resistance, that had seen its control of nearly 70 per cent of the country reduced to scattered and isolated parts of northern and eastern Sierra Leone, and had been all but pronounced dead, resurge with such power and destructiveness? In fact the RUF escaped from Freetown in February 1998 largely unscathed and far better armed than when it arrived in May 1997. Aware of the overwhelming firepower of the Nigerian troops and air force, the rebels carefully avoided confrontation with them and withdrew deep into the forests of Kailahun district (which had always been their most strategic redoubt). Nigerian Ecomog troops, who completely lacked counterinsurgency training, failed dismally to pursue the rebels to their hide-outs, preferring conventional assaults against towns like Makeni and Kabala (from where the rebels would withdraw without a fight) and dropping bombs from thousands of feet up, most often missing the targets. Battered but hardly beaten, steadfastly maintaining its often underrated command structure, the rebels regrouped in the Kailahun rainforests, bringing most of the SLA renegades who had fled with them under the command of the RUF War Council.

Bockarie explained the development in notes prepared for the detained Sankoh thus: 'Immediately Freetown and the Provincial Headquarters fell in the hands of Ecomog [the Nigerian-led intervention force]...the High Command [of RUF], J.P.K [Major Johnny Paul Koroma], senior officers, junior officers and the entire combatants held a forum and finally agreed to continue the struggle under one structure and command.'[7] In fact this was hardly a partnership. The soldiers who fled with the RUF to the Front's Kailahun positions were simply incorporated into the rebel force. Koroma was himself soon detained by Bockarie, who had become his new boss, after a quarrel over diamonds and money.[8]

Another rebel force, with no apparent close contact with Bockarie's Kailahun-based forces, was on the run in the north of the country under the command of Solomon Musa. Musa was a swashbuckling former army captain who had been a strong man in the NPRC but was forced to retire early and sent to Britain to study in 1994. He was very popular with the rank and file soldiers for his brashness and seeming ability to represent their views to the officer corps. When the junior officers staged the AFRC coup, they promptly invited him from Britain to join them. He soon became the Chief Secretary of State (in effect prime minister), and fled to the bush when the Nigerian forces drove the AFRC out of Freetown. Although he coordinated his efforts with those of the main rebel forces under the command of Bockarie—who had received significant supplies from Liberia and Burkina Faso—Musa operated almost autonomously. His forces, however, participated in the Bockarie-led attack that took Kono and routed the Nigerians in the district.

The operation that led to the capture of Kono illuminates many of the forces that made the Sierra Leone war so destructive and criminal: diamonds, mercenaries, international racketeers and the Liberian/Burkinabe connection. British newspaper accounts in January 1999 revealed that the RUF, through Liberia's President Taylor, its main sponsor, had contracted two British companies

[7] The Black Revolutionary Guards, 'To the Leader: Situation Report', undated handwritten notes (in author's possession).
[8] Major General Sam Bockarie, 'Letter to the Leader of the Revolution, RUF SL', 26 September 1999.

operating 'ageing' Boeing aircraft to ferry arms and 'white' mercenaries (including South Africans and Ukrainians) to rebel-held areas of Sierra Leone in exchange for diamonds.[9] These mercenaries helped train the rebels and participated directly in the attack on Koidu Town, according to eyewitnesses. A retired South African army officer on contract with Charles Taylor to train his Anti-Terrorist Unit provided most of the training for the RUF rebels and their renegade SLA allies, so that the rebels' offensives against Kono and Makeni and their early January 1999 invasion of Freetown looked like 'textbook South African army' tactics.[10] It turned out that central to these deals was an Israeli businessman described by one UN report as 'a business partner and confidant of Liberian President Charles Taylor'. Police records in several European countries reveal his involvement in organised criminal activities, arms trafficking and money laundering. On 22 December one final shipment of arms to the RUF by this man proved crucial in the catastrophic RUF attack on Freetown two weeks after. His BAC-111 flew weapons from Burkina Faso into Liberia, and from there they were ferried by helicopter into rebel-held parts of Sierra Leone.[11]

In tense Freetown, with its weak, barely functioning government, and an ill-paid and therefore unco-operative Nigerian army holding the fort, these events were not monitored: there was simply no capacity for that. Also troubling was the rift among the Nigerian army commanders leading Ecomog, and the lack of respect for these officers among the rank and file because of the apparent corruption of the officer corps. The commander of the Nigerian Ecomog force, called the Sierra Leone Task Force, Brigadier-General Ahmed Ahmadu, openly sparred with his predecessor who was now head of the shattered Sierra Leone Army, Brigadier-General Maxwell Khobe, a highly respected soldier who had led the offensive that drove out the AFRC junta. Soldiers' pay was delayed and when paid was largely skimmed off by the officers. Payroll theft was rampant. A large number of the frontline officers and soldiers were engaged in diamond mining, and as *The Economist* reported, these

---

[9] *Sunday Times*, 23 January 1999; also Ian Smillie, Lansana Gberie and Ralph Hazleton, *The Heart of the Matter: Sierra Leone, Diamonds and Human Security*, Ottawa: Partnership Africa Canada, 2000.

[10] Herbert Howe, *Ambiguous Order: Military Forces in African States*, Boulder, CO: Lynne Rienner Publishers, 2001, p. 221.

[11] *Report of the Panel of Experts Appointed Pursuant to Security Council Resolution 1306 (2000), paragraph 19, in relation to Sierra Leone*, p. 36.

soldiers 'made local deals with the RUF, in one place mining on opposite sides of a river bank.'[12] This was in Kono, and it was the main reason why the Nigerians were taken completely by surprise when Bockarie's forces attacked, killing many of them.

Sadly, there was no one in authority to step in and ensure order and discipline. Ecomog continued to reassure the worried Freetown population that all was under control, and journalists asserting otherwise were arrested and detained. In the first week of January 1999 Ecomog announced that its forces had killed 100 rebel soldiers who had dared attack their base in Hastings, about 15 miles from Freetown. Nigerian Alpha jets were used in the counter-attack against the rebels. Civilian survivors, however, reported that Hastings had been completely overrun by the rebels, who withdrew after the Alpha jets started to pound their positions, in the process losing dozens of their fighters. In fact it turned out that Ecomog was correct, but hardly in a reassuring way. That same week members of the United Nations Observer Mission in Sierra Leone (Unomsil), which had withdrawn in panic after the fall of Makeni, began to return to the country 'in view of the improving security situation', according to an announcement by the UN Special Representative in Sierra Leone, Francis Okello. The Kamajor militia group, the most determined foe of the rebel forces, also announced a string of victories against the rebels, beating them back from key areas in the Eastern and Northern Provinces. It turned out, however, that these victories were mainly against the RUF forces left behind by the main ex-SLA force under the command of Solomon Musa. It was in this state of confusion, claims and counter-claims that the rebel forces entered Freetown on 6 January 1999.

The rebels had infiltrated the city a week or so before, joining civilians displaced by their attacks on Hastings, Waterloo and the surrounding villages to flock into the city with their weapons wrapped in dirty bundles. It was a familiar RUF tactic, causing mass displacement by attacking villages and joining the movement of frightened villagers to infiltrate towns and cities; and it was one extremely difficult to counter. A small group had also fought its way to Mount Aureol, where Fourah Bay College is located. The area conveniently overlooks the east end of Freetown; a rugged bush road (which residents call a 'canal') from the top of the hills goes down to Savage Square, the heart of the east end. Freetown resi-

---

[12] 'Sierra Leone: Diamond King', *Economist*, 29 January 2000, p. 52.

dents appeared to have been taken completely by surprise and shocked by the speed of the rebel takeover of the city.

The attacks began at about 3 a.m., with shelling heard simultaneously in Calabar Town, Savage Square and Wellington. From the east end of Freetown the rebels moved straight to Pademba Road prison, where large numbers of RUF and ex-SLA soldiers, including Sankoh, had been detained after the ousting of the AFRC. A large number of these had faced or were facing treason charges. The rebels overpowered the small detachment of Nigerian troops guarding the prison and blasted open the gates, freeing and arming the detainees. Sankoh, however, had been quietly removed from the prison, on 23 December, and taken to an undisclosed place—a clear indication that the government and the Ecomog command were anticipating the rebel attack on Freetown at least two weeks before it happened.[13]

By 7 a.m. the rebels had taken over State House in central Freetown. A rebel spokesman was heard briefly announcing the overthrow of President Kabbah on a local FM station, but a Nigerian Alpha jet quickly blasted the station from the air. Instead President Kabbah broadcast a message on the state radio, affirming that he was still in control and urging residents to resist the rebels. In fact Kabbah had barely managed to escape this latest onslaught. He was ferried across the sea to Lungi, where the Nigerians maintained a strong garrison, a few minutes before the rebels—no doubt tipped off by someone in the President's camp—arrived in the area.

What happened next was a regime of horror lasting nearly two weeks and so intense and bizarre that it almost defies description. Most of the rebels who entered Freetown were ex-SLA soldiers loyal to Solomon Musa who had been killed a week before, reportedly by

---

[13] In testimony to the High Court in Freetown the Israeli Yair Klein said that both the Sierra Leone government and the Ecomog leadership knew that the rebels would attack weeks before the January invasion but decided not to put up resistance. It was hoped that such a dramatic attack, which would be contained, would finally convince the international community to come to the aid of the beleaguered government and peacekeeping force, and perhaps lead to the killing of a large number of the rebels' senior commanders, who had been very elusive. If this is true—and indeed Finance Minister James Jonah's statements to the BBC after the attacks would seem to indicate that it is—then there must have been a very curious underestimation of the RUF's capacity for terror and its reckless disregard for international opinion.

friendly fire (although Ecomog officers claimed they were responsible). However, except for the burning down of some houses in
Wellington and Kissy and the inevitable looting of shops, there was
at first a semblance of command and control among the rebels. But
after Kabbah spoke the rebels immediately armed thousands of
teenage RUF fighters, almost all of them wearing bandages on the
side of the head where incisions had been made to pack crack
cocaine under their skin. They seemed completely insane or delirious. They rounded up whole neighbourhoods, forcing frightened
civilians to stage a demonstration of welcome for them. Those not
showing enough enthusiasm were gunned down immediately. Hundreds were killed in this way.

The older SLA soldiers joined in after the Nigerians, recovering
from the shock of the surprise attack and the horrors of rebel carnage, counter-attacked in an operation they code-named 'Death
Before Dishonour'. This was just as well, since the rebel invasion
clearly represented a spectacular failure of the Nigerian military.
Realising that their grip on large parts of Freetown would falter, the
rebels dug in from central Freetown through to the far eastern end
of the city and for nearly two weeks attacked the homes of civilians,
killing those who refused to give them money or who looked well-
fed, or whom they simply disliked. There was a millenarian quality
to the terror: random, ecstatic and finally comprehensive. It was
also perversely inventive.

Edward Conteh, a middle-aged former seaman, had fled the city
to the Mount Aureol hills with his wife and eight children in the
first week of the rebel attack. A daring young man had killed a rebel
soldier he found raping his very young sister in his Fourah Town
home. In reprisal a group of the rebels stormed the area, indiscriminately killing seventy civilians. Conteh escaped with his family and
hid in the hills for three days. When he and his family were starving,
he decided to go into town to look for food. There he ran into the
rebels on 15 January. I met Conteh in July 1999 in the camp for
amputees, a depressing collection of tin and wood shacks housing
at the time about 300 people who had had their hands chopped off
by the rebels. The camps were based in Aberdeen, in the west of
Freetown, and there he told me his story. 'I ran into the rebels on
Kissy road. They had with them eleven civilians they had picked up,
three of them caught burying hands amputated by the RUF. I was
thrown among them. No one asked me any questions. The rebels
then gunned down nine of their captives and amputated three of
us,' he explained, seeing my eyes fixed on his stumped arms. 'The

rebels told us to go to President Kabbah since he has lots of medicines.' The rebels had heard that an aid agency was in the country
helping to sew up severed hands, so now they would bag all hands
they chopped off and take them away. It was not to eat them, as
many have alleged, but simply to deprive their victims of any chance
of having their hands back. Cruelty cannot explain that: this was
not rational violence. Victims begging to be killed were ignored:
the rebels were simply interested in chopping off the hands.

Two-year-old Memuna Mansaray was found hidden in a mosque
with her mother and grandmother at Wellington. The rebels shot
her mother in the shoulder and, leaving her for dead, grabbed
Memuna. They clinically cut off her left hand with a machete and
threw her on top of her mother. I also met Memuna at the camp for
amputees. She was living with her uncle, who was also amputated by
the rebels that same day. Her mother had died of her wounds, her
father had also been killed. By the time I met Memuna, in July
1999, she had become something of a celebrity, a living symbol of
the senselessness and barbarism of rebel warfare.[14]

Ghoulish games were played. In Calabar Town a group of teenage rebels raided the home of an elderly gentleman and dragged
him outside. A large hen was feeding in his garden. The rebels told
the old man to catch the hen for them. They were laughing but the
old man knew this was an order. He aimed carefully and sprang on
the hen. He missed. There was a burst of laughter and automatic
fire. The old man lay dead along with the hen. Events such as these
were not rare; indeed the rebel campaign in Freetown would have
been farcical had it not been so appalling. Take, for example, the
fate of Dr Dhaniya, a professor of agronomy at the University of
Sierra Leone. He was gunned down by the rebels because they found
an academic gown in his room. They probably mistook the gown
for that of a lawyer—a figure who clearly rated top of the list of
rebel demonology: it represented, for them, the dread of civil soci-

---

[14] President Kabbah took Memuna to Lome, capital of Togo, for the signing of the shambolic accord with the RUF in July 1999, and held her up
for the TV cameras immediately after signing the very unpopular and, it
turned out, unrealistic accord, declaring, 'I am signing this for victims
like this!' After the accord, however, Memuna was dumped back in the
horrible camp where I found her far away from the triumphant presidential hands. Memuna now lives in the United States, taken there by a US-
based charity. I last saw a picture of her standing with New York Senator
Hillary Clinton, her husband Bill and several other young amputees
from Sierra Leone. Prosthetics operations had been performed on them.

ety, of higher learning, the rule of law, and more particularly of those who had tried and condemned their leader Foday Sankoh for treason the year before. Before the rebels left, they also gunned down Dhaniya's wife and set the house ablaze.

No one knew how many women were raped but it must have been hundreds. Hundreds more, particularly teenage girls, were abducted as the rebels fled the superior fire-power of the advancing Nigerian forces. Two senior government ministers were abducted and murdered, and the homes of many others were burned down. In the first week of the fighting, the rebels burned to ashes 500 buildings, including government offices and private homes, in central Freetown alone, and one newspaper claimed that at the height of the fighting 550 bodies were cremated on one day.[15]

Rebel atrocities in Kissy, Wellington and Calabar Town, where they reigned supreme for over two weeks, were so gruesome that witnesses often avoid talking about them because of their sheer wantonness and incredibility. At night, because there was a blackout, the rebels would lock up whole families in their houses and set them ablaze, so that there would be light in the area. It was during this period, while the rebels were terrorising eastern Freetown and the Nigerians were advancing from the west, that a cruel twist of fate allowed the rebels to open a new phase of horror in the city: a group of them raided a World Food Programme (WFP) warehouse at Kissy looking for food, but instead discovered hundreds of brand-new machetes which had been brought in by the UN agency to be given to peasant farmers. Intended to be used for the cultivation of food, the machetes were now used by the rebels crudely and methodically to cut off the hands of people, including those of hundreds of people who could have used them to grow food.[16] The perversion was complete: the tragedy was brutally surreal. This was how the mass amputations inflicted on civilians began in Freetown in January 1999, violations which finally obtained for the long-drawn-out brutalities of the rebels international attention—and their ultimate undoing.

The New York-based rights monitoring group, Human Rights Watch, meticulously documented the atrocities in a graphic report that must have shocked even those who were familiar with the RUF's bestiality:

The rebel occupation of Freetown was characterized by the systematic and widespread perpetration of all classes of gross human rights abuses against

---

[15] *Africa Confidential*, 22 January 1999.
[16] Interviews in Freetown, July 1999.

the civilian population. Civilians were gunned down within their houses, rounded up and massacred on the streets, thrown from the upper floors of buildings, used as human shields, and burnt alive in cars and houses. They had their limbs hacked off with machetes, eyes gouged out with knives, hands smashed with hammers, and bodies burned with boiling water. Women and girls were systematically sexually abused, and children and young people abducted by the hundreds.

The rebels made little distinction between civilian and military targets. They repeatedly stated that they believed civilians should be punished for what they perceived to be their support for the existing government. Thus, the rebels waged war against the civilian population through their perpetration of human rights abuses. While there was some targeting of particular groups, such as Nigerians, police officers,[17] journalists, and church workers, the vast majority of atrocities were committed by rebels who chose their victims apparently at random...

It is difficult to ascertain the level of seniority within the RUF at which the perpetration of human rights abuses was ordered, though the widespread participation in abuses suggests that they must have been authorized at a high level within the RUF's command structures. Victims and witnesses frequently overheard commanders on the ground give orders to perpetrate atrocities, and there are very few accounts of individual combatants and commanders trying to halt the abuses. When witnesses reported that individual combatants did object and try to halt the abuses, those objecting were often met with death threats from their fellow rebels.

The atrocities were often planned and premeditated. Victims and witnesses describe well-organized operations to round up civilians who were later executed, attacked with machetes, or raped. On several occasions rebels gave advance warning that atrocities were to be committed later. Witnesses describe the existence of distinct units for committing particular crimes, like the Burn House Unit, Cut Hands Commando, and Blood Shed Squad. Some of these squads had a trademark way of killing, such as Kill Man No Blood unit, whose method was to beat people to death without shedding blood, or the Born Naked Squad, who stripped their victims before killing them.[18]

Calculated cruelty? Certainly. Yet the ecstatic character of such acts makes even cruelty meaningless. One gets the overwhelming impression of a kind of madness with no other 'method' than to experience a nihilistic frisson. That drive to undo, destroy and terrorise had been the RUF's signature quality all along, but it was the invasion of Freetown that stamped it permanently on the popular imagination. In less than two weeks nearly 100,000 people were driven

---

[17] Over 900 police officers were killed during the war.
[18] Human Rights Watch, *Getting away with Murder, Mutilation, and Rape*, New York, 1999.

from their homes and were camping at the National Stadium, to the west of the city, in conditions of utter dereliction.

Nigerian Ecomog soldiers had seen something like this before, in October 1992, in Monrovia, capital of Liberia. That was when Charles Taylor's National Patriotic Front of Liberia (NPFL) launched 'Operation Octopus', designed either to finally capture the city from the West African peacekeepers or to destroy it for all. Hundreds of homes were burnt down and thousands killed. The NPFL infiltrated in the weeks before the attack, and when it finally attacked it was with an orgy of looting, rape, arson and murder. But even the ghastliness of the NPFL attack pales besides the work of its imitators, the RUF, among whom were people who had taken part in the attack on Monrovia. The Nigerians' counter-offensive also followed the pattern of their response to Taylor's 'Operation Octopus': use of heavy artillery, naval guns and aircraft to bomb the heavily populated areas where it was suspected that the rebels were hiding, leading to many civilian deaths. Summary executions of suspected civilians by the Nigerian troops were common. Hundreds of innocent civilians were murdered in this way.

Some of these atrocities have been memorably documented by Sorious Samura in *Cry Freetown*, which was aired over and over by the BBC, the CNN and many of the world's TV networks. The documentary was, perhaps inevitably, one-sided, showing only the horrible activities of the Nigerian soldiers. But it correctly reflected the mood and behaviour of a large number of the beleaguered Nigerian soldiers as they pushed back, street by street, a highly dangerous, almost invisible, enemy that used civilians as human shields and wore civilian clothes. Needless to say, Samura's documentary, showing supposed Nigerian peacekeepers engaged in sometimes gratuitous acts of violence and atrocities against civilians they were supposed to be protecting, permanently damaged the image of the Nigerian military and enhanced the view of African conflicts as mindless savagery.

It took about three weeks, but the Nigerians, aided by the newly-armed CDF, beat back the rebels from Freetown, once again establishing a tenuous hold on the now battered capital. It was a Pyrrhic victory. Six thousand civilians and thousands of homes in Freetown had perished along with—as soon became evident—the whole brilliant novel concept of regional peacekeeping in Africa. Nigerian casualty figures have not been released, but at the height of the fighting in Freetown the British Foreign Secretary Robin Cook, who was no doubt in a position to know, let slip in an interview with the BBC a figure of 700 Nigerian soldiers killed since the rebel resurgence, which must count as among the highest losses a peace-keeping force has ever incurred in any theatre. Overall Nigerian losses in Sierra Leone are reckoned to have been over 1,000 killed and several thousands wounded, which is to say that more Nigerian troops died fighting the RUF than did soldiers of the Sierra Leone Army, which often collaborated with the rebels throughout the conflict. The Sierra Leone tragedy finally attracted serious international attention after the Freetown massacres, and a large UN force called Unamsil, made up of largely ill-equipped troops from poor countries, replaced the Nigerian-led Ecomog and incorporated some of the Nigerian troops.

How did it come to this? Were these atrocities a desperate, last-ditch attempt by the rebels to tilt the political balance in their favour—conquest by mutilation and rape—or were they simply a nihilistic, irrational exuberance in terror for the sake of terror? Or let us rephrase the question following Paul Richards, a scholar who has studied the Sierra Leone war more closely than most: How did the RUF, an organisation of mainly impoverished and 'alienated' young people, forge a view of reality in which it made sense to commit such atrocities on the very poor? The east end of Freetown was the most impoverished part of the city. It was also an area teeming with unemployed, marginal and 'alienated' (a rather too political word) youth, many scarcely distinguishable from the bulk of the RUF fighters in their background and economic circumstances. Was the wreaking of such horrible havoc on this area an instance of what Freud famously called 'the narcissism of minor difference'?[19] Or were the atrocities a rational, calculated effort of a group wanting to intimidate and thereby control the country by use of shock tactics—terror as spectacle?

War and terror

On 15 January 1999, while still resisting the Nigerian counter-offensive in Freetown, but now no doubt convinced that that its grip on

---

[19] Freud discussed the phenomenon in the context of 'communities with adjoining territories, and related to each other in other ways as well, who are engaged in constant feuds and in ridiculing each other as well.' 'It is always possible,' Freud adds, 'to bind together a considerable number of people in love, so long as there are other people left over to receive the manifestations of their aggressiveness.' See Sigmund Freud, *Civilization and its Discontents*, New York: W.W. Norton, 1961, p. 61.

the city was faltering badly, the RUF leadership issued an extraordinary statement through its 'legal representative' Omrie Michael Golley. This urbane and articulate British-trained lawyer was an unlikely spokesman for the illiterate ruffians who dominated the RUF. He had formerly been a 'special envoy' for the NPRC but had fallen out with Strasser in 1995 in disputed circumstances. After that he launched what he called 'an independent peace initiative', and was among the first from the outside world to visit Foday Sankoh in his forest enclaves in Kailahun district. The grimness of conditions there (as he told me in an interview in 1995) convinced him that it was time for the RUF to come out of the bush and start talking peace. But when news reached the NPRC of his visit to Sankoh, he was promptly denounced as a 'rebel collaborator'. The denunciation only made him more acceptable to the RUF, and himself more anti-government. Within a few years he had changed from a 'peace activist' to a virtual RUF spokesman, becoming the rebels' most eloquent public defender.

The heavily legalistic if rambling language of the 'independent peace initiative' suggested that Golley probably played a hand in drafting it. Entitled 'RUF Calls for Independent Investigations', the statement was an attempt to put the atrocities still going on in Freetown in context, and exculpate the RUF leadership from any part in them. The statement, chilling in its cold-bloodedness, had exactly the opposite effect.

The statement began with a jarring *non sequitur*. 'Human beings go to war when they feel they can no longer get action to be taken on their grievances by verbal articulation. [...] and in war, pent-up rage and the breakdown of law and order lead to untold atrocities.' The fact that the 'breakdown in law and order' is itself caused by the resort to warfare and the atrocities is not noted, but that is not the interesting point. 'Fighters tend to use this breakdown in law and order to unleash their angry negative emotions by committing untold atrocities. Unfortunately', the statement added, 'the brunt of these atrocities is usually directed against innocent civilians caught in circumstances beyond their control.' It mentioned the cases of Kosovo, Algeria and 'Laurent Kabila's Congo', instances where 'man's inhumanity to his fellow man are almost identical' with the case of the RUF's Sierra Leone. The choice of models itself, of course, speaks volumes, but it is the RUF's analysis of the widespread amputations of civilians that is of greater interest here.

The statement referred to 'a series of attacks on Northern towns by people calling themselves "RUF rebels"' in 1997 shortly after

'President Kabbah attacked the North as being responsible for the destruction of the southeast during the RUF war.'[20] The statement claims that these attacks were actually the work of the Kamajors. In those attacks 'villagers had their limbs hacked off'. However, 'in a very worthy point of note, the style of amputations was markedly different from the amputations previously done during the elections protest.' During the 1996 elections that brought President Kabbah to power, there was a wave of amputations mainly in the Eastern and Southern Provinces, but also in parts of the Northern Province; for the first time, the RUF was implicitly admitting that it carried out those amputations. And then came the chilling analysis:

Medical Personnel treating these amputees in early 1997 shortly after Kabbah attacked the North stated that the hands were cut off not at wrist as before but at a point through the palm. This signalled that whoever was doing these new set of amputations in the North, it was not the RUF.[21]

One has to pause for a moment to grasp the significance of the statement that the hands were cut off through the palm. The RUF was stating that it had a procedure, a standard method of crudely amputating human hands; any deviation from this procedure would be detected. The implication is that, far from the amputations being isolated, individual acts committed by wayward recruits, they were directly sanctioned by the RUF leadership, and members were trained to carry them out with clinical precision. There is a host of anecdotal evidence to bear this out. 'Operation No Living Thing' perhaps effectively began in Kodenbala, an obscure village hidden in the verdant wet forests of northern Sierra Leone, in April 1998. We have the exact account of a reporter who interviewed survivors of a dramatic rebel attack on that village the same month. According to a *Washington Post* reporter drawing on the accounts of

---

[20] Foday Sankoh came from northern Sierra Leone, and the RUF launched its war in southern and eastern Sierra Leone, areas bordering Liberia, from where the rebels came. President Kabbah's statement was impolitic but scarcely as sinister as the RUF statement rendered it: it was intended, it would seem, to trigger a more nationalistic response to the RUF carnage by 'shaming' the northern part of the country, then largely unaffected by the war and probably largely indifferent to it.

[21] The *Ninja* Website, January 1999. I found no evidence that the Kamajors, who admittedly have been accused of extrajudicial killings of suspected rebels and other forms of violence, inflicted amputations. The Truth and Reconciliation Commission (TRC) report of October 2004 suggested that some Kamajors did so, but on a small scale compared to the RUF.

survivors, the rebels attacked the village at dawn, gathered the villagers under a large tree and 'one man told us that "since you want a civilian government, we are going to cut off your hands or kill you",' one survivor recalled. The rebels then grabbed a six-year-old girl out of her mother's lap 'and stretched her on the ground. They held her arm down on a big root of a tree and a machete swept down, severing the arm below the elbow. Amid a scene of screaming, blood and confusion, Kamara (the girl's mother) remembers being seized next, and then the blow that severed her own arm.' Many other villagers were mutilated in this way.[22] Another reporter, also basing his account on interviews with victims, reported on the rebel atrocities, this time in Freetown in January 2001. He wrote in the *New York Times*, '"I asked them to kill me now," Mohamed Sesay remembered pleading after he was caught by rebels gripping machetes. But they ignored him. They held his arms flat on a tree stump. And he felt the machete fall on a wrist, then another. "This," the rebels told him, "is an example to show the president."'[23]

Most of the atrocities in Freetown, as we have seen, followed this pattern of wantonness and utter depravity. However, although the attacks were for the most part random, the rebels took time to make sure the mutilations especially had a signature quality, frighteningly recognisable and original. Earlier attacks on the rural peasantry in late 1993 and 1994, when the RUF faced defeat and near-destruction, included the cutting off of noses, fingers, lips and tongues, and the literal carving of the word 'RUF' on the bodies of unfortunate victims, who were then allowed to live. One of the earliest cases of mutilation—and the most dramatic at the time, in 1994—was the cutting off, at the wrist, of both hands of a volunteer soldier in Kono, who was then made to carry a message, strapped around his neck, to the NPRC, announcing that the RUF was still alive and active. The RUF had then just recovered from near-defeat, and had now adopted a strategy of randomly attacking villages, destroying them and withdrawing into the bush. So there was method in this apparent madness: the RUF always resorted to utterly repugnant acts of violence when it faced serious resistance or defeat. In such a situation it fell on the weak and defenceless, people whose support it had never really canvassed and who therefore showed no real sympathy for the group, but whom the RUF, quite bizarrely, then suspected of betrayal.

[22] *Washington Post*, 5 December 1999.
[23] Norimitsu Onishi, 'A brutal war's machetes maim Sierra Leone', *New York Times*, 26 January 2001.

The anthropologist Paul Richards got it right when he argued that the emergence of the Kamajor militia as 'a genuine grassroots movement' succeeded in further fuelling in the RUF a feeling of alienation, and may indeed have been partly responsible for the RUF's widespread resort to 'bizarre patterns of violence'. The RUF became something of a cult, its nihilistic leader Foday Sankoh assuming almost God-like characteristics among the young recruits, his overlordship more distant than hands-on—and therefore more endearing and enduring. But Richards clearly missed the point when he implied a wholly political quality to this reaction, arguing that the atrocities were the RUF's 'response, shaped by sectarian values, to a revival of patrimonial social forces (meaning the Kamajors) ranged against it.'[24] That the RUF, after its near-defeat in 1993 and its almost total rejection by Sierra Leoneans, had become something of a sect, driven by an 'enclavist' mentality which saw everyone outside the enclave as an enemy meriting brutal death, can hardly be doubted. This mentality was more an expression of desperation than of political calculation, however.

The fact is that the Kamajors, more motivated than the Sierra Leone Army (they were after all fighting to free their villages and land of the RUF insurgents and thus for their very survival), had quickly become a very serious military threat to the RUF, seeking them out in their forest hideouts and destroying some of their strategic strongholds in the process. The RUF's resort to ghastly violence was a result, it seemed, of their realisation that they now faced an enemy that was determined and strong enough to destroy them. In this regard Richards has argued that dramatic violence of the nature of the RUF atrocities was a despairing, last-ditch attempt by an essentially weak fringe political group, already obnoxious, to make a plea for attention or recognition. It brings to mind the philosopher George Santayana's acute description of fanatics as people who redouble their efforts when they lose sight of their aims, except that the RUF's aims have always been vague at best, leaving their obsessive looting activities and terror tactics to define them. And certainly desperation and confusion can hardly explain the bizarre style of the attacks themselves, or the insane energy with which they were carried out.

Victims of RUF mutilations in Freetown in January 1999 have told of how the rebels would ask them to chose between 'long sleeve' (having their hands cut off from the wrist) and 'short sleeve'

[24] Paul Richards, 'The New Political Violence in Africa: Secular Sectarianism in Sierra Leone', *Politique Africaine*, June 1998.

(having their arms cut off from the shoulders). The RUF's preferred weapon was a blunt machete, no doubt so that the operation
would be more painful. It also meant that the operation took more
time, which was perhaps strategically unwise because the RUF was
at the same time trying to fight off a brutal Nigerian and CDF offensive. This suggests an almost entirely psychotic quality to the atrocities. Observers would detect a slight difference in the amputations
and other types of atrocities from 1994 to 1996: the swiftness and
apparent selectivity of the amputations in Kono district (mainly
intended to scare off civilians from the RUF's diamond mining
operations), the amputations of peasants in Kailahun and Kenema
districts, once the nation's breadbasket (these, often done in the
harvest season, were intended to prevent peasants from harvesting
their rice farms), and the more general amputations of 1996 (clearly
intended to prevent people from voting). These atrocities of an
earlier, less ecstatic nature were, in that sense, terribly rational;
compared to them, the 1999 attacks, more desperate and more random, appear neurotic, not to say frenetic. They were so gruesome
that the perpetrators had to be drugged and made insane to be
able to carry them out.

Now, under what circumstances are certain types of violence
preferable to other types? What makes certain qualities of violence
or torture not only imaginable but quite effective and therefore, in
that perverse sense, rational? David Apter, one of the sober voices
in conflict studies, has cryptically summed up the supposed thinking behind some immensely violent group behaviour by saying, 'Ex-
tremism is testimony of provocation'. The question, however, is:
provoked by whom? The often defenceless victims, poverty-stricken
peasants condemned to subsistence and dereliction? Here again it
is necessary to engage the analysis of Richards, illustrating as it does
Apter's sententious judgement. The RUF's war, he writes, is a kind
of post-modern conflict in which the rebels have used terror as
spectacle: in a 'television age, the insurgents have used violence
and destruction as weapons through which to make concrete, and
visible to national and international audiences the issue of Atlantic
exploitation of forest society.' The extreme violence of the rebels
then is a statement to the world, 'Look what you have driven us
to!'[25] As a rationalist framework this is hard to beat. The problem is
that most of the RUF's terror activities were perpetrated far from

[25] Paul Richards, *Fighting for the Rainforest: War, Resources and Youth in Sierra
Leone*, International African Institute/James Currey (Oxford) and Heinemann (Portsmouth, NH), 1996.

the TV cameras, went largely unreported by the media, and were targeted at obscure communities with no apparent knowledge of, let alone any stake in, the great mechanism of 'Atlantic exploitation'. Throughout the conflict the RUF assiduously avoided targeting Westerners—people whose mutilations would undoubtedly have brought the attention of the world's media to the conflict long before. Those Westerners abducted, in 1995, were safely escorted into neighbouring countries and released.

The point is that violence-as-spectacle does not have to send any particular message; it could simply be driven by a certain ecstasy, a perverse satisfaction resulting from the infliction of inventive and unusual styles of torture. It is depravity as old as history. In the sixteenth century Montaigne reflected on this form of perversity in his lapidary essay 'On Cruelty':

I live in a season when unbelievable examples of this vice of cruelty flourish because of the license of civil wars; you can find nothing in ancient history more extreme than what we witness everyday. But that has by no means broken me in. If I had not seen it I could hardly have made myself believe that you could find souls so monstrous that they would commit murder for the sheer fun of it; would hack at another man's limbs and lop them off and would cudgel their brains to invent unusual tortures and new forms of murder, not from hatred or for gain but for the sole purpose of enjoying the pleasant spectacle of the pitiful gestures and twitchings of a man dying in agony, while hearing his screams and groans. For there you have the farthest point that cruelty can reach: 'That man would kill not in anger or in fear but merely for the spectacle.'[26]

That aside, Richards' fixation on 'rationality' can seem downright patronising, not to say pedantic. It certainly does little credit to his position to argue against description of the RUF's tactics as 'barbaric', a term which, as Stephen Ellis has noted in his excellent work on the Liberian war, has been freely used by victims of such tactics to describe the RUF. But surely to describe the atrocities as 'barbaric' is not to explain the motivation of the perpetrators and the psychology that informed the bizarre nature of the violence. For this reason Ellis's trenchant comments about the nature of warfare and the rules of engagement are interesting but hardly helpful in this regard:

When wars are fought according to rules, or at least within limits, which are widely understood by those affected, they may appear less barbarous to sur-

[26] Michel de Montaigne, 'On Cruelty' in *The Essays: a Selection*, translated and edited by M.A. Screech, Harmondsworth: Penguin, 1991, p. 169.

vivors than wars in which the participants have a sense that there are no rules, or that the ones previously in use are no longer being observed. Hence the perception that one war is more barbaric than the other is related not only to the number of victims, but above all to the observance or otherwise of rules, or at least unwritten norms, and the element of drama which is such an important aspect of war.[27]

His comments, however, are pertinent in one important respect. There is no point in arguing that wars are by their nature brutal, with death and destruction the main characteristics, or that so-called low-intensity conflicts—violence perpetrated by non-state actors operating within states and with no international legal standing—are always even more so. As the Yale scholar James Turner Johnson has noted in *Morality and Contemporary Warfare*,[28] this is a misconception that has strong roots in an instinctive pacifist mentality; it has little historical or instrumental basis. It could be found, for example, in the writings of the sixteenth-century Christian humanist Erasmus. He describes warfare in these unremittingly bleak terms:

Consider [war's] instruments, I pray you: murderers, profligates devoted to gambling and rape, and the vilest sort of mercenary soldier…Think, next, of all crimes that are committed with war as a pretext, while good laws 'fall silent amid the clash of arms'—all the instances of sack and sacrilege, rape, and other shameful acts, such as one even hesitates to name…Even so the worst evils fall upon those who have no stake in the war.[29]

In fact, the history of warfare shows the development, by almost every society, of certain rules of engagement, of what Johnson calls 'a just war tradition and its development into a natural law'. Johnson concludes his study with an important comment about 'contemporary warfare' and the tendency to interpret its tendency not to distinguish between military and civilian targets as somehow 'natural', and to be expected even by those who rigorously oppose it:

The particular nature of contemporary warfare leads to the recognition that the problems it raises are in fact not different in kind from those encountered repeatedly in the long pre-modern history of war, problems

---

[27] Stephen Ellis, *The Mask of Anarchy: The Destruction of Liberia and the Religious Dimension of an African Civil War*, London: Hurst, 1999, p. 22. These comments are made in relation both to the RUF and to the National Patriotic Front of Liberia, NPFL.

[28] James Turner Johnson, *Morality and Contemporary Warfare*, New Haven, CT: Yale University Press, 1999.

[29] Quoted in Johnson (note 28), p. 121.

which the traditional restraints sought to address and remedy. The rules protecting noncombatants, for example, is not some kind of intellectual or legal abstraction remote from the realities of war, but the result of cumulative response to earlier experience of warfare against noncombatants, and it makes little sense to capitulate to the idea that such warfare is somehow a necessary feature of twentieth century conflict, 'total war.'[30]

The fact is that some contemporary wars have been remarkably less brutal and destructive than others, and highly professional armies operating under the sanction of states have been known to perpetrate unspeakable atrocities, while some guerrilla armies have behaved remarkably professionally. The Japanese atrocities in Nanking, China, in 1937 and the American atrocities in My Lai, Vietnam, can appear incomprehensible when compared to the exceptional behaviour of the Cuban revolutionaries in their war against Fulgencio Batista, or the restrained conduct of Amilcar Cabral's guerrillas in their war against a murderous Portuguese colonial army in Guinea Bissau. Time and space cannot account for the difference either. At about the time when Castro's guerrillas were waging their war in Cuba, another insurgent group in Colombia was conducting atrocities remarkably similar to those perpetrated by the RUF. Carlos Leon's very disturbing account of some of those atrocities, happening between 1949 and 1958, was published in the *American Journal of Psychiatry* (May 1969).

The atrocities, which happened during the period known in Colombia simply as *La Violencia*, included mutilation such as the cutting-off of noses, tongues and ears, and the quartering or dismembering of victims. One man was crucified on a log, then killed by having nails hammered into his eyes; another had his teeth removed with pliers, and was then forced to walk with his previously sliced feet on a floor that had been covered with salt; recruits were forced to experiment with machetes on a prisoner or a dead body, and did so until some sort of exhilaration or climax occurred (after this perverse sexual ritual the body was cut up); pregnant women had their foetuses removed; there were frequent mutilations of breasts and castrations; one commando instructed his gang to bring him 'no reports but ears'; and of course the rape of women was common, as was the impaling of bodies and the drinking of victims' blood. The Colombian rebels' preference for beheading produced designs of decapitation that have striking similarities with the RUF's inventive styles of amputation that appeared in Freetown

[30] Johnson (note 28), p. 224.

in January 1999: there was *el corte de franela* (T-shirt cut), in which the machete sliced deep along the line where the throat joins the chest; *el corte de corbeta* (neck-tie cut), in which the machete cut via the incision under the mandible, through which the tongue of the victim was pulled out and made to hang outside like a neck-tie; *el corte de mica* (monkey cut), in which the victim had his or her head cut off and placed on the chest; and *el corte francés* (French cut), which involved peeling back the skin of the victim and thus exposing the skull, while the victim was still alive—'sometimes', Leon informs us with a truly macabre touch, 'a hose was used to spray the skull and make it look neater.'[31]

I have drawn attention to these graphic details for two reasons. First, to show that violence that is deemed unimaginable and inhuman can be appealing to some and therefore quite repeatable in certain circumstances. And second, to show that such violence, indeed almost every form of violence and inhumanity, is culturally neutral; it is not specific to 'cultures', 'races' or 'tribes' (I use these words loosely to capture their popular meanings). This last point is particularly important, because there have been volumes of depressing works discussing the 'peculiar savagery' of African wars and trying to ground the atrocities committed in such wars within a particular cultural framework, usually depicted as either barbaric or neurotic, and therefore triggering all kinds of racial anxieties. Works challenging such deliberate misconceptions are often overly defensive and therefore easily ridiculed. This is not to say that such works, or the issues they tap into, are not interesting in themselves; the point is that they often add more confusion than clarity. This has been exactly the result of the debate about the 'rationality' or otherwise of the RUF's terror tactics, and about the so-called 'New Barbarism' thesis.

The idea of analysing the RUF terror campaigns as either rational or not first started as reaction to the utterly feverish and simplistic account of poverty, depression and crime written in 1994 by the American journalist Robert Kaplan in *Atlantic Monthly*. Welding together the thesis of Martin van Creveld on post-Cold War wars of

---

[31] Carlos Leon, 'Unusual Patterns of Crime During La Violencia in Colombia', *American Journal of Psychiatry*, May 1969 I am grateful to the late Lemuel Johnson, a Sierra Leonean scholar at the University of Michigan, for drawing my attention to this fascinating paper, doing so with the characteristically terse remark that 'the similarities with Sierra Leone can only be regretted.'

non-state actors, Thomas Homer-Dixon's pessimistic environmental prognosis and Samuel Huntington's thesis on the unavoidable 'clash of civilizations', Kaplan described the war in Sierra Leone—and at the time in Liberia, following lightning stops in both countries—as anarchic, criminal (as opposed to political) violence that would lead to a Hobbesian state of nullity and terror. Both conflicts, Kaplan argued, were instances of 'New Age primitivism'. A quaint, heavily-loaded phrase; and Kaplan, a master of the sullen amplification, had more to say. The widespread armed violence in both countries, he wrote, was not war in the sense in which Clausewitz defined wars as a continuation of politics by other means. Instead, what was happening in Sierra Leone

....is a microcosm of what is happening in West Africa and much of the underdeveloped world: the withering away of central governments, the rise of tribal or regional domains, the unchecked spread of disease, and the growing pervasiveness of war.[32]

This kind of war is not politically motivated but criminally driven, with dispossessed urban youths—'loose molecules in an unstable social fluid'—wreaking vengeance on societies that have left them despairing and poor. Kaplan suggested that these armed youths were Africa's modern-day *écorcheurs* who were roaming and ravaging the countryside in a manner reminiscent of the armed mercenaries in Germany during the Thirty Years' War.

It must be stated that Kaplan's article derived much of its provocative force from the fact that it tapped into some of the key contemporary anxieties of Western academics, activists and policy makers: the environment (Western, especially European, ecological romance is still a very strong political rallying point), urban violence, youth, over-population and resource scarcity. These issues are no doubt serious, but the view that in much of Africa they have already reached crisis point is misleading, not to say mendacious. Poverty and unemployment or state neglect do not necessarily lead to organised violence or warfare; and the idea that unemployed youths in Africa are always restive, possessed by an inchoate revolutionary zeal—a determination to overthrow the corrupt and inept elite—is a dangerous romantic fantasy. As Yusuf Bangura insightfully noted, 'Processes of deprivation and alienation do not always

[32] Robert Kaplan, 'The Coming Anarchy: how Scarcity, Crime, Over-Population and Diseases are Rapidly Destroying our Planet', *Atlantic Monthly*, February 1994.

push their victims towards political violence, but towards apa-
thy...and the leadership of many violence-prone groups is often
drawn from individuals who could secure adequate livelihoods
from, or access to, the political systems they challenge.'[33] Charles
Ghankay Taylor, whose forces triggered the Liberian civil war, was a
well-educated member of the Liberian political elite and a former
junior cabinet minister of the government—President Samuel
Doe's dictatorship—against which he started the war. The point is
that initiating organised violence against a state, any state, requires
considerable resources and often outside support, factors not associated with poor alienated youth.

Richards was the first to challenge the Kaplan thesis in a book-
length study of the war, a large part of which was devoted to refut-
ing the vigorous misconceptions of the cavalier American journalist. In *Fighting for the Rainforest* Richards suggests that what appeared
as random and anarchic violence in Sierra Leone was in fact the
highly organised and ideologically-driven campaign of a group of
'embittered pedagogues' who were motivated to replace Sierra
Leone's backward 'patrimonial system' with 'a revolutionary egalitarian one'. Richards offers his book as a refutation of what he calls
the 'New Barbarism' thesis—Kaplan's contention that the violence
was an atavistic throwback to a pre-modern, pre-colonial era of
large-scale banditry and anarchy. The Sierra Leone war, he writes,
'must be understood partly as "performance", in which techniques
of terror compensate for the lack of equipment.' War is always horrible and destructive, whether fought with machetes or computer-
guided bombers, so that 'it makes no sense to call one kind of war
"barbaric" when all that is meant is that it is cheap.' The RUF's
employment of tactics such as mutilation of its victims should be
seen as rational in the light of its lack of sophisticated equipment
which would make killing more efficient—and at a distance. In any
case the RUF's terror was the product of the 'intellectual anger of
an excluded educated elite.'[34]

Richards does not seriously address the RUF's deliberate and
consistent targeting of civilians, athough this aspect of its 'total war'
approach in a country that its members claimed as their own—and
which the RUF's leaders claimed they wished to govern in a 'revolutionary, more democratic' way—must surely be of great moral and

---

[33] Yusuf Bangura, *The Search for Identity: Ethnicity, Religion and Political Violence*, Geneva: UNRISD Occasional Paper, November 1994, p. 25.
[34] Richards (note 25), pp. xiii–xxix.

practical interest. Surely the principle of discrimination is fundamental to every form of warfare, and especially warfare that claims
to be 'just' and aimed at a 'revolutionary' purpose? The Protestant
theologian Paul Ramsey has written with great penetration on
responsible warfare and on what he calls the 'principle of discrimination' as 'shorthand for "the moral immunity of non-combatants
from direct attacks"'. Ramsey employs what he calls the 'rule of double effect', and argues that the 'death of an innocent man might be
brought about, without guilt to the agent, as the unavoidable yet
indirect effect of an action whose primary intention and physically
independent effect was to secure some good,' but that 'military
action should, in its primary (objective) thrust as well as its subjec-
tive purpose, discriminate between directly attacking combatants
or military objectives and directly attacking non-combatants or
destroying the structures of civil society as a means of victory.'[35]

Richards, on the other hand, seems concerned less about moral
issues than about efficacy; and as an excuse for his evidently fatuous
view, it must be stated that his book was published in 1996, long
before much of what we now know about the RUF became common knowledge. At that time the RUF was operating deep in the
wet forests of eastern and southern Sierra Leone, emerging in small
bands to raid villages and set up deadly ambushes. Sankoh was a
mysterious, disembodied voice occasionally heard on the BBC African Service, and he was seen neither on TV nor by almost anyone
else outside his group. The other excuse, or rather motive, was a
need to debunk the transparent but highly influential misconceptions about the conflict that Kaplan paraded as insights, and there
can be no doubt about Richards' determination to do so. By representing the war as the bellwether of post-Cold War crises that will
lead to the ultimate doom of much of the so-called Third World,
Kaplan was saying that these places were beyond salvage. He even
believed that it was harmful for the West to try giving a helping
hand. This kind of thinking clearly appealed to many in the United
States which was still reeling from the effects of the botched mission in Somalia in 1992. As a result, the US State Department had
Kaplan's article faxed to every one of their embassies around the
world. Some analysts believe that the Clinton administration's failure to react to the Rwandan genocide was largely influenced by
Kaplan's pessimistic prognosis (President Clinton once declared

[35] Paul Ramsey, *The Just War: Force and Political Responsibility*, New York:
Charles Scribner's Sons, 1968, pp. 428–9.

himself an admirer of Kaplan's writings, and is said to have taken Kaplan's earlier book on the Balkans, *Balkan Ghosts*, on a visit to Europe during the Kosovo crisis).

Even so, Richards' spirited defence of a group that was already notorious for apparently gratuitous attacks on the rural peasantry, wanton arson and rape, and which had favoured no one with a coherent explanation of its activities, made many Sierra Leoneans livid. In Yusuf Bangura's review of the book (to which we referred earlier) the Sierra Leonean scholar took issue with what he believed was Richards' uncritical reading of the RUF's propaganda tract, *Footpaths to Democracy*—published in 1995, long after its campaigns started, and clearly meant to appeal more to Western environmental activists than the Sierra Leoneans it claimed it wanted to 'liberate' from corrupt politicians—which presented the group as revolutionary. Bangura lamented, 'The resource exploitation, vandalism and random and barbaric violence are either ignored or not properly investigated.' Bangura concluded that the RUF was a criminal organisation that used 'barbaric' methods against the country's citizens; the effectiveness of this method, in terms of giving the RUF significance, does not make it any less criminal.[36]

However, the question remains: why did an organisation, which claims to be fighting to improve the lot of the country's derelict poor, target the very poor for its most vicious atrocities? How did it forge a view of reality or political or social responsibility that justified such horrendous activities?

It is tempting, given the gap between the rhetoric of the rebels and the profoundly bizarre nature of the atrocities they committed, to seek a deeper understanding of their actions. Ellis does this effectively in his study of the Liberian civil war in which he focused on the 'religious dimension' of the conflict. Whatever one's views of the functions of religion in human life, it is hard to disagree with Ellis' conclusion:

There is no doubt that some of the acts of war in Liberia which had been considered particularly atrocious contain, at least in the view of many Liberians, references to known repertoires of spiritual symbols…These symbols, while recognizable, are sufficiently distorted or abused as to cause widespread disgust. Most notably, these repertoires are those relating to religion. Many of the main protagonists in the war have claimed, some with

---

[36] Yusuf Bangura, 'Understanding the Political and Cultural Dynamics of the Sierra Leone war: a Critique of Paul Richards' "Fighting for the Rainforest"', *Africa Development* (Dakar: CODESRIA, vol. XXII, nos 3–4, 1997).

obvious sincerity, to have been in direct communication with God at various stages of their bloody careers. This is not just a personal quirk, but is situated in a history in which religious belief has functioned as a mainstay of political and social order...[37]

Stephen Ellis convincingly illustrates the profoundly important role religion had always played in Liberian political life, which, controlled (until 1980) by a largely corrupt and aloof Americo-Liberian elite—religious confession to many of them was more than a show of fealty to the Supreme Being, it was a matter both of identity and of rationale for discrimination and criminal appropriation—was always inherently more brutal and mercenary than its neighbours'. It became even more so after an army sergeant, a 'native' Liberian from the long-oppressed hinterland of the country, Samuel Doe, seized power in 1980 in one of Africa's most bloodthirsty coups, demonstrating, in bold relief, the congruent corruptions of both oppressor and oppressed that have been such a marked feature of societies in transition in much of the so-called Third World.

However, such an interpretation would be dubious at best when adopted to understand the nature of the mainly copy-cat violence of Sierra Leone's war. Mariane Ferme's otherwise erudite book, *The Underneath of Things: Violence, History, and the Everyday in Sierra Leone* (2001),[38] produces this effect when she falls for the seductions of deeper cultural readings of a war that was so perversely modern in its origins and many of its trajectories. Ferme, aiming to probe 'not only questions of origins ("How could this occur?") but also issues of a socio-cultural nature, examining institutions, values, and views of self and sociality that sometimes are associated with violent outcomes', is convinced that a purely anthropological approach can lay bare the true character of Sierra Leone's violent recent history. Her argument is so fascinating that I am obliged to quote it at some length, if only to show how ultimately unhelpful the approach is:

The point is to understand how the visible world (as it appears, for instance, in ritual, political, and domestic appropriations of public space) is activated by forces concealed beneath the surface of discourse, objects, and social relations. Such forces manifest themselves in everyday conflicts through the potential disruption of the deceptive order of ordinary appearances. For example, what appears on the surface as generous action toward friends, family, and strangers may suddenly change into a violent

[37] Ellis (note 27), pp. 22–3.
[38] Mariane Ferme, *The Underneath of Things: Violence, History and the Everyday in Sierra Leone*, Berkeley: University of California Press, 2001.

encounter with the enemy...Material objects themselves may be invested with potent forces, influencing the people who come into contact with them, and thus becoming potential sources of conflict. Hence the necessity of understanding not only how everyday conflicts arise but also how they crystallize and develop unpredictably, and in contestable ways. Specific, potent social and political roles, discursive forms, and objects exist within the cultural and historical repertoire of this region to operate such mediations. These figures and sites of mediation are themselves the legacy of struggles where the effective use of ambiguity has been—and continues to be—more productive than the pursuit of social ideals of transparency.[39]

Ferme is an anthropologist with a superb, almost native understanding of the rural community in southern Sierra Leone—an area then largely unaffected by the war—that she studies. Her sensitivity to the nuances of this society cannot be questioned. She speaks the language of the area, Mende, well, and has lived among the people for considerable periods of time. The problem begins when she applies extrapolated findings from this small rural community to a war whose main trajectories are hardly 'traditional' in the sense of being driven by indigenous factors and ideas. She acknowledges this, though rather tangentially, when she writes that the war's 'local resonances with a traditional hunting lore must not blind us to the new global alliances between covert business interests and the organization of terror.'[40] However, Ferme's emphasis on the material culture of the war obscures its core quality: that it was a brutal war of pillage masterminded and driven largely by people whose philistine calculations and strategy were perversely modern in the starkest sense of the word.

I aim to understand the RUF's violence by focusing on three aspects of the rebel phenomenon: its composition; its thoroughly mercenary character; and a social/political context in which impunity, for those who can exercise or have a capacity for organised violence, had almost become the norm.

One of the most interesting theses linking the composition of the RUF to its abysmal behaviour as an insurgent group is Ibrahim Abdullah's notion of the 'lumpen' character of the RUF, to which we referred earlier. Abdullah, a social historian, has suggested that the RUF's predisposition to wanton violence was the result of the group's core class composition. The RUF, he argued, is made up of socially uprooted and criminally disposed youths whom he called 'lumpens'. From this 'social class' there emerged, after decades of a

[39] Ibid., p. 2.
[40] Ibid., p. 5.

corrupt and ultimately failed one-party system, what he called a 'lumpen youth culture'—a despairing anti-social movement of drug addicts, petty thieves and gamblers, growing up mostly in the slums of Freetown. People from this group formed the core leadership of the RUF, which is why the group was pathologically disposed to criminal violence and terror. The 'mutilation, murder and rape of innocent women and children by the RUF are acts that are incompatible with a revolutionary project,' Abdullah argues. 'The "revolutionary" acts...were committed again and again precisely because of the social composition (of the RUF)...A lumpen social movement breeds a lumpen revolution.'[41]

Abdullah's argument is seductive, not only because of its elegant ideological anchor. The RUF was undoubtedly dominated by ill-educated—indeed largely uneducated—young men with extremely confused and demagogic notions of statecraft. Many of these young men were unemployed (and probably unemployable) before the war, and lived lives often bordering on criminality. Many can surely be described as 'lumpens'. However, Abdullah's argument that the RUF war was a 'revolt'—a revolt of lumpen youths—suggests, completely wrongly, that there was an internal uprising of these so-called 'lumpen youths', one which would have happened whether there was any outside influence or not. Abdullah's description of 'lumpen youth culture' reads like a classic listing of the miseries of the urban poor, but, as we have noted earlier, while the idea that the neglected poor will surely take up arms against the oppressive elites may appeal to romantics it is not true. It is certainly not true of the Sierra Leone war. People like Sam Bockarie and Issa Sesay (who was the last 'interim' leader of the RUF) may be correctly described as 'lumpen', but Sesay was recruited into the RUF in Liberia by an ageing former army photographer who himself was a protégé of the Liberian warlord Charles Taylor.

The point is that it is very easy to provide causes for poor people; and in a country with such limited opportunities as Sierra Leone, mercenary warfare—armed violence not driven by any political or social project—can easily seem like a legitimate option. The more pertinent point about the RUF was that it was overwhelmingly dominated by very young people, a large number of them teenagers or in some cases pre-teenagers—a whole generation of whom literally grew up within the group. Sierra Leone's National Committee for

---

[41] Ibrahim Abdullah, 'Bush Path to Destruction: The Origin and Character of the Revolutionary United Front (RUF/SL)', *Africa Development* (Dakar: CODESRIA), vol. XXII, nos 3–4, 1997, pp. 45–76.

Disarmament, Demobilisation and Reintegration (NCDDR) on 9 January 2002 said it had disarmed 18,354 RUF combatants, almost half of them children. NCDDR chairman Francis Kai Kai told me that the other half were also very young, a large number having grown into adulthood within the group. Many of these children were orphans who had seen their parents killed, and who now looked up to the rebel leadership as some kind of surrogate parenthood.

Dr Edward Nahim, a Freetown-based psychiatrist who, as head of the Children Associated with War (CAW) project, was certainly in a position to know, argues that most of the atrocities associated with the RUF war, 'particularly of the playful, random types', were committed by children or those in the RUF who grew into adulthood within the group.[42] Dr Nahim is a soft-spoken middle-aged man who was the head of West Africa's oldest psychiatric hospital at Kissy in Freetown. He suggested that a large number of the children fighting within the RUF were abducted and then inducted into the group through the use of violence and drug abuse. Drug use, he said, was 'out of control' among the rebels, and largely accounted for much of the violent barbarism of the RUF. As he told a British newspaper in 1995, 'It is usually a combination of marijuana, alcohol and gunpowder. Over time the soldiers become delirious. They don't know what they are doing.'[43] One former boy RUF soldier, in an interview with the same newspaper, positively concurred. 'Our superiors put gunpowder in our food and gave us brown pills which they called cocaine to take with our drink. The drugs make your heart strong, make you feel that you are not afraid of anything.' Another, interviewed by the *Sunday Times*, was more forthright. 'We killed many. When we were afraid, we smoked cannabis mixed with the residue of gunpowder from bullets. It made us brave and we didn't care about killing.'[44] Surely, as Camus quotes Pisarev, the 'theoretician of Russian nihilism', as saying, the 'greatest fanatics are children and adolescents.'[45]

Child participation in the RUF, and particularly in the roguish Sierra Leone army and the civil defence forces, was sometimes voluntary, as Peters and Richards have argued,[46] but even when this

---

[42] Personal interview, Freetown, April 2001.

[43] 'Boys in arms find peace a trial', *Independent*, 28 September 1995.

[44] 'Machete rule makes hell of Sierra Leone', *Sunday Times*, 31 December 1995.

[45] Camus (note 3), p. 149.

[46] Krijn Peters and Paul Richards, '"Why we fight": Voices of Youth Combatants in Sierra Leone', *Africa*, 68 (2), 1998.

was the case, Dr Nahim has listed four factors that could have influenced such a grim decision: 'Revenge' ('children have seen their parents killed'), 'New Image' ('It has been popular to wear the military uniform....which represents power'), 'Masochism' ('With a gun a child becomes a superman') and 'Security' (food security, that is)—the result being pretty much the same. According to Nahim, because children have 'not yet formed a stable identity', they are highly impressionable and therefore prone to literalism and exaggerated abuse. Child combatants, he argues after an extensive experience with many of those already disarmed, are prone to a 'neurotic state', violent and utterly unstable. They develop 'loss of hope and trust in people, in self and in the world', and are beset, when deprived of the illicit drugs they have been used to, by 'constant fear, depression and extreme sadness, frustration and suicidal feelings or feelings of anger and revenge or resignation.'[47]

This analysis was made in 1993, just over two years after the war started and before some of the worst atrocities associated with it were committed. It meant, therefore, that far from being an expedient measure taken as things got out of hand or became more difficult for the RUF, the recruitment of child combatants was a deliberate and even necessary part of the RUF's military campaign. So much so that the policy is almost celebrated within the RUF as an ideology. The chorus of the RUF's anthem, which was always sung as a matter of ceremony and as part of the inductive process, makes reliance on child combatants its principle by stating, 'Go and tell my parents, they may see me no more/When fighting in the battlefield I'm fighting forever.' The anthem states that 'Every Sierra Leonean is fighting for his land', including, of course, the children, who, however, needed a lot of prodding to do so, as we know from eye-witnesses' accounts. In the early stages of the war abducted children were made to commit atrocities against family members, then the letters 'RUF' were cut into their bodies, after which the wound was rubbed with lime to prevent it from being effaced. Paul Richards has provided a chilling and entirely credible account of how some of these children were inducted into the rebel group.

Villagers report being required to witness the terrifying spectacle of public beheadings in which the victim's neck was cut, working from back to front with a blunt knife. The purpose of these atrocities seems to have been to

---

[47] Dr E. A. Nahim, 'Children Associated with War Project—Executive Summary', Freetown, 1993.

bring about the irrevocable break between conscripts and their communities. Subsequently, youth conscripts could not escape for fear of reprisals.[48]

Richards calls this process 'de-institutionalization'. From this point the mass amputations in Freetown in 1999—by most eye-witness accounts committed largely by child combatants high on drugs—become quite comprehensible, and Richards' sympathetic comment that such children were 'human rights abusing products of human rights abuse'[49] fits. The question then arises: why did the RUF have to do this? Why, with the degree of resentment and poverty in Sierra Leone, did the RUF not attract willing, politically motivated recruits in numbers large enough to wage a more organised insurgency campaign? Why didn't it even try?

An answer to these questions bears directly on our second point in the analysis of the RUF's violent pathology: its essentially mercenary character.

A once fashionable rendering of the origins of the RUF war went like this: A hundred or so lightly armed guerrillas with a great revolutionary zeal to overthrow the corrupt one-party state of President Momoh crossed into the country from Liberia in March 1991. They were led by an ageing ex-army corporal whose main grudge against the APC tyranny was that it had imprisoned him for a long time for a failed coup plot, and he was determined both to seek revenge by mobilising disgruntled Sierra Leoneans to overthrow that tyranny and then to establish a more just and fair regime. But the campaign went septic, largely because it was dominated by Burkinabe and Liberian mercenaries 'on loan' from Charles Taylor: unenthusiastic about politics, they forced the campaign to devolve into an opportunity to loot and murder at will, creating a cycle of violence from which there was to be no turning back.

This highly discredited account was, of course, based on anecdotal evidence, but as such accounts go, it contained a grain of truth. The problem is that it overstated the political motivation of the 'insurgency' and greatly understated the role of the outside forces that actually created it. Foday Sankoh, from the very start of the war the unmistakable leader of the RUF, certainly had deep grudges against the APC dictatorship, but he never once articulated any political aims or influences beyond complaints about

[48] Paul Richards, 'Rebellion in Sierra Leone and Liberia: A Crisis of Youth?' in O. Furley (ed.), *Conflict in Africa*, London: Tauris, 1995, p. 158.

[49] Paul Richards, 'Demobilizing the RUF in Sierra Leone', undated discussion paper (in author's possession).

corruption and the lack of democracy. It has thus been left to journalists and scholars to carry out the dubious task of speculating, from the incoherent and contradictory ranting of Sankoh and other RUF spokesmen, about what the political influences on the RUF might be, and then describing the RUF as being under such influences, which according to one obtuse reading were predominantly Pan-Africanism.[50] A journalist who actually interviewed Sankoh before writing—unlike some scholars who long became 'experts' on the RUF without bothering to talk to any of the rebels—marvelled at the vagueness of Sankoh's political ideas but was still able to discern from his fulminations 'the broadest of influences, from the ideals of the Boston Tea Party and the French Revolution to the Communism of Cambodia's Pol Pot.'[51]

My argument is that however much Sankoh's complaints against the rotten political system echoed those of many Sierra Leoneans, and however determined he was to wrest control of the state from the successive governments he fought, his lack of political maturity and serious political organisation ensured that he remained nothing more than a functionary within a vast network of warlord economies that was controlled by Charles Taylor and his principal supporter, Blaise Compaore of Burkina Faso. Abdullah and Muana may well be right to argue that the RUF did not 'possess the kind of leadership that would be necessary to designate it as a warlord insurgency',[52] but that is only true if one completely ignores, as they do, the RUF's crucial Liberian link. Liberia had, once Taylor established control over the timber and diamond producing regions in the early stages of his insurgency, been transformed into a quintessential warlord economy and remained so even after its war was declared over and Taylor emerged as the elected President. It was the antithesis of a bureaucratic state—it was more or less the warlord President's personal fiefdom.[53] The RUF's own efforts were essentially a sub-warlord system.

The influence of the Liberian warlord connection has been palpable throughout Sierra Leone's war, especially at the early stages

---

[50] Ibrahim Abdullah, 'Bush Paths to Destruction' (note 41).

[51] Howard French, 'African Rebel with Room Service', *New York Times*, 23 June 1996.

[52] Ibrahim Abdullah and Patrick Muana, 'The Revolutionary United Front: A Revolt of the Lumpenproletariat' in C. Clapham (ed.), *African Guerrillas*, Bloomington: Indiana University Press, 1998.

[53] See William Reno, *Warlord Politics and the African State*, Boulder, CO: Lynne Rienner, 1998; 'In ruined Liberia, its despoiler sits pretty', *New York Times*, 20 February 2001.

and more crucially at the end. When the rebels entered Kailahun and Pujehun districts, they targeted in particular ethnic Mandingo and Fula traders, two groups that were being exterminated with compulsive zeal in Liberia by Taylor's NPFL. In Kailahun district the rebels slaughtered at least sixty civilians, almost all of them Mandingo and Fula traders. In Pujehun, upon taking over the bucolic and long-neglected town, they murdered forty-six people, sixteen of them Fula traders and the rest Mandingos.[54] These murders were clearly an extension of the NPFL's ethnocide in Liberia, and caused great alarm and panic among people in those areas, leading to mass displacement and flight. This development only fuelled anger and resentment among the RUF troops, who now made their campaign of destruction more comprehensive and random. Once the RUF took control of the diamond-rich Kono district, first in 1993 and for much longer periods in 1995 and 1997, the dynamic of a warlord-type insurgency began to take hold: it remained so until the end of the war, with the Liberian connection its most decisive factor, and with Sierra Leone diamonds being the mainstay of the warlord economy (more on this in Chapter 8).

The RUF was thus largely conceived as a mercenary enterprise, and never evolved beyond banditism: it never became a political, still less a revolutionary organisation. This is why, I argue, it was so excessively brutal, and why it had to resort to the mass recruitment of children—people who had no political consciousness or social responsibility, and about whom it could therefore not reasonably be said to have acted in any political sense—as the vanguard of its campaigns. It was, one might say, the RUF's original sin, and it led to more. Atrocities against civilians, including mutilations of all sorts, were from the time it started its war a mark of the RUF's campaign, but mass amputations—the RUF's signature contribution to guerrilla warfare—started later in its faltering war effort, and were mainly carried out by its child combatants. By resorting to one of the few uses of mass amputations in history the RUF, which had no serious backing among the population it claimed to be fighting to liberate, was able to project power in great disproportion to its actual size and capacity for military combat.

The atrocities, however, were carried out within a particular social space and time, and the fact that they were executed so openly—Bockarie announced his 'Operation No Living Thing' on the BBC World Service, as we have seen—suggests something much

---

[54] Amnesty International, *Sierra Leone: The Extra-Judicial Executions of Suspected Rebels and Collaborators*, London, 1992.

more than wilful bestiality: it would suggest that the perpetrators clearly felt they were beyond reproach, perhaps that there was simply no mechanism that could hold them to account for their crimes. This perhaps also explains why senior RUF members, in conversations since the ceasefire, have always appeared genuinely bewildered by the setting up of a Special Court to investigate some of the atrocities associated with the war and to prosecute those responsible for crimes against humanity. For them there was a war, and what happened during that period did so because of that immutable fact. Sankoh once put it in plainer terms than anyone could. In answer to a question about charges of atrocities against his forces, he replied, 'When two elephants are fighting, who is going to suffer?' he said with a smile… 'The grass, of course. I cannot deny it.'[55]

This unabashed attitude to violence mocks the elegant anthropological readings of Ferme, who has interpreted the often laughable sartorial inventiveness of the RUF—plainly an aspect of the young fighters' drug-induced ecstatic state—as part of the process of 'concealment' and then 'assuming a new identity to carry out…acts of violence legitimately and with impunity.'[56] The rebels' unusual dress code has been much commented upon, and there has been a tendency on the part of Western academics to read too much into it, unlike journalists who often found it either bewildering or simply hilarious. Ian Stewart, the Associated Press writer who in January 1999 in Freetown survived a RUF bullet wound to the head, still remembered, long after the traumatic experience, that the rebel who shot him was 'dressed in American-style jeans, rubber flip-flops, and a jaunty black bowler hat like one of the droogs from Stanley Kubrick's film *A Clockwork Orange*.'[57] Ferme, on the other hand, sees much more in this, describing the often ghoulish attire as 'masks', suggesting an atavistic throwback to an older, more authentic ritual of warfare:

The mask confers on its wearer the ability, through assuming a new identity, to carry out…acts of violence legitimately and with impunity, because his or her real identity is concealed. This aspect of masking has always been put to use in war, and particularly in this region's civil wars, where cross-dressing, masks, and amulets have played key roles in the material culture of war.[58]

[55] French (note 51).
[56] Ferme (note 38), p. 3.
[57] Stewart (note 2), p. xvii.
[58] Ferme (note 38), p. 3.

This may have been true historically, but certainly the bizarre styles of clothing that the rebels wore during their campaigns cannot in any way be called 'masks'; they were not intended to be such. The atrocities were often committed with no attempt to cover them up, and RUF commanders were sometimes even happy to be photographed committing them.

An understanding of this kind of mentality would require a related inquiry: Why was it that the RUF, which many agree was a group of self-interested and even criminal characters, could inflict such terror and violence on the population while the state and its agents were so ineffective in meeting the challenge? The answer, I argue, can be found in the nature of the state itself, the corruption and emasculation of its institution by nearly three decades of near-criminal misrule, the destruction of all legitimate political opposition, the lack of opportunities for political dissent, and the culture of political thuggery that was the bedrock of the corrupt one-party state that ran Sierra Leone for over two decades.

7

FROM 'U-NASTY' TO 'MODEL PEACEKEEPING'

'Impartiality and the use of force only in self-defense should remain the bedrock principles of peacekeeping. Experience shows, however, that in the context of intra-state/transnational conflicts, consent may be manipulated in many ways. Impartiality for the United Nations operations must therefore mean adherence to the principles of the Charter: where one party to a peace agreement clearly and incontrovertibly is violating its terms, continued equal treatment of all parties by the United Nations can in the best case result in ineffectiveness and in the worst may amount to complicity with evil. No failure did more damage to the United Nations peacekeeping in the 1990s than its reluctance to distinguish victim from aggressor.' (Brahimi Report on UN Peace operations[1])

In the eleven years of extremely dirty war in Sierra Leone, the country's long-suffering and courageous citizens remember a number of 'watershed' events—the NPRC coup of 1992, the hard-fought-for democratic elections of 1996, the highly destructive AFRC coup of 1997, to name a few—but none dominates the popular imagination as much as the January 1999 attacks on Freetown and, flowing directly from that, the Lome Accord of July 1999. The January 1999 attack, which left in its wake thousands killed or mutilated and a city in ruins, revealed the utter ghastliness of the so-called rebel war as well as the frightening helplessness of ordinary Sierra Leoneans in the face of such blatant violation and suffering. With the vulnerability of the elected government once again tragically exposed, Western governments, particularly the United States, began to place

---

[1] *Report of the Brahimi Panel on United Nations Peace Operations*, October 2000. The full report can be found at http://www.un.org/peace/reports/peace_operations.

156

enormous pressure on the Kabbah administration to negotiate a settlement with the RUF and thus end the war. It was their way of avoiding intervention—at the time when their military forces were active in trying to curb the genocidal campaign in Kosovo—in an African conflict, while pretending to be doing something.

US President Bill Clinton and his Secretary of State Madeleine Albright sent the administration's Special Envoy for Africa, the Reverend Jesse Jackson, an African-American with very little bureaucratic influence or power in Washington, to West Africa to do the dirty work. Ryan Lizza of the *New Republic* has told the story of this contemptible attempt at peace making in an article that exposed in devastating detail the hypocrisy and lack of commitment of Clinton's policy on Africa.[2] Under mounting pressure from Jackson a reluctant President Kabbah and other West African leaders were brought together in Lome, capital of Togo, to hammer out yet another peace agreement. 'I had grave misgivings about it, and didn't want to go,' a suave and angry President Kabbah told this writer in April 2002. 'I knew, from my past dealings with Sankoh, that it won't work. Sankoh is the most treacherous and evil man I have had to deal with in my over 40 years of public service. His words simply can't be trusted. But we had no choice. Here were these world powers telling us that "look, now is your chance. If you don't cooperate, we will never be there for you." We were in a box. We wanted UN intervention, but that was not possible unless we had some kind of peace agreement. So we agreed to go.'[3]

Sankoh, who was then in gaol, condemned to hang for treason by the High Court of Sierra Leone, was released. In July 1999 the Sierra Leone government and the RUF—but no representatives of the renegade soldiers—met and signed the Lome Accord which, like the Abidjan Accord, announced a cessation of hostilities and granted amnesty to all parties involved in, and for all crimes committed during, the war. The Accord further made Sankoh chairman of a commission on strategic minerals, which was 'charged with the responsibility of securing and monitoring the legitimate exploitation of Sierra Leone's gold and diamonds, and other resources that [were] deemed to be of strategic importance for national security', effectively giving him official control over all the diamond mines in the country. The position also gave him 'The Status of Vice-President of Sierra Leone [which] therefore [made him] answerable

[2] Ryan Lizza, 'Where Angels Fear to Tread', *The New Republic*, 24 July 2000.
[3] Interview in Freetown, April 2002.

only to the President of Sierra Leone.' The Lome Accord finally gave Sankoh and 'all combatants and collaborators' during the decade-long war 'absolute and free pardon...in respect of anything done by them in pursuit of their objectives, up to the time of the signing of the [Lome] agreement.'[4]

The agreement scandalised Sierra Leoneans and the human rights community around the world. Peter Takirambudde, head of the Africa programme of the New York-based Human Rights Watch, spoke for many when he characterised the agreement as 'a major retreat by all parties—the United Nations, the Clinton administration, the others', adding: 'For the rest of Africa, where there are rebels in the bush, the signal is that atrocities can be committed—especially if they are frightening atrocities. The lesson to other rebels is that half measures will not do.'[5] The chagrined and embarrassed UN representative at the talks, while broadly endorsing the Accord, publicly condemned the amnesty agreement and appended a disclaimer to the article granting blanket immunity. That left open the possibility that the odious article would be reviewed in due course. The head of the UN High Commission for Human Rights, the outspoken Irish ex-President Mary Robinson, made this possibility clear when she announced that the United Nations did not recognise the amnesty aspects of the agreement.

But the ebullient Jesse Jackson was undaunted. He had President Clinton telephone Sankoh for an encouraging chat,[6] and hailed the agreement as a personal diplomatic triumph. Jackson went on to compare Sankoh to Nelson Mandela, averring that both were freedom fighters. Even the donor-driven and near-paralytic Kabbah administration could take it no more: when Jackson announced that he would be visiting Sierra Leone in mid-2000 to negotiate the release of UN peacekeepers abducted by the RUF (more on this presently), the Sierra Leone government announced that his safety would not be assured, so great was the anger of the ordinary citizens against the flamboyant American diplomatic hustler.

In the wake of this dreadful agreement Western attitudes towards Africa came under renewed scrutiny. Why was it that the RUF, which was demonstrably more brutal than all the militias in the Balkans, could be treated as victorious freedom fighters while the likes

[4] *The Lome Accord* (published by the Government of Sierra Leone, Freetown, July 1999).
[5] Steve Coll, 'The Other War', *Washington Post*, 9 January 2000.
[6] Ibid.

of Milošević would be hunted down as war criminals? Steve Coll of the *Washington Post* put it this way:

The violent campaign against civilians carried out by rebel forces in Free-town last January not only failed to stir American and European govern-ments, it set the stage for a United Nations-endorsed rebel triumph. Early last summer, as NATO declared victory in Kosovo, West African nations, the United States, Britain and the United Nations provided diplomatic and financial backing for a peace agreement that delivered amnesty to the rebels...In other words, notwithstanding what happened in Freetown last January—or, rather, because of what happened—the rebels achieved some-thing like victory.[7]

Coll puts the blame for this brutal double standard in the West's treatment of Africa and other parts of world, particularly disadvan-taged areas of former Eastern bloc countries, on racism, but in the particular case of Sierra Leone, he identified a more immediately potent factor: Kaplan's *Atlantic Monthly* article in which he de-scribed the Sierra Leone war as 'increasing lawlessness that is far more significant than any coup, rebel incursion, or episodic experi-ment in democracy', arguing that such 'criminal anarchy (has emerged) as the real "strategic" danger'. Well, Sierra Leone was of no discernible strategic value to the United States or Europe, so why bother? Kaplan's dismissive thesis, Coll writes, 'took hold with many members of Congress, diplomats and foreign policy analysts', for it 'seemed to capture their own gathering revulsion and exhaus-tion with post-Cold War challenges America faced in the Third World, especially in violent corners of Africa. Americans and Euro-peans watched passively during Rwanda's genocide in 1994', a trag-edy that saw hundreds of thousands of Africans die 'in a killing spree far greater in scale than anything (that took) place in Sierra Leone.'[8]

However, Western failure to get involved militarily in African cri-ses is rooted in a more profound pathology. There is the element of horror-fatigue, of course, and there is a lingering racism that in-fects the attitude of Western policy makers. The end of the Cold War amplified all of these factors: Africa, once a strategic battle-ground, lost this status as far as the West was concerned. Even as the Somalia disaster unfolded the United States watched coldly as vari-ous militia groups ravaged Liberia, America's own creation and until the end of the Cold War one of its most important allies on the

[7] Ibid.
[8] Ibid.

continent, hosting a CIA listening post and the Voice of America's relay station for Africa. In the absence of this crucial strategic or geopolitical interest, external interventions in civil wars in African countries were often two-track, focusing on the brokering of 'peace agreements' on the one hand and the provision of humanitarian assistance on the other. This approach assumes, as a matter of course, that leaders of the fighting factions are rational political actors driven by legitimate grievances—poverty and technological under-development are often seen as sources of legitimate griev- ances in themselves—who will take advantage of whatever peace accord is brokered and then settle down as respectable political players with a stake in the new *status quo.*

There has been a paralysing lack of interest in the commitment of what has been, since the founding of the United Nations, an inte- gral aspect of peace building and maintenance: troops from other parts of the world to keep the peace. Most Western nations, who control the mechanisms of the United Nations, have shown an almost obsessive lack of interest in getting their troops involved in Africa's myriad conflicts. The exception was France. That Euro- pean nation, whose sense of 'national grandeur and power'—to quote Rachel Utley's seductive phrase[9]—has been dependent upon a projection overseas of its potential to exercise unmistakable influ- ence, has since the 1960s militarily intervened in at least nine Afri- can countries. France intervened in Mauritania, Senegal, Gabon, Cameroon and Chad in the 1960s; in Chad again, as well as in Mauritania, the Central African Republic and Zaire in the 1970s; in Chad twice more in the 1980s; in Togo in 1986; and finally— and most controversially—in Rwanda in the 1990s. These interven- tions earned France the title 'the gendarme of Africa'.[10] In fact, in early 2001 French President Jacques Chirac was a prominent proponent of intervention in Guinea, during a time when Liber- ian-supported guerrillas were ravaging the southeastern parts of that country; and France still maintains significant military bases in Senegal and Djibouti.[11] Unlike other former colonial powers, especially Britain, France continued to regard many of its ex-colo- nies in West Africa, with the exception of Guinea, as its traditional sphere of influence and maintained a policy of *rayonnement* towards

[9] Rachel Utley, '"Not to do Less but to do Better…": French Military Policy in Africa', *International Affairs*, vol. 78, no. 1 (January 2002), pp. 129–46.
[10] Ibid.
[11] Ibid.

them.[12] France's military aid to Africa was 800 million French francs in 1984, and in 1990 it had 6,600 troops stationed there.[13] This military presence was a source of great disquiet among other, non-French-speaking African states, especially the West African regional power Nigeria, which viewed the intrusive French presence in West Africa as a kind of 'Trojan Horse' strategy and the recipient African nations as neo-colonial client states.[14]

In the 1980s rhetoric about 'neo-colonialism' in West Africa could still draw audiences. But for much of the 1990s and since the beginning of the new millennium the demand has been for greater Western involvement in the region to check the hugely destabilising wars started by Charles Taylor's 1989 incursions into Liberia. It took the murderous January 1999 attacks on Freetown—6,000 killed, thousands mutilated and abducted, a large part of the city torched—and the odious Lome Accord to generate this kind of involvement, and even then in a largely circuitous and ad hoc manner. Before Lome the United Nations had a limited involvement with Sierra Leone. The UN Secretary General had maintained a Special Representative in the country since 1994, and after the signing of the Abidjan Accord in 1996 the organisation, as one of the 'moral guarantors' of the agreement, consented to send 900 troops to monitor the ceasefire and help in the disarmament and reintegration programme outlined therein. However, the force was never sent, because the United States vetoed its deployment on the grounds that there was no agreement about this in Sierra Leone: Foday Sankoh expressly condemned the idea, and instead insisted, both in Abidjan and after the signing of the Accord, that the government must terminate its contract with Executive Outcomes and expel it from the country.

A few months after the government, under pressure from both Sankoh and donor agencies, complied with this suspect demand, the coup of 1997 happened, precipitating a more profound crisis than had hitherto been seen in the country. After the reversal of the coup the United Nations created the United Nations Observer Mission in Sierra Leone (Unomsil), on 13 July 1998, with seventy Military Observers. The force was mandated to monitor the security

---

[12] Tony Chafer, 'Franco-African Relations: no Longer so Exceptional', *African Affairs* vol. 101, no. 404 (July 2002), pp. 343–63.

[13] Adekeye Adebajo, *Building Peace in West Africa: Liberia, Sierra Leone and Guinea-Bissau*, Boulder, CO: Lynne Rienner, 2002, p. 37.

[14] Adebajo (note 13), p. 31.

situation, oversee the disarmament and demobilisation process, and ensure the observance, by all sides to the conflict, of international humanitarian law. The Lome agreement, for which the United Nations was also a 'moral guarantor' (minus the amnesty provision), called for a more active UN participation—in view of the still highly volatile situation in the country—and a 'transformation (of) and new mandate for Ecomog'. The 12,000 Nigerian troops still in the country were expected to remain in the months following the signing of the Accord to support the disarmament, demobilisation and reintegration programmes, and to ensure the delivery of humanitarian assistance throughout the country.

Shortly after Unomsil deployment, the United Nations took steps to enforce an arms embargo on the RUF. In quick order the UN mission called attention to Liberia's role in continuing to support the RUF, especially its recalcitrant and psychotic commander Sam Bockarie. In October 1999, after an agreement was hammered out between the United Nations and the Nigerian-dominated Ecomog, the United Nations expanded its troops to 6,000: 3,000 from the Nigerian forces already in the country, 2,000 from India and 1,000 from Guinea. The new UN force, which replaced Unomsil, was called Unamsil (UN Mission in Sierra Leone), and was authorised by Security Council Resolution 1270, passed on 22 October 1999. In November Kenyan troops arrived to join the UN mission. But the UN forces were lightly armed and appeared in no mood for actual combat duties. Britain had fifteen unarmed military observers with Unamsil; they were charged with helping to supervise the disarmament of the RUF. Shortly after the arrival of the Kenyan contingent, the RUF attacked and disarmed hundreds of Kenyan troops; they also seized 500 AK-47 rifles and tons of ammunition from the Guinean contingent.

In November 1999 Sam Bockarie, who was against the Lome Accord in the first place, declared that he was once again ready to start a fight to the finish. 'I'm envisaging another serious battle in Sierra Leone,' he said. 'I told my men to clean all their barrels and wait.'[15] It appeared that there was a serious rift between Bockarie, blamed by many for the atrocities in Freetown in January 1999, and Sankoh, who was in gaol at the time and was now, in his beguiling, crooked way, actively trying to present a new, more polished and nationalistic image to people in Sierra Leone. In December the dispute erupted in a gun battle between Sankoh's loyal supporters and

[15] Coll (note 5).

Bockarie's. When all was over, eight of Bockarie's senior aides lay dead, killed by Bockarie himself. Sankoh, now settled in his highly lucrative position of diamond czar, dismissed Bockarie's activities in patrician terms ('he is my son; he will come back'), and proceeded to busy himself with making secret deals with shady foreign diamond miners and dealers. By December 1999 Nigeria's President Olusegun Obasanjo, expressing disappointment at the lack of international support for regional peace operations in West Africa— as well as honouring a campaign pledge he had made to withdraw Nigerian troops from Sierra Leone—declared that he was accelerating the withdrawal of the entire Nigerian contingent from Ecomog in Sierra Leone. Unamsil reacted by asking the Security Council for more troops.

In Sankoh's new role as Vice President and diamond czar, with many important and not-so-important foreign visitors knocking at his door, the delusions of grandeur that had always underlined the warlord's brutal policies became starkly apparent. During a visit to a Unamsil disarmament centre in Makeni in January 2000 Sankoh berated the Kenyan Unamsil soldiers, telling them that they were stooges being used to cause problems in an African country and that they were not needed. He evoked the United Nations' alleged complicity in the death of the Congo's Patrice Lumumba, and declared that he would not be facing the same fate at their hands. He clearly regarded himself as the freedom fighter Jesse Jackson had claimed he was. He then launched into an insulting personal attack on Kofi Annan, calling him 'a nuisance in Africa, being used by World War power [*sic*] against his own brothers.' He told the Kenyan troops: 'We don't trust you, you are not neutral. You always work in the interests of colonial masters.'[16] And then, a little later on the same day, in the presence of the UN soldiers, he told a gathering of his RUF fighters—Makeni was now one of the RUF's most important bases, and the rebels patrolled the streets, armed, alongside Unamsil soldiers—to cooperate with the disarmament process.

---

[16] Three weeks later, in an interview with the BBC on 14 February, Sankoh continued his attacks on the United Nations in no less vehement terms: 'The people sitting in the United Nations pass resolutions without even informing the leadership of the RUF. Without consulting us. Look, in the Lome Peace Accord, we agreed that Ecomog should be transformed into a peacekeeping force and we have been working with Ecomog troops, especially the Nigerians. We have nothing against them. They are our brothers.'

He said these words in English. Quickly after that, speaking in Temne and Mende (Sankoh spoke both languages fluently), he told the fighters not to disarm at all.[17]

Earlier, on 17 October 1999, when US Secretary of State Albright visited Sierra Leone, Sankoh kept her waiting for several hours before he turned up for a meeting at the US Embassy, blustering. He objected to being requested to visit the Secretary of State at her own embassy, and made clear that as he was the new strong man in the country, visiting dignitaries must call on him—as Secretary Albright had called on President Kabbah.[18] In fact Kabbah was also present at the meeting. The architects of Lome may by now have concluded that they had made a grave miscalculation: Sankoh was clearly not playing along. In February 2000, when Sankoh flew to South Africa ostensibly to get medical treatment—but probably to meet his shady contacts in the Byzantine world of diamond trading—the reaction was swift. The UN Security Council mounted pressure on the South African authorities to have Sankoh sent back to Sierra Leone. A humiliated Sankoh arrived in Freetown vowing to strike back.

The Unamsil force was under the command of the Indian Major-General Vijay Jetley, a serious but aloof (some say arrogant) officer who became extremely unpopular with the Nigerian contingent as well as with the RUF. The Special Representative of the UN Secretary General (SRSG), in effect the political head of Unamsil, was the Nigerian ambassador Oluyemi Adeneji, and Jetley's deputy was another Nigerian, Brigadier-General Mohamed Garba, all in deference to the large proportion of Nigerian troops in Unamsil and Nigeria's historic role in the country as an intervention force. Relations between the Indian commander and his Nigerian deputy were very strained, with the Nigerian accusing Jetley of a racist preference for consulting with Indian commanders rather than with Garba, and of a tendency to deploy the African contingents in areas where their exposure to danger was greater than that of the Indian troops.[19] In addition to these problems, the mandate of the force was murky at best, and widely misunderstood in Sierra Leone.

---

[17] Interview with former RUF fighter, Freetown, April 2001. Sankoh dismissed the Unamsil as 'just enjoying the girls on the beaches' etc.: Excerpts of interview on the Sierra Leone Web, 15 February 2000.

[18] Interview with an official who attended the meetings, Freetown, April 2001.

[19] Interview with Unamsil informant, Freetown, September 2002.

As the surrender of arms by the Kenyans and Guineans showed, many Unamsil soldiers were not briefed before their deployment that they could use force to resist assault by the factions they were to disarm. Jetley himself explained the matter this way:

Most units under my command…had not been properly briefed about their mandate…[and did not] have the mental aptitude or the will to fight the rebels when the situation so demanded, and resorted to handing over their arms on the slightest danger to their life. This aspect enabled the rebels to gain a moral ascendancy and thereby emboldened them to take on the UN…[20]

Consequently, progress on the disarmament process was very spotty. In May 2000 Unamsil announced that it had disarmed 24,042 combatants (of 45,000 reckoned at the time to be with the RUF and other militias), but that the combatants turned in only 10,840 weapons. That same month the Nigerian Ecomog troops completed their withdrawal, the announcement of which precipitated an immediate crisis, one of the biggest in the UN's peacekeeping history. The RUF, until then pretending to cooperate with the UN force in the disarmament and reintegration process, suddenly began more sustained attacks on Unamsil soldiers, culminating in the ambush and abduction of 500 newly-arrived Zambian troops. An account of how this crisis developed has been insightfully provided by Major Phil Ashby, a British soldier who was one of the Military Observers.[21] According to Ashby, the UN mission was constantly harassed by the RUF to start with. The RUF behaved as if it was entirely in control of the country. Teenage ruffians, armed with rifles, would rough up UN soldiers, and Unamsil, under orders to avoid fighting, was reduced to humiliating negotiations with individual RUF commanders.

Things came to a head when a RUF commander, Colonel Augustine Gbao, invaded one of the demobilisation camps on the grounds that Unamsil had disarmed some RUF fighters without first clearing it with him. Gbao had some UN soldiers and military observers tied up, beaten and then later detained. When the Zambian troops arrived they were sent without adequate briefing to relieve the UN forces, but 'their orders were ridiculously vague and they were

[20] Major-General Vijay Jetley, 'Report on the Crisis in Sierra Leone', a leaked memo to the UN, September 2000. The full report can be found at the Sierra Leone Web: http://.sierra-leone.org/jetley0500.html.
[21] Major Phil Ashby, *Unscathed: Escape from Sierra Leone*, London: Macmillan, 2002.

poorly equipped.' The 500 Zambians headed to Makeni, where the UN soldiers were held along with twenty-five armoured vehicles: 'On paper, this was a strong and well-armed unit,' Ashby observes. 'But in years of civil war, the RUF had learnt how to ambush armoured columns.' And this was ideal guerrilla terrain:

> The road to Makeni, though made of tarmac, was narrow with jungle on both sides. So, unable to move off the road, only the front vehicle in the column could engage targets ahead. In effect, the firepower of twenty-five armoured cars was reduced to one. If the rebels could physically block the road, the column would not be able to turn round, and would get stuck like a lobster caught in a lobster pot. To confuse things further, the Zambians had terrible communications. Those at the front of the column could not even talk to their Colleagues at the back, let alone the outside world.[22]

The Zambians were stopped by the rebels near Makeni, the rebels probably suspecting that the force was heading towards Kono, their chief diamond mining centre (the RUF commanders had earlier clashed verbally with Jetley over the Unamsil commander's 'single-minded' determination to deploy in the diamond district[23]). The rebels tricked the Zambians into entering Makeni in small groups, allowing the RUF to disarm them all, group by group, and then have them stripped naked and detained. The rebels then donned the Zambian army uniforms and continued to assault other Unamsil units. It was a disaster beyond belief. Ashby and his men were also put under siege, but in the dead of night managed to escape to Freetown. The UN mission was on the verge of total collapse. A group of Unamsil soldiers surrounded Foday Sankoh's compound in Freetown, but they were clearly not in control of the situation. Sankoh, however, was, and at the time was planning a takeover of the government, which was to have been carried out with the arrival in Freetown of thousands of RUF fighters, many of them dressed in UN army uniforms. Britain promptly sent in 650 more military personnel.

Sankoh's plot was foiled after civil society organisations coordinated a huge protest march on his compound on 7 May, and then the Sierra Leone Army, heeding a call by the apparently reformed former junta leader Johnny Paul Koroma, mobilised against the RUF with the support of the British troops. During the stand-off at Sankoh's house soldiers opened fire on the unarmed demonstrators. Sankoh had armed guards at the house, but the house was sur-

[22] Ibid., p. 169.
[23] Interview with Augustine Gbao, Freetown, September 2002.

rounded by Nigerian Unamsil soldiers. Many observers, including participants in the demonstration I have spoken to, believed the shooting was started by the Unamsil troops, who appeared frustrated by the sheer size and determination of the crowd (there were attempts to break through the Unamsil soldiers by the crowd, who were determined to arrest Sankoh themselves).[24] Twenty-one civilians, including a journalist, were shot dead. It was a bloody moment and in the general confusion Sankoh, dressed as a woman, escaped, but emerged later to be shot in the leg and captured by a pro-government soldier.[25] The humiliated warlord, now a shadow of his former self, was charged with the murder of the demonstrators in a Freetown court.[26]

After this disaster the UN mission went into a tailspin, and Sierra Leoneans could only watch in scorn during the UN's long negotiations with rebel commanders to have the Zambians released. The RUF moved the Zambians to Liberia and had them handed over to President Taylor, who had been projecting himself as a peacemaker since the Zambians were captured. The Liberian leader then had the Zambians flown to Freetown, demonstrating even to the most credulous that he was clearly the boss of the RUF show. Unamsil became a despised force, the acronym altered by the locals to read 'U-nasty'. The peacekeepers were called 'Beach-keepers', since many of them frequented the stunningly beautiful beaches of Freetown, and Paddy's Beach Bar, a popular seaside haunt in the west end of Freetown also frequented by the UN forces, became known as the 'Second HQ of U-Nasty'. Pios Foray, a radical journalist in Freetown, put it this way: 'The early Unamsil was a terrible failure. They came, observed, and ran away. They simply made a fool of UN peacekeeping.'[27] The contempt was not confined to Sierra Leone. In a blistering article on the Sierra Leone crisis in the prestigious *New York Review of Books*, the American journalist James Traub wrote of the beleaguered UN mission:

The mission in Sierra Leone now looks like a ludicrous attempt to apply the loftiest set of moral principles in a sadistic and predatory world. It is

[24] Interviews in Freetown, January 2001.
[25] 'Sierra Leone: Special Report—"I am the Scorpion. I captured the Lion"', *Guardian*, 17 May 2000.
[26] The trial was suspended after Sankoh was charged with 'greatest responsibility' for crimes against humanity during the war by the UN-mandated Special Court for Sierra Leone.
[27] Interview in Freetown, September 2002.

another case of precisely the kind of ruinous naivete that the UN has been accused of suffering from in Bosnia and Rwanda. But it is worth remembering that it was the Clinton administration…who forced on President Kabbah the grotesque shotgun marriage with Foday Sankoh in the first place. It is at least as absurd to believe that Sankoh would be satisfied by power-sharing as to believe that the RUF could be conquered by a campaign of friendly persuasion, or that the rebels would be intimidated by the peace-keepers' modest show of force…

…Secretary-General Annan, fully aware of the limitations of UN peace-keeping, sent off UNAMSIL with a Security Council mandate more suitable to Cyprus than to the nation of chaos he must have known Sierra Leone to be. And the Department of Peacekeeping Operations shipped off a force of soldiers with hardly any idea how to engage in peacekeeping because most of the soldiers that knew about it wanted no part of it. Did anyone really have much confidence in what they were doing?[28]

Schism within the UN staff in Freetown quickly bubbled to the surface in the cruel form of a secret memo that Jetley had written to his superiors in New York but which was leaked to the *Guardian* in Britain. Jetley reviewed the crisis for which he largely blamed the Nigerians. The memo is worth quoting at some length:

Peacekeeping operations are a combination of diplomacy and tact. Generally in African countries the Peace Accord signed is shaky and fragile. In a mineral-rich country like Sierra Leone, politics has a very major role to play in finding solutions to civil wars. In my case, the Mission Directive given to me and which I tried to follow implicitly directly conflicted with the interests of not only the warring factions but also of the major players in the diamond racket like Liberia and Nigeria. As an Indian, and having no hidden agenda to promote, I became a victim of the machinations of these countries. By placing their stooges in the right places they have not only tried to scuttle the peace process but also try and denigrate me and the country I represent, to promote their own personal ambitions and personal interests.[29]

Jetley went on to note that the Nigerian army was 'interested in staying in Sierra Leone due to the massive benefits they were getting from the illegal diamond mining,' and accused Brigadier-General Maxwell Khobe, the Nigerian officer who led the assault that ousted the AFRC, of receiving 'up to 10 million dollars to permit the activities of the RUF'. He accused both Adeniji and his own deputy Garba of involvement in similar diamond corruption and

[28] James Traub, 'The Worst Place on Earth', *New York Review of Books*, 29 June 2000.
[29] Jetley (note 20).

sabotage, and claimed that the Ecomog force commander Major General Kpamber was 'also involved in the illegal diamond mining in connivance with RUF leader Foday Sankoh'. Jetley suggested that the RUF's assault on Unamsil soldiers, which markedly spared the Nigerian units, may have been instigated by the Nigerians to discredit him, and pointed at the timing of the kidnap of the Zambian unit—just after Nigerian Ecomog units completed their withdrawal—as suggesting that the RUF acted in agreement with the Nigerians.[30]

It was well known that senior Nigerian officers, including Khobe, were involved in diamond mining and smuggling, and the behaviour of the Nigerian forces on the day of the massive civil society demonstration was clearly repulsive, even suspect, but it looked like a stretch to suggest that the Nigerians had forged such intimate and highly improbable ties with the RUF. In any case, these sweeping and highly damaging allegations were hotly denied by the Nigerians, who called for the recall of Jetley. Garba announced that as the largest unit in the Unamsil force, the Nigerians would henceforth not take orders from him. General Victor Malu, Chief of Staff of the Nigerian forces, declared the Indian general was merely trying, by levying these allegations against them, 'to justify his ineptitude, inaction and inefficiency in the leadership of a multinational force.'[31] Unamsil appeared to be in its death throes.

The controversial, not to say disastrous episode of the kidnapping was traumatic for the United Nations. Not since the Congo crisis in the early 1960s had they faced such a serious existential challenge—and in a region that acutely needed the world body as a guarantee of its very survival. Sierra Leone had now become an unlikely test case for the United Nations' relevance. The UN Secretariat quickly deployed a team of highly experienced peacekeeping personnel to review the Sierra Leone mission, and on the basis of their recommendation, confusion regarding the mandate of the force and its rules of engagement was sorted out (the force was now to act more robustly to protect itself and ordinary civilians). A new commander of higher rank, the respected Kenyan Lieutenant-General Daniel Opande, was appointed to replace the controversial Jetley. The United Nations also authorised an increase in troop strength from 11,000 to 13,000 and later to 23,000, the largest UN

[30] Ibid.
[31] Chris McGreal, 'UN to bolster peacekeeping force', *Guardian*, 13 September 2000.

force ever deployed. The draft resolution tabled in the Security Council in September 2000 for the increase in troop size noted 'with concern serious shortfalls in capacity encountered by Unamsil in the recent past with regard to command and control, equipment, training and preparation of military personnel and the implementation of rules of engagement,' adding that the success of the mission would depend on 'an effective command and control structure and capacity, a single chain of command and the commitment to implement the mandate.' The mandate should include rapid and robust response to hostile activity, and action to extend 'state authority, restore law and order, and further stabilize the situation progressively throughout the entire country.'[32]

Recognising the role that the RUF diamond mining activities, including Sankoh's secret diamond deals (discovered when his house was ransacked, and the documents found there made public) had played in precipitating the crisis, the United Nations also set up a Panel of Experts to look into the role of diamonds in the conflict and Liberia's continuing links with the RUF. The Panel subsequently recommended targeted sanctions on Liberia, and on the RUF, which covered its diamond sales, weapons purchases and travel by senior Liberian officials, including President Charles Taylor. And member states, particularly Britain, provided better fighting equipment and logistical support for the UN force on a bilateral basis.

Changes were also effected within Unamsil's own rather bloated and largely inefficient bureaucracy. Alan Doss, a senior UN administrator and among the most experienced in the UN system, was sent to join Unamsil as deputy to Adeniji to undertake an overhaul of the entire management and support system. Unamsil also now assumed responsibility for 'defence stores' for the African contingents, encouraged inspection by the staff of contingents' defence headquarters, and approached non-force-contributing countries for equipment and logistic support. A study undertaken by the International Policy Institute of King's College, University of London, of peace operations (including the Sierra Leone peace process) in 2002–3—in which this writer participated—concluded:

The kidnapping of Unamsil soldiers and evident disregard for the terms of 'Lome'...marked a change in the approach of the UN force. During the two months that followed the May events UNAMSIL engaged in a number of skirmishes. The UN mission began killing RUF combatants as the military situation required. These aggressive tactics peaked with Operation

[32] Ibid.

Khukri on 15–16 July 2000...Khukri, undertaken to free Indian UNAMSIL troops still trapped as a result of the events of May, was war-fighting. A considerable number of RUF troops were alleged to have been killed. There was one Indian fatality.[33]

The operation was led by the Indian contingent, which had been augmented with additional troops and helicopter gunships shortly after the May crisis, and also benefited from the support of UK Special Forces in planning assistance. The Indian contingent, however, would shortly be withdrawn after Jetley was sacked, to be replaced by a highly efficient, disciplined and more conciliatory Pakistani force of over 4,000 troops. By early 2001, with sufficient troops now on the ground and the mission beginning to gain *gravitas*, Unamsil began serious work to correct the negative local and international perception of the mission. This task fell to the Public Information unit headed by an energetic and resourceful former journalist and Africa hand, Margaret Novicki, an American. Novicki and her staff, including Patrick Coker, a Nigerian, and later Kingsley Lington, a Freetown-based journalist, started a highly effective radio programme, regularly issued press releases and met local and foreign journalists. They also made jingles explaining the role of Unamsil that were broadcast on local radio stations, and embarked on what Novicki called 'community liaison', including networking with local groups to explain exactly what peacekeeping implied. 'This kind of coordinated public information strategy was really Kofi Annan's initiative,' she told me. 'Before Annan, no one in the United Nations thought seriously about it. Public perception of the United Nation mission is often as important in its ultimate success as the kind of resources available for it. And the singularly tragic event of May 2000 made this all the more compelling.'[34] Before long, people stopped using the terms 'U-nasty' and 'Beachkeepers'. Unamsil was on the road to gaining support.

The disarmament programme accelerated under Unamsil's new command, which was now better coordinated, and dealing with a more pliable RUF leader, the young and enterprising diamond smuggler Issa Sesay. By January 2002 72,490 combatants, both RUF and CDF, had been disarmed and a total of 42,000 weapons and 1.2 million rounds of ammunition collected. In interviews I conducted

---

[33] 'A Review of Peace Operations: A Case for Change', a report by the Conflict, Security and Development Group, International Policy Institute, King's College London, 2003, p. 77.

[34] Interview in Freetown, September 2002.

in Freetown in late 2002, former RUF combatants universally praised both General Opande and Adeniji for their conciliatory approach, and suggested that this was what finally convinced them to cooperate with the disarmament and reintegration programme.[35] But clearly there were two other, more important factors accounting for the RUF's late cooperation with the UN mission: its defeat by Guinean forces when its forces attacked Guinea's forest regions—which are rich in diamonds—at Taylor's instigation in late 2000 and early 2001,[36] and the massive show of strength by the British troops after the May 2000 crisis and the UK's sustained and more visible presence in the country thereafter.

The incursions into Guinea began in September 2000, as more international attention focused on Sierra Leone after the May crisis, with units of the RUF attacking a number of Guinean border towns immediately to the south of the capital Conakry. The area was then home to thousands of Sierra Leonean refugees who had fled from attacks by the RUF in their country. Not long afterwards the RUF attacked Guinean towns and villages in the 'Parrot's Beak' area of the country, emerging from Sierra Leone and points along the Liberian border, causing great destruction and dislocation, including that of thousands of Guineans and as many as 75,000 Sierra Leonean refugees who had been living on the Guinean side of the border for several years. Guinea responded proportionately. After the initial attacks began Guinea, with help from the United States (which maintained an annual C-JET military training programme with the Guinean army) and France, its former colonial master, acquired some armoured helicopters and some old MiG fighter bombers which it used to pound rebel bases in both Sierra Leone and Liberia. Guinea also helped to train over 1,000 Donsos (the Kono name for Kamajors or hunter-militias) from Sierra Leone's Kono district, deploying them against the RUF. The British, who had made an open-ended commitment to Sierra Leone, and now sensed the danger an escalation of the war would pose to them, also provided intelligence and other support to the Guinean army.

[35] Interview with Eldred Collins, RUF's Public Relations Officer, and with Augustine Gbao, the RUF's Chief of Security and many others, Freetown, September 2002.
[36] See Lansana Gberie, *Destabilizing Guinea: Diamonds, Charles Taylor and the Potential for Wider Humanitarian Catastrophe*, Ottawa: Partnership Africa Canada, 2001.

The Guineans battered both the RUF and its Liberian allies, and early in 2001, when the Donsos launched attacks against RUF-held positions in the diamond-rich district (where they were busy mining diamonds even as the United Nations was struggling to restructure its mission in Freetown), the RUF could only muster fifty fighters in reinforcement, and in an odd ironic twist appealed to Unamsil to deploy in the area to prevent it being completely overrun by the Donsos.[37] Earlier reports stated that Taylor had called up RUF fighters in Sierra Leone to help defend his position against Liberians United for Reconciliation and Democracy (LURD), a new anti-Taylor Liberian rebel group armed and deployed by the Guinean authorities in response to the Taylor-orchestrated attacks against Guinea. This movement of the RUF—some reports said about 2,000 of the hard-core fighters—back to Liberia helped significantly to make the ones remaining in Sierra Leone more vulnerable and therefore more amenable to UN demands.

Of no less importance was the intervention of the British forces, operating independently of Unamsil but in obvious support of the mission and the Sierra Leone government, following the May 2000 crisis. As we have noted, the UK's dramatic intervention helped to prevent a coup by Sankoh and the complete scuttling of the UN mission. Shortly after Sankoh went into hiding the British Joint Deployment Force, which included the 1st Parachute Regiment and 42 Commando of the Royal Marines, deployed in Freetown to secure the airport at Lungi to conduct 'Non-Combatant Evacuation', essentially evacuation of non-Sierra Leoneans, particularly Western nationals. British Chinook helicopters participated in the operation. The evacuation was completed within forty-eight hours. Six hundred British paratroopers were then deployed to guard Sierra Leone's 'vital grounds', which included the airport, the seaport and Freetown itself. The British press dubbed the operation 'Mission Creep', because it was the effective beginning of more sustained British military involvement in the Sierra Leone conflict.

The British deployed the Parachute Regiment's Pathfinder Platoon near Lungi under the command of Sergeant Stephen Heaney. That week RUF troops, trying to capture the airport, attacked the platoon at night but were repulsed; over twenty of the rebel force, which outnumbered the British five to one, were killed, with the British sustaining no casualties. The operation helped convince the

---

[37] Interview with former British army commander in Sierra Leone, Brigadier Jonathon Riley, Freetown, April 2001.

RUF, if this was needed, that it was up against a very powerful enemy indeed. Sankoh's arrest less than two weeks after this incident completed the demoralisation of the RUF. The UN mission had been saved from imminent collapse.

Not long after this a group with a particularly nasty reputation, styling itself the West Side Boys (actually remnants of Koroma's People's Army and hardened convicts released from Pademba Road prison during the January 1999 attack on Freetown), captured eight British soldiers and held them hostage. Always high on drugs and cheap gin, the West Side Boys had been harassing civilians and the ill-armed Unamsil units, and were in the habit of abducting young women to be used as sex slaves in their bush hideouts. After capturing the British soldiers they demanded fresh elections before they would release the troops, and called for the resignation of President Kabbah. Their leader was Major Kallay, one of the soldiers who plotted and carried out the AFRC coup, and although Johnny Paul Koroma, now in Freetown and heading the 'Lome'-created Commission for the Consolidation of Peace, dissociated himself from the thuggish and brutal band, it was clear that the West Side Boys were nostalgic about those junta days. During negotiations to free the hostages, the renegade forces foolishly demanded food and communications equipment from the British, which they were given, but which in turn were used to pinpoint their location in the bush. British paratroopers, guided by SAS units long hidden in the bush, launched a commando raid against the West Side Boys on 10 September 2000, killed 26 of them, captured their leader and freed the hostages. The whole West Side Boys gang had been destroyed. It was a demonstration of power that greatly impressed the RUF and certainly helped change its mind about starting another round of fighting.

By September 2000 British troop strength had reached 1,000, and the British government announced that it was stepping up a retraining programme for the Sierra Leone army; by early 2001 4,500 army personnel had been retrained. The United Nations brokered yet another ceasefire agreement with the RUF. On 13 November British marines staged a massive military exercise around Freetown. The British commander announced publicly that the exercise was intended to 'remind the leadership of the RUF to honour that agreement'. The RUF announced that it now had an 'interim leader' in Major Issa Sesay, a boyish and taciturn former close Sankoh aide, and effective disarmament began shortly thereafter. It officially ended in January 2002, and in May general and presidential elections were conducted across the country. Kabbah once again emerged victorious, with over 70 per cent of the votes cast. Sierra Leone was once again declared at peace.

However, the British intervention was not limited to military matters. Through its Department for International Development (DFID) the British government virtually bankrolled the Sierra Leone government through the entire process. Britain, the biggest foreign donor to Sierra Leone, sponsored the UN Security Council resolution which led to the increase in Unamsil's troop strength, the setting up of the Panel of Experts and the imposition of sanctions on Liberia and the RUF, all of these making the rebels effectively impotent, bereft of foreign backing.

At the height of the fighting in Freetown in January 1999, after Britain pledged £1 million in additional humanitarian assistance to Sierra Leone, and sent the frigate HMS *Norfolk* with 3 tons of medical supplies and equipment for Connaught Hospital in Freetown, Foreign Secretary Robin Cook announced that Britain's goal was to 'restore a stable, integrated Sierra Leone', and in a forceful tone called on Taylor to 'withdraw support' for the rebel forces.[38] By its actions after May 2000 Britain certainly matched rhetoric with action. Its longer-term commitment to Sierra Leone—particularly to 'Security Sector Reforms', which included rebuilding the army and the police force—is an example of a creative 'nation-building' process. An expatriate British police officer, Keith Biddle, paid by DFID, headed the Sierra Leone Police force from 2001 to 2003. Under Biddle's efficient command, Britain provided new uniforms, vehicles and other logistical support for the police, and upgraded officers' pay. The Sierra Leone Police is certainly in many ways far more professional, more effective and less corrupt than it was before British intervention.

Britain has also set up an anti-corruption unit in Freetown that has exposed corrupt practices by government officials, including senior cabinet ministers, one of them being sacked as a result. The aim is virtually to rebuild the collapsed state institutions in the country, a job that is often sneeringly referred to (in the United States) as 'nation-building', but which is a necessary component of peacekeeping in collapsed states wracked by violent conflict, as the United States itself has discovered in Afghanistan. Significantly enough, Britain has drawn on its former imperial resources for this task: former British colonial officials in Sierra Leone participated

[38] The Sierra Leone Web, http://sierra-leone.org/slnews0199.html

in discussions concerning Britain's strategies in the war-wracked country, and a former colonial District Officer has returned to the country to engage in chieftaincy rehabilitation,[39] a job the British think is necessary to restore the legitimacy of the state. The British have rebuilt, in a grand way, the Supreme Court of Sierra Leone, and helped restore other state structures. The DFID-funded community rehabilitation project, in which dozens, perhaps hundreds, of small model houses are being built in villages and towns destroyed during the war, is also a highly commendable step in state-building.

Many Sierra Leoneans, especially the older ones—betraying a nostalgia for the peaceful colonial days—speak affectionately of the British role in Sierra Leone, belated though it was, and rather less affectionately of the Nigerians and Guineans whose crucial interventions, resource-starved though they were, were of a far more committed nature. Why has Britain, which was a late-comer to the West African crisis, become the most highly praised for bringing peace to Sierra Leone? As we noted earlier, before Britain's intervention, Nigeria was the leading foreign factor in both Liberia and Sierra Leone, and if there was any contest for hegemony in the region, it was between Nigeria (which was strongly allied to the English-speaking nations of the region) and France (which continued to maintain a near-neocolonial relationship with several of its former colonies, with the exception of Guinea). The answer has to do with timing, resources and experience. Britain entered the fray when Nigeria was obviously exhausted, and when the reputation of Nigerian forces was at its lowest. Almost every observer concluded, after the January 1999 attack on Freetown, that the Nigerian-led force had failed, and failed disastrously. And no one failed to notice that it was the robust presence of the British troops that prevented the total collapse of the UN mission and a relapse into violence.

Britain's development assistance also contrasts sharply with Nigeria's commitment. Nigeria is itself a poor country with many problems; it simply cannot afford the kind of aid programmes the British have brought to Sierra Leone. As for France, its reputation has always been questionable in the Mano River region of West Africa, which consists of Sierra Leone, Guinea and Liberia. France was known to have backed—through Côte d'Ivoire and Burkina Faso, and for the hardwood timber trade—Charles Taylor's cata-

---

[39] William Reno, 'The Failure of Peacekeeping in Sierra Leone', *Current History*, May 2001, pp. 219–25.

strophic incursions in the region. France's previous wretched treatment of Guinea, after the latter opted for independence in 1958, has not been entirely forgotten either. Perhaps more important, if there have been questions about the integrity of the regimes that France has militarily backed in West Africa, it is almost universally agreed that the RUF of Sierra Leone was such a depraved and brutal force that militarily crushing it would raise no controversy anywhere—indeed would only be praised.

How Britain's recent interest in West Africa will play out in the future balance of power and hegemonic interests in the region is hard to tell at the moment, but the recent initiatives seem to indicate an era of cooperation between the two great powers in their dealings with Africa. In 1997 France's Defence Minister Richard said that France would work in Africa 'in close liaison with other European or Western countries already providing military assistance, especially Britain'; and at the Franco-British summit in Cahors in February 2001, the two nations made a joint commitment to work on peace and security issues in Africa, including a determination to reduce conflict, jointly supporting efforts to limit trade in small arms and prevent natural resources, such as 'conflict diamonds', from fuelling wars[40]—this last commitment was made in recognition of the role that smuggled diamonds played in underwriting the wars in Sierra Leone and Angola. France actually provided transit facilities and some technical support in Senegal during the evacuation of foreigners from Sierra Leone by British troops. Nigeria's great influence in the region, alas, will almost certainly be limited if these two powers, with incomparably greater resources and more experience in military and other interventions, sustain their interest and cooperation in West Africa.

After the end of the disarmament process and the conduct of successful elections in Sierra Leone in 2002, the UN mission in the country was being advertised as a sterling success story, which is largely justified. But the main reason given for this success by UN officials in Freetown in various interviews I have conducted with many of them—the conciliatory 'softly-softly' approach towards the RUF adopted by Adeniji and Opande, in contrast to the more confrontational style of Jetley—can hardly stand up to scrutiny. The RUF did not become suddenly cooperative because Unamsil adopted an attractive policy. The paternalistic approach of Adeniji and Opande certainly helped, but mainly as a face-saving mecha-

[40] Utley (note 9).

nism for an essentially defeated and demoralised RUF—defeated by the Guinean forces and the CDF, and demoralised by the capture and public humiliation of its messianic leader Foday Sankoh, as well as the sustained and 'over-the-horizon' presence of a powerful British military throughout the latter stages of the disarmament process.

On 7 March 2000 Secretary General Annan appointed a panel to undertake a study of the United Nations' past peace operations. This was two months before the kidnapping of UN peacekeepers in Sierra Leone. The panel, headed by the Algerian diplomat Lakhdar Brahimi, therefore clearly drew on lessons learned by Unamsil. In its October 2000 report it noted that the United Nations 'must not apply best-case planning assumptions to situations where the local actors have historically exhibited worst-case behavior. This means that mandates should specify an operation's authority to use force.' The Brahimi Report then made reflection's on the United Nations' past peacekeeping experience which the authors presumably considered profound, not to say reasonable, but which only indicated that they were themselves still to grasp the fundamental nature of the kinds of insurgency or warfare that predatory groups like the RUF represent:

It should have come as no surprise to anyone that some of the missions of the past decade would be particularly hard to accomplish: they tended to deploy where conflict had not resulted in victory for any side, where a military stalemate or international pressure or both had brought fighting to a halt but at least some of the parties to the conflict were not seriously committed to ending the confrontation. UN operations thus did not deploy in post-conflict situations but tried to create them (*sic*). In such complex operations, peacemakers work to maintain a secure local environment while peace builders work to make that environment self-sustaining. Only such environment offers a ready exit to peacekeeping forces, making peacekeepers and peace builders inseparable partners.[41]

What the United Nations' experience in Sierra Leone clearly showed is that this distinction between 'peacekeepers' and 'peace builders' is very strained indeed: it is a distinction without a difference. The traditional conception of peacekeeping, which is steeped in the United Nations' long-past experiences (the deployment in the Sinai peninsula in the 1950s, for example), emphasises agreement between warring states before peacekeepers are deployed. But there are few inter-state conflicts these days—in conflict-ridden

---

[41] Report of the Brahimi Panel (note 1).

Africa only one conflict in the 1990s, the war between Ethiopia and Eritrea, was clearly inter-state; the rest were intra-state or a hybrid of the two types of conflict (warfare in the Democratic Republic of the Congo drew in over half a dozen African armies while still maintaining the character of an internal insurgency). So the tidy deployments known as 'sheriff's posses' are hardly an option in conflicts like those in Sierra Leone, Liberia or the Congo. In that kind of conflict—whose ending is, after all, the whole idea of 'humanitarian intervention', a seductive phrase used even by UN bureaucrats these days—the affected state virtually collapses, and the continuation of the conflict is itself a correlate of this collapse. The peacekeeping forces sent into such situations must be ready for battle, for some form of combat is a virtual certainty. As Traub puts it:

We live in an era of collapsing states; and now governments declare war on factions, often ethnic, as in Kosovo; or factions try to murder their way into power, as in Liberia and Sierra Leone; or in the absence of any state at all, as in Somalia. The new contestants find the UN's principles quaint; they aren't much swayed by international public opinion, and they often derive tremendous economic benefits from war. They can't be reasoned with; they can only be stopped. You can't go into places like Sierra Leone unless you are prepared to shoot people when you are provoked; you can't go unless the explicit idea is to stop the bad guys. But the UN can't live by that truth.[42]

One can only hope that the UN Security Council and the bureaucrats at the organisation's plush New York offices, still steeped in the thinking of a tidier, more conventional past, have learned the hard lessons from the Sierra Leone experience.

[42] Traub (note 28).

8

DIAMONDS AND THE RUF's WAR

'Where are our diamonds, Mr President? Where is our gold, NPRC?
RUF is hungry to know where they are. RUF is fighting to save Sierra
Leone.'[1] (RUF 'anthem')

'Ours was not a civil war. It was not a war based on ideology, religion
or ethnicity, nor was it a 'class war'... It was a war of proxy aimed at
permanent rebel control of our rich diamond fields for the benefit of
outsiders.' (Ahmed Tejan Kabbah, President of Sierra Leone.[2])

It is a mark of the mercenary character of the RUF's war that nearly
ten years after it began observers were still struggling to find not
just a coherent explanation for its remarkably brutal nature—demonstrated by the amputations—but also the motivation behind waging the war itself. 'What was driving the rebels to such depths of
depravity?' was a question that usually came accompanied by 'What
do they hope to achieve by doing it?' There is another question,
however, that would have yielded more rewarding results: what could
possibly have sustained the level and intensity of violence that plagued such a materially poor country? Attributes that usually foment
prolonged violence even in bankrupt states—'tribalism', religion,
ideology and big power interests—were all distinctly lacking in the
Sierra Leone. Yet the violence was perpetrated with fanatical intensity and depravity.

It was not until 2000 that a satisfactory and widely accepted explanation was found, by three researchers working for a small Canadian NGO, Partnership Africa Canada, with an eye to influencing

[1] RUF/SL, *Footpaths to Democracy* (published by the RUF), p. 1.
[2] 'Kabbah on Diamond War', *New Vision* (Freetown), 27 September 2001,
quoting from the President's convocation speech at Southern Connecti-
cut State University, New Haven, after the University conferred on him an
honorary doctorate in 2001.

Western policy towards the largely neglected crisis in Sierra Leone. That explanation focused on Sierra Leone's rich alluvial diamond deposits, and the lust they aroused in predatory players, local as well as international. This apparently simple explanation, focusing as it does mainly on the political economy of the conflict, has gained such influence and wide acceptance—the former US ambassador to Sierra Leone, John Hirsch, even entitled his insightful 2001 reflections on the Sierra Leone conflict *Diamonds and the Struggle for Democracy*[3]—that it needs to be analysed to be properly understood. How did diamonds—which have no value whatsoever to the average Sierra Leonean beyond their attraction to foreigners—come to be held responsible for fuelling the decade-long conflict in the country?

Throughout much of the 1990s, as we have seen, the war was a largely mysterious affair that attracted attention around the world mainly because of its brutality. Robert Kaplan in 1994 dismissed it as 'anarchic' criminal violence, and its extreme brutality as a throwback to an ancient, deeply primitive past. This interpretation was rightly rejected by more serious observers and academics. Yet some of these attempts to explain the war, notably Paul Richards' *Fighting for the Rainforest* (1996), were scarcely more helpful, as we have seen. However, the explanation that focuses on diamonds—as both the fuel for the war and the motivation for the RUF's leaders and principal foreign backers—is now widely accepted.

This explanation was first perfunctorily suggested by William Reno in his *Corruption and State Politics in Sierra Leone* (1995), which focused on the then military government, the NPRC, and its hiring of mercenaries to fight off the RUF. In Reno's analysis diamonds only appear as the means to pay the mercenaries and the principal concern of the NPRC: the junta wanted to keep the diamond fields, the main earner of Sierra Leone's foreign exchange, from falling permanently into the hands of the RUF. The same approach was adopted by the Canadian Brigadier Ian Douglas in his otherwise incisive 1999 paper 'Fighting for Diamonds—Private Military Companies in Sierra Leone'.[4] Much the same is true of an important

---

[3] John Hirsch, *Diamonds and the Struggle for Democracy*, Boulder, CO: Lynne Rienner, 2001.

[4] Ian Douglas, 'Fighting for Diamonds—Private Military Companies in Sierra Leone' in Jakkie Cilliers and Peggy Mason (eds), *Peace, Profit or Plunder? Privatisation of Security in War-Torn African Societies*, Johannesburg: Institute for Security Studies, 1999, pp. 175–200.

paper on the predatory and criminal nature of the NPRC by Arthur Abraham, a respected historian and a former minister in the junta's cabinet. The role of diamonds in the RUF's own campaigns went largely unexamined. As an insider Abraham was able to provide a convincing insight into the ghastliness of the regime he once served as Minister of Education, by focusing on how the NPRC's preoccupation with illegal diamond mining activities led it to a criminal manipulation of the still largely contained war. Abraham writes:

The involvement of the army on a large scale in Kono (from late 1992 on) probably brought a change for the worse in the official prosecution of the war. Diamonds were introduced into the war equation.[…] While senior military officials were busy helping themselves to the resources of the state, the less privileged soldiers felt resentment and found ways of helping themselves as well. This was partly responsible for the Sobel phenomenon…As the war continued, Sobels operated in broad daylight posing a major security problem.[5]

Abraham, like Reno, saw the diamond issue purely in terms of the nefarious activities of the NPRC, and how this led to an informal collaboration between their foraging army and the RUF forces. The 'senior NPRC officials (civilians and soldiers), busy enriching themselves, could not satisfy the wants of the ragamuffins they had put under arms, and so turned a blind eye to the misdeeds of the Sobels,' Abraham wrote. 'The Sobels attacked towns under the guise of rebels and looted property; they could "sell-game"—government forces withdraw from the town, leaving arms and ammunition for the rebels behind them.' Abraham noted that with 'this kind of collaboration' the NPRC people had an 'interest not only in looting to enrich themselves, but in creating the impression that the rebels were a formidable enemy. This way, the war would keep going to the benefit of both the NPRC and the RUF.'[6]

This absence of a serious analysis focusing on the RUF's economic preoccupations was both surprising and telling. That the RUF was both predatory and capable of mercenary brutality was not in doubt. Its practice of sexual violence, including gang rape of young girls (the preference being for virgins, as an excellent report by the Human Rights Watch documented[7]) and sexual slavery, was known

---

[5] Arthur Abraham, 'War and Transition to Peace: A Study of State Conspiracy in Perpetuating Armed Conflict', *Africa Development* (Dakar: CODESRIA), vol. XXII, nos 3–4, 1997, p. 103.

[6] Ibid., pp. 103–4.

[7] Human Rights Watch, *Sierra Leone: 'We'll Kill you if you Cry': Sexual Violence in the Sierra Leone War*, vol. 15, no. 1 (A).

for years, as was the systematic looting of villages and towns that fell under its control. It was also clear that the RUF carried out its most coordinated and ferocious campaigns in the diamond-rich regions of eastern Sierra Leone, which were among its earliest targets. And it was widely remarked upon that the RUF did not articulate a coherent political platform even after years of warfare, which was a source of great frustration for diplomats and professional conciliators with an interest in brokering peace in the ravaged country. Charles Taylor's support of the RUF, much denied by the Liberian warlord, was also widely remarked upon. The problem was connecting the dots to present a coherent picture of the RUF's activities as well the dynamics of its relationship with Taylor. The main difficulty, of course, was that both the RUF leadership and areas under its control were inaccessible to outsiders, including journalists. As a result the RUF war was dismissed by many commentators as 'senseless' and therefore incomprehensible.

Then in January 2000 Partnership Africa Canada (PAC) published a report which put much of the blame for the war—'this enormous human tragedy'—on diamonds. *The Heart of the Matter: Sierra Leone, Diamonds and Human Security* recounted the corrupting of Sierra Leone's diamond industry, with legal exports falling from a peak of 2 million carats per year in the 1960s to less than 50,000 carats by 1988. Sierra Leone's despotic president during much of this period, Siaka Stevens, tacitly encouraged illicit mining, becoming involved himself in criminal or near-criminal activities. The situation only worsened when the RUF war started, and by 1999 formal diamond mining had completely collapsed. Throughout the war, however, while there were hardly any government-supervised diamond exports, the diamond business was thriving across the border in Liberia, a country with very little diamond production of its own. Between 1994 and 1999 Belgian figures alone registered more than $2 billion worth of diamonds imported from Liberia, although at the very best of times Liberia never surpassed $10 million in exports of its own diamonds.

The PAC researchers found that throughout much of the conflict the RUF's diamond mining activities were extensive and well-coordinated, and that within those operations shady business interests, including those with connections to organised crime, and almost all of them with bases in Taylor-controlled Liberia, were active. The RUF maintained special armed mining units which supervised mining operations, employing mainly captives and illicit freelance miners. The miners worked in conditions of servitude—

indeed often at gunpoint. Laggard captives and those caught stealing were shot. Diamond theft was ranked next only to 'disloyalty' to Foday Sankoh or 'treason' in the RUF's scale of serious offences, and the RUF leadership preferred to use children in their illegal mining operations because they were less likely to steal. A former commander told this writer that hundreds of people may have been shot for attempting to steal diamonds mined under the RUF's watch.

The Heart of the Matter concluded that Charles Taylor was the principal beneficiary from this criminal business, having trained, armed and mentored the RUF for the purpose of plunder more than for any geostrategic and political calculations. Taylor himself had funded his own quest for power and economic control in Liberia from the country's rich hardwood timber reserves, making hundreds of millions of dollars in the process. But Sierra Leone diamonds would prove even more lucrative. It was a classic case of warlord politics—exporting violence for the main purpose of stealing. The PAC report noted that 'only the economic opportunity presented by the breakdown of law and order could sustain violence at levels that have plagued Sierra Leone since 1991… it is ironic that enormous profits have been made from diamonds throughout the conflict, but the only effect on the citizens of the country where they are mined has been terror, murder, dismemberment and poverty.'

The PAC report showed conclusively that there was virtually no oversight of the international movement of diamonds. Both large and small companies were colluding in the laundering of stolen diamonds. The official diamond industry was later to estimate the volume of 'conflict diamonds'—diamonds mined and traded by rebel groups—at different times as being between 4 and 15 per cent of the world total, but even the low figure represents a significant volume of cash considering the $7.5 billion annual trade in rough diamonds. In fact it is estimated that as much as one-fifth of the world's rough diamond trade may be 'illicit' in nature, characterised by theft, tax evasion and money laundering. Given the secretive and unregulated nature of the international diamond trade, it was a simple matter for the RUF and its Liberian backers to move millions of dollars' worth of diamonds into the legitimate trade and use the proceeds to buy the weapons and drugs needed for the young and depraved fighters.[8] By laying bare the political

[8] Ian Smillie, Lansana Gberie and Ralph Hazleton, *The Heart of the Matter: Sierra Leone, Diamonds and Human Security*, Ottawa: Partnership Africa Canada, 2000.

economy of Sierra Leone's decade-long war, the PAC report found an explanation for the dynamics of the conflict and the reasons for its intensity, its apparent 'senselessness' and its almost intractable nature. That explanation helped to shift discussion of the war, in academic, journalistic and policy-related circles, away from complacent and racist explanations evoking notions of mindless African savagery and nihilism to more easily grasped and appreciated trajectories: resource exploitation, criminal appropriation and power.

The report received widespread publicity, and major newspapers, radio and television stations around the world—in Canada, Britain, Belgium, the United States, Japan, Australia and African countries—carried stories highlighting its findings. The reaction of major interested governments around the world was also positive. The Canadian Foreign Minister, Lloyd Axworthy, a Harvard-trained political scientist who had made human security the linchpin of his policy, welcomed the report and used it in his extensive advocacy on behalf of Sierra Leone in the UN Security Council and elsewhere. In quick order his Department organised a one-day seminar on the economic dimension of civil wars, to which he invited the authors of *The Heart of the Matter* (this writer was the rapporteur) and leading scholars who were interested in the issue, and appointed David Pratt, Member of Parliament for Nepean-Carleton, as Special Envoy for Sierra Leone, a role that allowed the Canadian government to be more actively involved in the Sierra Leone peace process and to play a central role in the debate about reforming the corrupt international diamond industry.

The British government, Sierra Leone's most important foreign ally and biggest donor, took the report with equal seriousness. Shortly after it was launched, the British Foreign Office minister Peter Hain visited Sierra Leone, where he referred to the report in a stirring speech to parliamentarians and civil society activists: 'I am determined to look for ways to stamp out the theft of Sierra Leone's diamonds, and the way they have been used to fund conflict.[...] Why is it that the government of Sierra Leone derives almost no revenue from diamond sales? And why am I being told that the Liberian annual diamond exports are beyond its diamond mining capacity?'[9] On his return to London Hain reported the extent to which diamond mining by the RUF was central to the lack of progress in

[9] See the Sierra Leone Web (archives) at http://www.sierraleone.org/slnews0100.html.

the peace process, and called for a more active deployment of the UN force in the RUF's diamond mining areas:

I want to see the United Nations peacekeepers, in particular the Indian battalion which I saw camped at the main airport outside Freetown, deployed across the country where they ought to be, which is the eastern side of the country where the RUF rebel combatants have been, and are still in large numbers; where the diamonds are and where a lot of trouble has occurred.[10]

A few months later, when the UN force finally declared that it would deploy in the diamond-rich Kono district, the RUF became more aggressive, which led to the fateful kidnap of UN peacekeepers in May 2000 by RUF commanders. As a result of this brazen act, the British government quickly convinced the UN Security Council to appoint a Panel of Experts to investigate the RUF's diamond mining activities and the activities of its foreign supporters, which led to targeted sanctions against Liberia and a marked weakening of the RUF's funding and support bases.

The political economy of civil wars in Africa has recently received considerable academic and policy-related interest. Perhaps the most comprehensive treatment of the issue can be found in *Greed and Grievance: Economic Agendas in Civil Wars*, a collection of essays by well-known academics in the field.[11] The book explores how 'economic considerations often shape the calculations and behavior of the parties to a conflict, giving rise to a particular war economy and a distinctive dynamic of conflict.' Perhaps the most succinct statement of the book's major arguments is made by David Keen in a paper that was published elsewhere but whose argument he restates even more vigorously in this book:

Conflict can create war economies, often in regions controlled by rebels or warlords and linked to international trading networks; members of armed gangs can benefit from looting; and regimes can use violence to deflect opposition, reward supporters or maintain their access to resources. Under these circumstances, ending civil wars becomes difficult. Winning may not be desirable: the point of war may be precisely the legitimacy which it confers on actions that in peacetime would be punishable as crimes.[12]

[10] Ibid.

[11] Mats Berdal and David M. Malone (eds), *Greed and Grievance: Economic Agendas in Civil Wars*, Boulder, CO: Lynne Rienner, 2000.

[12] David Keen, 'The Economic Functions of Civil Wars', Adelphi Paper 320, Oxford University Press for the International Institute for Strategic Studies, 1998.

Keen's elegant and seductive argument can be summed up thus: for 'rebel' groups like the RUF and Angola's UNITA, warfare for pillage became an end in itself, a *raison d'être*. But it is in the activities of Charles Taylor, perhaps Africa's most successful and ruthless warlord-politician, that one can find the true apotheosis of criminal warlordism. After seven years of destructive warfare Taylor finally agreed to a UN- and ECOWAS-supervised disarmament and then an electoral process in 1997. He then used his stolen wealth to bribe voters, and his rebel-thugs (a large number of whom were not disarmed, such was the shabby way in which the process was conducted) to intimidate those he could not bribe. The elections were a largely farcical affair and the results were never really in doubt. Many voters, fearful that Taylor would resume the war if he lost, voted for him: one of the election slogans in favour of Taylor was: 'He killed my ma, he killed my pa, but I'll vote for him.' Taylor organised bus trips to refugee camps in Guinea, from where traumatised Liberian refugees and some Sierra Leonean ones, bribed with food and the promise that the war would finally be ended if Taylor were elected, were bussed to Liberia to vote.

Taylor's chief challenger, the sophisticated Ellen Johnson-Sirleaf (who had supported Taylor in the early stages of the war[13]), was simply out of her depth. Her supporters were intimidated and she herself faced death threats. Taylor emerged the overwhelming winner. But even after being in office as President for five years, he continued to function in a foraging mode, operating the quintessential warlord economy and either actively refusing to rebuild formal state institutions that were destroyed during the war that he himself had started, or destroying those still that existed. In the words of a Human Rights Watch report of 2002,

After five years in office, President Charles Taylor's government continues to function without accountability, exacerbating the divisions and resentments fueled by the war. Taylor has steadily consolidated and centralized power by rewarding loyalists and intimidating critics. State power is regularly misused by high-ranking officials to further the political objectives of the executive branch, to avoid accountability, and for personal enrichment. State institutions that could provide an independent check on the Taylor administration…remain weak and cowed.[14]

It might be argued that there are quite a number of African governments that did not begin as rebel insurgencies but which can

---

[13] Author's interview with Mrs Johnson-Sirleaf, Abidjan, December 2002.
[14] Human Rights Watch, *Back to the Brink: War Crimes by Liberian Government and Rebels*, vol. 14, no. 4 (A), May 2002, New York.

behave with similar ghastliness, but it is hard to imagine any other government, even in crisis-ridden Africa, that actively foments warfare, including mass killings and orchestrated invasions of neighbouring states, as Taylor undoubtedly did. It has now been established, by UN investigators as well as independent observers, that fighting around Monrovia in February 2002, ostensibly spearheaded by Liberians United for Reconciliation and Democracy (LURD), was actually the work of Taylor's own forces, the President personally directing it in order to declare a state of emergency and frighten opposition politicians away from the country ahead of planned elections in 2003.[15] Taylor's earlier adventures, in Sierra Leone and Guinea, have been well documented, and were directed principally towards pillage rather than political ends.[16]

This kind of predatory and criminal warlordism, involving as it does a political leadership that operates at the head of a government enjoying some kind of international recognition, is often overlooked in discussions on the political economy of conflict. Even Paul Collier's sweeping World Bank report *The Economic Causes of Civil Wars* focused almost entirely on the link between 'natural resource predation' and internal 'rebellions'. Collier argues forcefully that civil wars are caused or perpetuated by the abundance of primary and 'lootable' commodities in poor and weak states around the world, and adds:

Rebellions either have the objective of natural resource predation, or are critically dependent upon natural resource predation in order to pursue other objectives. These, rather than objective grievances, are the risk factors which conflict prevention must reduce if it is to be successful.[17]

The problem is that, as we have seen in the case of Sierra Leone's war, some of these conflicts are hardly 'rebellions' or 'civil', and the

---

[15] Interviews with Amos Sawyer, former Liberian President, and with Conmany Wesseh, a Liberian exiled activist, Abidjan, February 2002; also with Corrine Dufka, researcher for Human Rights Watch, Freetown, March 2002.

[16] See, for example, *Report of the Panel of Experts appointed pursuant to Security Council Resolution 1306 (2000), Paragraph 19, in Relation to Sierra Leone*, December 2000; and Lansana Gberie, *Destabilizing Guinea: Diamonds, Charles Taylor and the Potential for Wider Humanitarian Catastrophe*, Ottawa: Partnership Africa Canada, 2001.

[17] Paul Collier, 'Economic Causes of Civil Conflict and their Implications for Policy', The World Bank, 15 June 2000, available at http://www.world-bank.org/research/conflict/papers/civilconflict.htm

regional dimensions, in the form of cross-border instigation and support, are their most crucial trajectories.

The dynamics of war and peace in Sierra Leone from 1999 to 2002 showed the extent to which the RUF's—and Taylor's—preoccupation with looting Sierra Leone's diamonds overrode every other consideration, including that of ultimate survival. Although the PAC report made the connection between the RUF's access to the diamond mines and its fundamental lack of interest in peace, this was only slowly grasped by outsiders and the Unamsil peacekeeping force. When elements of this 17,000-man force—the largest UN force in existence—began what looked like a probe into the RUF diamond areas, they were stopped in their tracks; 500 were abducted and humiliated, provoking a major crisis, as described earlier. The crisis abated only after robust military intervention by British troops.[18] The United Nations subsequently imposed targeted sanctions on Liberia: a ban on Liberian diamond sales and on travel by Liberian officials, including the President, and tougher weapons sanctions.

However, for over a year afterwards the United Nations almost pedantically avoided interfering directly with the RUF's diamond mining operations. A large Pakistani force was finally deployed in Kono District in June 2001, but the RUF still continued large-scale mining operations throughout that year.[19] Many of the miners were clearly RUF captives operating in conditions that can only be described as indentureship.[20] RUF export operations took a variety of forms. Some diamonds continued to leave through Liberia. Some reports alleged that Unamsil personnel had become involved in RUF diamond trading, naming Lebanese traders and RUF officials with whom they were dealing.[21] The *Washington Post* reported in November 2001 that operatives from the international Islamic terror group Al Qaeda visited RUF-held diamond mining areas several times and arranged diamond buying deals worth millions of dollars; this is discussed in greater detail below.[22] A UN Expert

[18] See Brian Urquhart, 'Some Thoughts on Sierra Leone', *New York Review of Books*, 15 June 2000.
[19] Author's observation, September 2001.
[20] See 'RUF, Unamsil, Lebanese in Diamond Deal', *Standard Times*, 24 March 2001.
[21] Douglas Farah, 'They fought for nothing, and that's what they got', *Washington Post*, 1 September 2001.
[22] Douglas Farah, 'Al Qaeda cash tied to diamond trade: sale of gems from Sierra Leone rebels raised millions, sources say', *Washington Post*, 2 November 2001.

Panel reported that the then 'interim' leader of the RUF, Issa Sesay, flew to Abidjan late in 2001 with 8,000 carats of diamonds which he sold to two dealers of undisclosed identity. Apparently these dealers were 'using a Lebanese businessman' who ran errands for them between Abidjan and Monrovia.[23]

It was clear that diamonds had become indispensable for the RUF: the gems are of an alluvial and widespread nature in Sierra Leone, and trade in them was highly unregulated internationally. Lacking political support and a motivating ideology, the RUF was able to enhance its power and political significance by criminally expropriating valuable resources with which to acquire weapons and hire mercenaries. The UN Panel of Experts, appointed after the abduction of UN peacekeepers by the RUF in 2000, to investigate 'the link between trade in diamonds and trade in arms and related matériel' that helped sustain the RUF war effort, found conclusively that diamonds constituted 'a major and primary source of income for the RUF' in 'sustaining and advancing its military ambitions.' The Panel found that the 'bulk of the RUF diamonds leave Sierra Leone through Liberia' whose President Charles Taylor sold them to dubious contacts, pocketed most of the proceeds, and arranged weapons and other deals (including drug purchases) for the RUF. The United Nations estimated the RUF's diamond exports as being 'from as little as $25 million per annum to as much as $125 million per annum.'[24]

The report was a solid amplification of the PAC's findings. Soon afterwards targeted sanctions were imposed on Liberia and the RUF, and similar sanctions were imposed on Sierra Leone's diamonds until a UN-monitored certification system was introduced in September 2000. The Kimberley Process, a forum that aimed to devise an international system of oversight, began to meet on the initiative of South Africa, home to the world's largest diamond company, De Beers.[25]

If there were any doubts about the toxicity of the 'conflict' diamonds nexus when the Kimberley Process started, they were dispelled by the *Washington Post* article of 2 November 2001 (see note 22).

---

[23] *Report of the Panel of Experts appointed pursuant to Security Council Resolution 1395 (2002), paragraph 4, in relation to Liberia*, p. 25.

[24] Ibid.

[25] A final agreement to regulate the rough diamond trade was signed at Interlaken, Switzerland, in November 2002, and the UN Security Council adopted the agreement in January 2003.

The article, which received widespread attention, deserves to be quoted at some length. Written by longtime war correspondent Douglas Farah, it stated that the Al Qaeda network 'reaped millions of dollars in the past three years from the illicit sale of diamonds mined by [RUF] rebels in Sierra Leone,' and that one of the RUF's senior officials acted as 'a conduit between senior RUF commanders and the buyers from both Al Qaeda and Hezbollah, a Shi'ite Muslim organisation linked to Lebanese activists who have kidnapped numerous Americans, hijacked aeroplanes and carried out bomb attacks on US installations in Beirut.' The West African Shi'ite Lebanese community has strong sympathies with Hezbollah, which is 'active in all these countries and...deeply involved in many businesses across the [West African] region.' Three senior Al Qaeda officials paid visits, arranged from within the RUF command, to RUF-held areas of Sierra Leone at different times in 1998 and later. There they received diamonds in exchange for cash.

The RUF official alluded to above was said to be connected to Al Qaeda through two Lebanese diamond dealers with longstanding family and business ties in both Sierra Leone and Liberia. Interestingly, five months before the *Washington Post* article appeared, and three months before the terrorist attacks on New York and Washington, the names of these two dealers were quietly placed on a travel ban announced by the UN Security Council. The ban also affected senior Liberian government officials and 'other individuals providing financial and military support' to armed rebel groups in countries neighbouring Liberia, in particular the RUF of Sierra Leone.[26]

After the junta was unseated by Nigerian troops in February 1998, Sam Bockarie took over effective command of the scattered RUF and AFRC forces as they regrouped in the diamond areas of eastern Sierra Leone. The embattled RUF was desperate for cash and other support, and trading with the Lebanese resumed. The replenished RUF attacked and took over Kono district in December 1998.

An important aspect of the Al Qaeda-RUF 'conflict' diamonds business was the role of West Africa's Lebanese diaspora community. In Sierra Leone the Lebanese overwhelmingly dominate the diamond industry and much of the service and retail sectors. For well over a century in West Africa the Lebanese have failed (or rather refused) to integrate into their host societies, concentrating almost wholly on trading. A large number of the more successful have continued to maintain close ties to the politics of the Middle

[26] UN Security Council, Press Release SC/7068, 4 June 2001.

East, a reality that only compounds their image in much of West Africa as exploitative and corrupt. Lacking serious local political ties, the Lebanese in West Africa have over the decades since independence shown no scruples about working with unsavoury political and other groups as long as money could be made. It was therefore not surprising that a number of key Lebanese figures in the region were implicated in the 'conflict' diamond trade with the RUF.

UN report S/2000/1195 in 2000 found that in 1997 Sam Bockarie had appointed a Lebanese, Mohamed Hedjazi, as an agent to negotiate with any companies for prospecting licenses or anything else to do with the mining and buying of diamonds. This was just after the AFRC coup, and Hedjazi, who was in Freetown at the time, became the official face of the AFRC's diamond business. However, the same report added, concerning Lebanese connections in Taylor's sanctions-busting and diamond dealings with the RUF:

A key individual is a wealthy Lebanese businessman named Talal El-Ndine. El-Ndine is the [Liberian] inner circle's paymaster. Liberians fighting in Sierra Leone alongside the RUF, and those bringing diamonds out of Sierra Leone are paid by him personally. Arms shippers and brokers negotiate their payments in his office in Old Road, Monrovia. El-Ndine also brings foreign businessmen and investors to Liberia, individuals who are willing to cooperate with the regime in legitimate business activities as well as in weapons and illicit diamonds.[27]

After the 1997 coup in Sierra Leone, which resulted in the killing of several Lebanese in Freetown, a large number joined their compatriots who had already fled to neighbouring countries—Guinea, The Gambia, Liberia and Côte d'Ivoire. At the time of the coup there were over 30,000 Lebanese living in Sierra Leone, almost all of them traders and many engaged in the diamond trade or businesses linked to it. After the coup was reversed in 1998, some returned. However, many remained in their new-found homes, but maintained their business contacts with Sierra Leone. Significantly, during these years diamond exports from The Gambia skyrocketed; with no known diamond deposits, it was recorded as the origin of $420 million worth of diamonds imported into Belgium between 1996 and 1999. Some of the Belgian importing companies were directly connected to firms operated by the same Lebanese families in Sierra Leone. The same was true in Côte d'Ivoire, suddenly a major exporter despite the dysfunctionality of its own small diamond industry.

[27] UN Security Council, Report S/2000/1195, 20 December 2000, p. 37.

When the two major diamond mining areas, Kono and Tongo Field, fell to the RUF, Lebanese diamond traders in these areas simply moved to Kenema, Bo and Freetown, and many were able to continue buying diamonds as usual, even though official exports had dwindled to almost nothing. A *New York Times* reporter suggested in January 2001 that RUF diamonds were probably being sold to at least forty Lebanese-run shops in Kenema.[28]

A mining ban was finally enforced in December 2001, a step that accelerated the disarmament process, completed a month later in January 2002. National presidential and parliamentary elections followed in May 2002. Foday Sankoh was in gaol, charged with the murder of unarmed demonstrators outside his house in May 2000, and therefore prevented from participating in the polls. The RUF made timid protests over this to the United Nations and the Sierra Leone authorities, but finally settled on a compromise candidate, Alimamy Pallo Bangura, a former university lecturer and diplomat. Bangura first shot to prominence in 1994 after the NPRC appointed him Sierra Leone's ambassador to the United Nations. In 1996 he was recalled by President Kabbah because of doubts over his loyalty and competence. After the AFRC coup he was appointed by the junta as Foreign Minister, but he was arrested, detained and charged with treason after the coup was reversed in 1998. He was convicted and condemned to hang, but released in the general amnesty after the Lome Accord. After that he emerged as one of the spokespersons of the new political arm of the RUF, the Revolutionary United Front Party (RUFP).

In the national elections in May 2002 hundreds of thousands of Sierra Leoneans, some with hands hacked off (the handiwork of the rebels), turned out to vote. It was a memorable moment. Lacking fingers, crudely amputated voters used the stumps of their hands to cast their votes. No one had any doubt that the RUF would lose, but the extent of their loss was nonetheless striking. The RUFP received less than 2 per cent of the vote; its presidential candidate actually received fewer votes than the number of RUF combatants who had handed in weapons—probably a reflection of the fact that a large number of the ex-combatants were still below the minimum voting age of 18. But cracks within the RUF had become evident shortly after the enforcement of the mining ban, with mutual recriminations between some RUF commanders. The journey of Gibril

[28] Noritmisu Onisha, 'Africa diamond hub defies smuggling rules', *New York Times*, 2 January 2001.

Massaquoi to become a senior official in the RUF mirrors many of those who later became important figures within the rebel group. He was a teacher at St Paul's Secondary School in Pujehun when the rebels attacked and occupied the town in 1991. He was abducted along with dozens of students from the school and forcibly enrolled in the movement. Because of his education, however limited, he quickly rose to prominence among the largely illiterate rebels and became one of their spokesmen.

Sierra Leone, it appeared, had been saved from the fate that befell Liberia: sustained terror and paralysis. A murderous rebel group had been overwhelmingly rejected at the polls and was in a state of virtual disintegration. No one could describe the rebels' fate better than Gibril Massaquoi himself. 'We fought 10 years for nothing,' he told a Western reporter. 'After 10 years of destruction, we had no message for the people.'[29] Massaquoi, it turned out, had already taken steps to defect and join the ruling Sierra Leone Peoples Party (SLPP). When this writer visited the RUFP offices in Freetown in November 2002, the place was almost derelict and the only senior party member on duty was Eldred Collins, who described himself as Publicity Secretary.

'We will wait patiently for the next elections,' Collins told this writer. 'We are exhausted, our people are exhausted, but the struggle is not over. Come next elections we will make a better impression. The politicians will foul up.' However, there was anxiety in his voice. He was worried that the Special Court would be 'biased against' ex-RUF members. 'They say all we did was commit atrocities, that we are responsible for all the mutilations and destruction,' he said. 'Yes, there were excesses on our part. I was not part of the military wing; I was only a political organiser. But I know that although our men committed many atrocities, other forces were also involved. The Sierra Leone Army was worse.'

I thought that, like Massaquoi's verdict, this was as good an epitaph for the RUF as could be given by anyone. But this sudden lapse into paralysis and self-doubt, resulting from its disastrous electoral defeat, still raised questions. Was the RUF's failure and almost complete self-annihilation the result of the crucial loss of its messianic leadership through the imprisonment of Foday Sankoh? Or was it due to its mercenary character, which made it so vulnerable once it was deprived of its crucial access to diamond resources and con-

---

[29] Douglas Farah, 'Once-mighty rebels are biggest losers, results spell demise for splintered RUF', *Washington Post*, 16 May 2002.

fronted by a powerful, countervailing force in the form of UN and British soldiers? But why, after the disarmament, did the RUF fail to function as the coherent and organised force it had been during ten years of bloody warfare?

I put this question to Pallo Bangura in September 2002. Bangura, an urbane middle-aged political scientist, was living quietly in a modest house with friends and extended family members on Campbell Street in Freetown. His wife, whose parents were closely connected to the ruling SLPP elite, had abandoned him because of his RUF links, and he was clearly a broken man. When I met him Bangura affected the tone of a disinterested analyst, speaking unctuously about the 'climate of vilification and hate' which he felt was 'negative to the reconciliation process'. He spoke of the RUF simply as 'a phenomenon'. He said that the key to the RUF's prolonged survival and ultimate failure was its leader Foday Sankoh. 'People always underestimated him, but it was clear to me, and I should think to everyone else who knew him, that Sankoh was a man of great charisma. The thing was that he understood the politics of patrimonialism far more than those in power at the moment. He grew up in it. President Kabbah is a bureaucrat, Western-trained and with a mentality steeped in the workings of the UN,' he said. 'He simply does not understand, as Sankoh did, that in impoverished African societies, where state-provided social services are almost non-existent, the leader ensures loyalty and support by giving out, by appearing to share what he possesses. This Sankoh understood very well. He showed great generosity with his personal wealth to visitors and supporters, and there were a lot of people who preferred his down-to-earth style to Kabbah's aloof and bureaucratic attitude.'[30]

I felt, in spite of myself, that Bangura was right—that Sankoh represented that curious (almost Freudian) phenomenon of the long-time political opponent who subconsciously imbibes all the vices of the dictator he detests and despises, the hatred becoming deeper as the opponent realises that he is no better than the dictator. Sankoh had been obsessed with, and hated, the corrupt Siaka Stevens and his APC for decades, but because of his limited education and experience Stevens' tactics were the only ones Sankoh was familiar with. Those tactics combined political violence with corruption; patrimonialism was the bedrock of Stevens' rule. Sankoh knew from experi-

---

[30] By early 2003 Bangura had volunteered to teach for free at a secondary school in Freetown. It was, he said, 'a sacrifice,' and gave the impression that it was temporary. He was looking for a job that would pay better.

ence that the tactics worked. Lacking the imagination and political maturity to articulate new ideas and doctrine, he simply settled on the belief that he was better equipped to engage in a more down-to-earth—and therefore more effective—form of patrimonialism, having attracted mainly underdogs to his movement, many of whom had known nothing but the APC's violent kleptocracy.

Cyril Foray, a history professor and Stevens' first Foreign Minister (he resigned from Stevens' government in the early 1970s on a matter of principle), put it this way—leaving out the uses of patrimonial politics and focusing on the effects of violent, predatory politics:

The idealization of violence by Mr Stevens and his political cohorts produced a belief among a whole generation of young Sierra Leoneans (some of them future RUF recruits) that violence pays, that it is or can be a way of life, and that it is the shortest and most effective route to achievement and success.[31]

With control over vast diamond wealth, Sankoh showed great generosity to the many supposed supporters who visited his palatial residence in Freetown in 2000 after he was made Chairman of the Strategic Minerals Commission, giving out thousands of dollars to visitors and hundreds of bags of rice to displaced people—displaced and reduced to penury by his war. In doing so he clearly cut a figure of a penitent who cared, in contrast to the effete and crass political elite in Freetown. While one can only guess what might have happened had Sankoh campaigned as the RUFP presidential candidate, there is little doubt that he would have done far better than Bangura. There can also be little doubt that with him at the helm the RUFP, whose young members still called him adoringly '*papay*' (our father), would have stuck with him to the last. Defection would certainly have been minimal.

The lesson this holds for Sierra Leone and similar African states is that there is no alternative to the building of strong bureaucratic states that function at the social level, effectively providing services like education and thereby employment, and avoiding the kind of corrosive corruption and misuse of public funds that are such a mark of the continent's misgovernment. It is a hard lesson and the tragedy is that Sierra Leone's political elites, in the form of the SLPP in power after the end of the war, appeared, like the Bourbons, to have learned nothing and forgotten nothing.

---

[31] *Newsway*, vol. 4, 1998, p. 12. Based on an interview with the author in London, 1998.

9

EPILOGUE

THE RECKONING

'What is important is not that...political gangsters should be made to suffer, but that they should be made to discredit themselves. Fortunately they do so in many cases, for to a surprising extent the warlords in shining armor, the apostles of the martial virtues, tend not to die fighting when the time comes. History is full of ignominious getaways by the great and famous. Napoleon surrendered to the English in order to get protection from the Prussians, the Empress Eugénie fled in a hansom cab with an American dentist, Ludendorff resorted to blue spectacles, one of the more unprintable Roman emperors tried to escape assassination by locking himself in a lavatory, and during the early days of the Spanish Civil War one leading Fascist made his escape from Barcelona, with exquisite fitness, through a sewer.'
(George Orwell 'Who are the War Criminals?'[1])

'Another gathering, another conversation, with another man. Mellowed by a goblet of Rémy Martin, I ventured an opinion about the sacrificial predilection of being; the necessity of oblation of men by men to men. "War is the excuse," I said. I was playing with words, true, but, oddly, the exchange petered into mumbles of "Never Again."'
(Adhiambo Owuor, 'The Weight of Whispers'[2])

The headquarters of the Revolutionary United Front Party (RUFP), tucked creepily amidst rows of retail shops on a busy Freetown

---

[1] George Orwell, 'Who are the War Criminals?' in George Orwell, *Collected Essays, Journalism and Letters of George Orwell*, vol. 2: *My Country Right and Left 1940–1943*, edited by Sonia Orwell and Ian Angus, Harmondsworth: Penguin, 1978, pp. 368–9.

[2] Adhiambo Owuor, 'The Weight of Whispers', *Kwani?* (Nairobi, 2003). This is a beautiful short story depicting the travails of a refugee family fleeing the Rwandan genocide. It won the prestigious Caine Prize for African Writing 2003. *Kwani?* is a Kenyan literary magazine.

street, is painted bright yellow and, above the cavernous entrance, sports a carefully painted portrait of a crouching lion. The rhetoric is not an idle one. The lion is a kind of totemic figure for the once dreaded members of the RUF, and it is the symbol of their leader Foday Saybanah Sankoh, whose petty army spearheaded the destructive decade-long armed conflict. The ugly building housing the offices stands almost opposite the once-elegant City Hall of Freetown, which was vandalised and torched by the rebels in January 1999. People walk past the two structures and hardly notice; shopkeepers and vendors sell their wares nearby as they have always done. It is as though the decade of terror and destruction was just one long nightmare from which people have now woken and which they prefer not to think about any more.

President Tejan Kabbah is not a man known for histrionics, but in a speech celebrating the hard-won peace he gave vent to the complacent feeling of amnesia or simple exhaustion in which the country has seemed so enmeshed since the disarmament of 70,000 fighters and the conduct of the widely praised polls. 'Who can forget the flames of peace that rose above the piles of weapons at Lungi on January, 2002?' he said. 'Who can forget the jubilation, the excitement, as well as the tears of joy that streamed down the faces of many of our compatriots as they witnessed or heard about the symbolic declaration of the end of nearly 11 years of an agonising rebel war? And who can forget the words "*Di whar don dohn*"? Yes, the conflict is over, at last! And a new dawn of re-awakening and hope, and of opportunity.'[3] It was time, the President said, to move on. It was time, it seemed, for business as usual.

A 'new dawn of re-awakening and hope, and of opportunity': the optimism is chastening. Business as usual, however, is hardly an option in the severely traumatised and battered nation. The signs of destruction could be seen almost everywhere in its picturesque but badly scarred capital, with its stunningly beautiful beaches and lovely hills that appear from afar to cast a protective shield over the small brick and wooden buildings sprawling nonchalantly beside the Atlantic Ocean: burnt down little houses, hastily built camps with blue plastic covers, and in the west end suburb of Aberdeen, about a mile from the popular Lumley Beach, a sprawling camp of tin and wood huts housing two hundred and thirty crudely amputated men, women, children and their families—the RUF's signa-

[3] Kabbah's speech can be found at: http://www.sierra-leone.org/kabbah.html

ture contribution to modern warfare. Estimates of the number of people amputated throughout the war vary, but as many as two to three thousand may have been victims, more than half of them dying of their wounds. It was the gruesome pictures of these amputees, many children and women, on the world's TV screens and newspaper front pages that helped to finally focus international attention on the atrocious war in Sierra Leone in 1999 and 2000.[4]

So the tactic that made the RUF so notorious and feared was what also led to its ultimate undoing. Michel Foucault, in his penetrating study of the history of torture and punishment, writes of the double-edged effects of the 'theatrical representation of pain'—or 'punishment-as-spectacle'—as serving both to frighten onlookers into a state of dumb submission and to spread 'a confused horror... (that enveloped) both executioner and condemned; and, although it was always ready to invert the shame inflicted on the victim into pity or glory, it often turned...violence of the executioner into shame.' It was the reason such a system was ultimately rejected.[5]

I visited the amputees' camp early one morning in November 2002. The residents had an association, the War-affected Amputee Association. Sahr Momodu Tarawalie was its Secretary General. A former school teacher whose left leg was blown away by the rebels in an ambush in the Kono district on 17 April 1998 (like many other victims of the war, he remembers the exact moment when he encountered his mutilators), Tarawalie spoke in anger about the anguish of suddenly finding himself disabled and lacking support. 'There are things that are very difficult to talk about,' he said. 'It is a life of constant terror and frustration...But there is this talk of reconciliation, this talk of forgiveness. I am all for reconciliation but how I can forget this,' he said, pointing at the stump under his trousers. 'I will live with this for the rest of my life.'

What people like Tarawalie so desperately yearn for, over and above the practical needs of living in an impoverished and harsh environment, is sustained peace and stability. But even these are threatened by events inside and around Sierra Leone, the wider regional dynamics of destabilisation from which Sierra Leone's own war derived. Reports in April and May 2002 indicated that hundreds of ex-RUF and ex-CDF combatants were hired by the falling

[4] See Steve Coll, 'The Other War', *Washington Post*, 9 January 2000.
[5] Michel Foucault, *Discipline and Punish: The Birth of the Prison*, New York: Vintage Books, 1979, p. 9.

regime of Charles Taylor and by his rebel opponents, Liberians United for Reconciliation and Democracy (LURD), to fight in Liberia's intensifying civil war. This was probably merely a case of mercenarism, and there was little evidence of cohesion or coordination among the disparate forces in Liberia. But many ex-combatants in Sierra Leone remained unemployed and disillusioned by the failure of the government and the United Nations to be fully forthcoming in terms of their reintegration benefits, kept on hold by the failure of the donor community to make good on their pledges. It may not bode well for the future of Sierra Leone.

Since Taylor launched his war in Liberia in 1989, Sierra Leone's fortunes have been intimately tied to those of Liberia, as its decade-long war was a derivative of Liberia's. Cross-border attacks from Liberia into Sierra Leone continued into 2003, and the situation seemed more threatening to Sierra Leone and the entire region, with widespread violence breaking out in Côte d'Ivoire after a failed coup there in September 2002. Soon afterwards, three rebel factions emerged in that country, two of them, comprising mainly former RUF and Liberian soldiers, operating in the western parts of Ivory Coast.

In reaction to these brazen acts of over-reaching the Ivorian authorities decided to arm and provide other support to a new Liberian faction called MODEL, and Guinea too increased its support for LURD. By July 2003 these rebel forces were besieging Monrovia with a far greater determination and strength than was hitherto possible. Taylor was forced out of power and into exile in Nigeria in August 2003. The UN-mandated Special Court in Sierra Leone had already indicted Taylor, and it announced that the indictment was still extant even with Taylor out of power. Interpol declared Taylor a 'wanted' person.

As for former combatants of the RUF and their comrades in the so-called People's Army, life shortly after the official end of the war appeared to be far better than that which their victims in the Amputee Camp were living. About 2,230 of them, including ex-rebels and renegade soldiers who had gained personal notoriety for mass murder and amputations, were reintegrated into the 'new' Sierra Leone Army, which was put together by the British as part of the DFID-sponsored Security Sector reforms. Some of those who were not reintegrated received substantial assistance to start different projects in their home towns and villages, and others have drifted back to the diamond mining areas to mine illicitly and unsupervised. Issa Sesay, a former street-side peddler of junk items in Abidjan (where he was recruited into the RUF by Foday Sankoh), was in November 2002 in Freetown, driving around in an expensive four-wheel-drive vehicle, and in January 2003 even received a medal for peace from President Kabbah. However, a few months later he was indicted by the Special Court, and was arrested and detained pending his trial for war crimes and crimes against humanity.

Gibril Massaquoi received funding from a government agency to start an agricultural project in his home town Pujehun. However, by an interesting twist of fate he was shortly afterwards recruited as a star witness by the Special Court, and was in early 2004 secured in an undisclosed location by the court, pending his testimony against his former comrades in the RUF. Dozens of former senior RUF commanders, like Fayia Musa and Phillip Palmer, were in Côte d'Ivoire in December 2002, apparently lying low. Augustine Gbao, former Chief Security Officer of the RUF and the man who captured 500 UN peacekeepers (of the Zambian contingent) in Makeni in May 2000, received funding from the same government agency that supported Massaquoi, also to start an agricultural project in his home district, in his case Kenema.

Gbao, a bearded middle-aged man with beguiling looks, was an officer in the Sierra Leone police, which he quit in 1983 as a sub-inspector. He joined the RUF in 1991, no doubt recognising an opportunity to settle scores with senior officers he perceived as 'corrupt and tribalistic'. I met Gbao in September 2002, in Freetown, several months before he was arrested and indicted by the UN-backed court for crimes against humanity, and he proudly explained what the RUF war was all about. 'We were fighting for justice and responsible government,' he said, 'and although we did not win militarily, we feel successful because people in this country have become more aware of their rights and the responsibility of their government. I am very proud of this achievement.' He added, 'Our struggle was about awareness…We have to encourage the youth to feel a part of this country. If that's done, this country will be free.'

Awareness, freedom: high words echoing the elegant quote from Frantz Fanon that opens the RUF's *Footpaths to Democracy*: 'Every generation must, out of relative obscurity, discover its mission, betray or fulfil it.' There is similar parroting of phrases from hard-headed revolutionary thinkers of other generations and in different situations in the little booklet, the deep corruptions of mimicry:

We are fighting for a new Sierra Leone. A new Sierra Leone of freedom, justice and equal opportunity for all. We are fighting for democracy and by democracy we mean equal opportunity and access to power to create wealth through free, commerce, agriculture, industry, science and tech-nology. Wealth cannot be created without power. Power cannot be achieved without struggle. And by struggle, we mean the determination, the human-istic urge to remove the shame of poverty, hunger, disease, squalor, illiter-acy, loafing and hopelessness from this African land of Sierra Leone, blessed with minerals, forests, rivers, and all that is required to restore the dignity, prestige and power of the African as an equal competitor on the world stage.[6]

The booklet—which is neither chiliastic nor particularly inspira-tional—exhibits a hodgepodge of influences, ranging from ideas of Enlightenment Europe, of Romantic writers and their cranky rhet-oric about the 'Noble Savage' to Fanon, Mao and Castro. 'We moved deeper into the comforting bosom of our mother earth—the forest,' it says. 'The forest welcomed us and gave us succour and sustenance. The forest continues to be our main sources (*sic*) of survival and defence to date.' These statements appear to be less about the strategic value in purely military terms of the thick rain forest of eastern Sierra Leone, which provided a base for the RUF throughout its campaigns, than a fake-romantic view of nature: they are gestures to European liberal environmental activists. The booklet then fulminates about the supposed schism and resent-ment that governs the relationship between rural peasants and the corrupt capital city-based elite, again rhetoric aimed at Western lib-erals (the booklet never circulated in Sierra Leone and could hardly have been noticed by the poor rural peasants anyway, many of whom are illiterate): 'No more shall the rural countryside be reduced to hewers of wood and drawers of water for urban Free-town. That pattern of exploitation, degradation and denial is gone forever. No RUF/SL combatant or civilian will countenance the re-introduction of that pattern of raping the countryside to feed the greed and caprice of the Freetown elite and their masters abroad.'[7]

Footpaths to Democracy reads like an ambitious adaptation of the *Basic Document of the RUF/SL*—itself an adaptation of a pamphlet written by Panafu activists in the early 1980s—which circulated clandestinely in 1991, shortly before and after the war started. The document, like *Footpaths*, was a curious period piece, virtually no more then an angry tract bemoaning the corruption and excesses of the APC one-party state. These documents did not set out a coherent political programme, but tapped into the deep-seated

[6] RUF/SL, *Footpaths to Democracy* (published by the RUF), p. 7.
[7] Ibid., p. 5.

resentment among the country's impoverished masses towards the demented and bankrupt APC one-party state. The underlying theme seemed to be that with the APC overthrown, everything else would fall into place. Such a shallow, almost sub-literate 'agenda' can easily be misappropriated by mercenary elements, which was exactly what the RUF did.

Like many other insurgent groups on the badly exploited continent of Africa, the RUF used this hazy rhetoric to bamboozle some liberal Westerners with an interest in social justice and thereby mask their true motivations, which were demonstrably pillage and the delinquent wish to exercise tomcatting powers over rural peasants, and to rob and terrorise a whole nation. And it is no accident that the man who penned these words for them was not even a Sierra Leonean—he was a Ghanaian exile living in London. It all makes using the limp label 'rebel' so inappropriate to describe insurgent groups like the RUF.

In the 1960s the words 'liberation movements' and 'guerrillas', with their appropriate romantic evocations, were used to describe genuine freedom fighters like Amilcal Cabral who took up arms against repressive European colonial powers in Africa. The post-independence insurgents like Uganda's Yoweri Museveni, who wrested power from successive tyrants, were also appropriately described as 'second liberation' fighters. Since such labels clearly do not fit groups like the RUF, UNITA and the NPFL, the catch-all word 're-bel' was applied. When that word was used by Albert Camus, it was with the explicit qualification of describing a largely intellectual, often narcissistic, indulgence possible only in industrialised Western societies with a surfeit of freedoms and opportunities but also with a lot of doctrinal resentment. Camus explicitly rejected the promiscuous use of violence. His rebel is someone 'who says no, but whose refusal does not imply renunciation'. For Camus, whose experience of the brutal war of liberation in Algeria profoundly influenced his thinking,

Rebellion cannot exist without the feeling that, somewhere and somehow, one is right. It is in this way that the rebel...says yes and no simultaneously. He affirms that there are limits and also that he suspects—and wishes to preserve—the existence of certain things on this side of the borderline. He demonstrates, with obstinacy, that there is something in him which 'is worthwhile...' and which must be taken into consideration. In a certain way, he confronts an order of things which oppresses with the insistence on a kind of right not to be oppressed beyond the limit that he can tolerate.[8]

[8] Albert Camus, *The Rebel*, New York: Vintage Books, 1956, p. 13.

I have used the word 'rebel' myself—interchangeably with 'bandit', which I prefer—because it has gained such common usage that it would be a distraction to bicker on the point in the text. If the RUF war suggested anything positive, it was agitation; it never became— and was evidently never intended to become—a revolutionary struggle in the sense of, as Gérard Chaliand has put it, 'a new underground political infrastructure...constructed patiently by middle-ranking cadres.'[9] It was what Chaliand has called 'banditism': an inchoate group driven by simple resentment and the urge to pillage and destroy.

It was this group which issued this self-defining statement in its moment of ultimate triumph:

For the past six years or so, we have been living in an environment of hatred and divisiveness. We looked at our brothers and killed them in cold blood, we removed our sisters from their hiding places to undo their feminity (*sic*), we slaughtered our mothers and butchered our fathers. It was really a gruesome experience which has left a terrible landmark in our history.

But the atrocities that occurred must not be taken out in the context of a personal vendetta. They were the result of a rottenness of a system which could not be uprooted except by brutal means. We did not take to the bush because we wanted to be barbarians, not because we wanted to be inhuman, but we wanted to state our humanity to a society that looked at us as sub-humans. The APC had spread its tentacles so deep that had the RUF not emerged, we wonder if we would not have still been under the yoke of that wretched regime.

In the process of cleaning the system, however, we have wronged the great majority of our countrymen. We have sinned both in the sight of man and God.[10]

The statement was broadcast on the Sierra Leone Broadcasting Service (SLBS) radio by Eldred Collins, the RUF's spokesman, shortly after the RUF was invited to join the calamitous AFRC coup in May 1997. It was meant as a confession and as a way of asking the nation to forgive their wanton excesses. As subsequent events demonstrated, including the brutality of the AFRC, the destructive resurgence of rebel activities in 1998 and the catastrophic attack on Freetown in January 1999, that confession did not lead to contrition. The use of violence for the purpose of terror, control and criminal expropriation was indeed always the linchpin of the RUF's

[9] Gérard Chaliand, *Guerrilla Strategies: An Historical Anthology from the Long March to Afghanistan*, Berkeley: University of California Press, 1982, p. 15.
[10] *African Sierra Leone Progress* (a New York-based Sierra Leonean newsletter), July 1997.

strategy; it would take overwhelming force to keep the compulsion in check.

In a fascinating paper entitled 'Humiliation, Betrayal and Violence in Civil Wars,'[11] David Keen applies the work of Omer Bartov[12] to explain the violent pathology of the RUF in the context of a feeling of alienation and humiliation which the young, impoverished recruits had towards the wider, uncaring and repulsively corrupt society, which created the need to reconstruct a collective new identity that would make their environment more enabling and acceptable. Keen writes:

It is difficult to understand the civil war in Sierra Leone without looking carefully at the role of shame and humiliation. This has been connected to, among other things, the abuse of power by local chiefs, to deficiencies in the educational system, and to dysfunctional politics at the national level.[13]

This view—that an iniquitous and shabby state and its elite drove dispossessed and alienated people to violence and vandalism—is, as I have argued, a seductive but largely unhelpful one. A more significant factor can be deduced from an astute earlier observation by Keen: 'Significantly, the number of outright battles between properly armed troops in this war has been small, and largely restricted to the areas most rich in diamonds. The great majority of violent acts have been against civilians.'[14] How violence of such magnitude was perpetrated for so long and for purposes no higher than criminal appropriation and power is one of the disturbing questions thrown up by insurgencies like that of the RUF. But it is in fact an old question.

Licensed cruelty and pillage: it is about the quest for wealth and control in societies essentially in transition. Joseph Conrad, in his famous novel *Heart of Darkness* (first published in 1902), which is about the ghastly Belgian empire-building in the Congo, describes events which strikingly resembles the campaign of the RUF. The story's narrator, who is on his way inland to take control of a river steamer, suddenly finds himself at a rugged trading post on the

[11] David Keen, 'Humiliation, Betrayal and Violence in Civil Wars', paper presented at the Franco-British Seminar on Conflicts in Africa (Centre for Defence Studies, London, 4 July 2001). In author's possession.
[12] Omer Bartov, *Mirrors of Destruction: War, Genocide, and Modern Identity*, Oxford University Press, 2000.
[13] Keen (note 11).
[14] David Keen, 'A Rational Kind of Violence', *Oxford Development Studies*, vol. 25, no. 1, 1997.

Congo river where sixteen or twenty Belgians of the Eldorado Exploring Expedition are camped. All around them terrible things are happening—peoples hand's being hacked off, men brutalised to death, others simply wasting away in the general degradation—but the Belgians don't even notice. And the narrator says of them:

> The only real feeling [among them] was a desire to...earn percentages... Their talk was the talk of sordid buccaneers, reckless without hardihood, greedy without audacity, and cruel without courage; and there was not an atom of foresight or of serious intention in the whole batch of them, and they did not seem aware that these things are wanted for the work of the world. To tear treasure out of the bowels of the land was their desire, with no moral purpose at the back of it than there is in burglars breaking into a safe.[15]

The description would perfectly fit the RUF.

The twentieth century began and ended with great upheavals and the mass destruction of human lives, and behind most of the calamities was some form of ideology or nationalism, some form of pretence to a higher purpose. People killed convinced that they were doing the right thing, or that every act of arson or murder was an affirmation of their rectitude. It was a century when, as Camus noted, 'man, through lack of character,' took 'refuge in doctrine' and then 'crime reason(ed) about itself.' And as soon as crime reasons about itself, 'it multiplies like reason itself and assumes all the aspects of syllogism.'[16] But there were always exceptions: there have been those who killed thousands of people for the crass purposes of usurping power or looting state treasuries or simply in the perverse pleasure of causing destruction. Such forces cause states to atrophy, leading to more violence and terror. In his controversial book on Stalin, the British novelist Martin Amis[17] quotes the Soviet dissident writer Solzhenitsyn as saying: 'The imagination and spiritual strength of Shakespeare's evildoers stopped short at a dozen corpses. Because they had no ideology.' Amis adds sardonically, 'This is more-or-less true of Iago, Claudius and Edmund (to take only the major tragedies). But we are left staring at the fact that Macbeth did not stop short—that he was, indeed, a usurping dictator who ruled by terror...' In insurgent groups like the RUF, we saw an organisa-

---

[15] Joseph Conrad, *Heart of Darkness* and *The Secret Sharer,* New York: Bantam Books, March 1981, p. 50.

[16] Camus (note 8), p. 4.

[17] Martin Amis, *Koba the Dread: Laughter and the Twenty Million,* Toronto: Alfred A. Knopf, 2002.

tion without any legitimacy or pretence to ideology carrying out a sustained campaign of violence that would lead to the near-total destruction of a whole nation. All that was missing in this tragic drama were the three witches…

Post-conflict justice and reconciliation

A report issued in 2003 by the Conflict, Security and Development Group at the International Policy Institute of King's College London makes a point which captures quite trenchantly the general feeling of most observers about the need for post-conflict 'closure' in the form of 'transitional justice' mechanisms in Sierra Leone:

The conflict in Sierra Leone was a war of great brutality. Civilians, by the thousands, were targeted for terror campaigns. Children were press-ganged from their communities and made to commit acts of terrible violence against those they would traditionally venerate. Belligerents exhibited little respect for international humanitarian law or other standards applied to waging war. Perpetrators and victims were often members of the same community, and violations of the person and the dignity of victims were unspeakably vicious. In post-conflict Sierra Leone, these matters had to be addressed publicly in order for it to be seen that the war had come to a close. Without the designation of those responsible—at all levels—and a public acknowledgement of their roles, social structure would likely remain unsettled and public faith in the solidity of the peace would be undermined.[18]

The same point has been made in another way in a *Citizen's Handbook* issued to educate ordinary Sierra Leoneans about the workings of two instruments of 'transitional justice'—the Truth and Reconciliation Commission, TRC, and the UN-Sierra Leone Special Court—set up during the disarmament process:

Experience from other countries, like South Africa, indicates that it can be useful to have bodies like courts and truth commissions, which examine the past. If the past is forgotten and not confronted, it may be difficult to change things and prevent such crimes from happening again. We can move forward only if we address the conditions that caused the war. It also requires punishing those with the greatest responsibility, to show that people cannot mastermind terrible acts in our country and get away with it. We also need to understand the experiences of both victims and perpetrators,

[18] 'A Review of Peace Operations: A Case for Change', a report by The Conflict, Security and Development Group, International Policy Institute, King's College, London, 2003.

and help communities to heal. We must deal with the past so that we can enjoy the future.[19]

The Lome Accord, to compensate for its despicable amnesty article, made provision for the setting up of the TRC. Article XXVI of the Accord states:

A Truth and Reconciliation Commission shall be established to address impunity, break the cycle of violence, provide a forum for both parties and perpetrators of human rights violations, to tell their story, get a clear picture of the past in order to facilitate genuine healing and reconciliation.

Following the signing of the Accord, the UN High Commission for Human Rights worked intensely with the Sierra Leone government to prepare for the setting up of the TRC, and on 10 February 2000 the Sierra Leone Parliament passed an Act legally setting up the Commission. The Act made provisions to compel persons to appear before the Commission where Commissioners were convinced that this would be necessary to get important statements from them. The Act clearly describes the purpose of the TRC as an instrument designed to create 'an impartial body of historical record' of the war and to 'help restore the human dignity of victims and promote reconciliation.' The TRC was required to conduct a year-long nation-wide process of collecting testimonies and research, and to foster 'inter-change(s) between victims and perpetrators'. At the end of the year, the Commission was to present a report to the Sierra Leone government, which would then share the findings with the UN Security Council.

A budget for the exercise was initially set at $10 million, but this was reduced to $6.5 million after potential donors complained that the earlier figure was too high. The cash-strapped Sierra Leone government was to contribute only a small fraction of this. All seemed set for work to start, with Commissioners already earmarked, when suddenly the RUF abducted UN peacekeepers in May, forcing the government and the donor community to suspend the process indefinitely.

The May 2000 events forced the government and the architects of the Lome Accord to rethink the amnesty provisions. On 6 June 2000 President Kabbah wrote to the UN Secretary General requesting the organisation's assistance in setting up a 'Special Court' which

[19] Paul James Allen, Sheku B. S. Lahai and Jamie O'Connell, *Sierra Leone's Truth and Reconciliation Commission and Special Court: a Citizen's Handbook* (Freetown, 2003), p. 48.

would specifically 'try Foday Sankoh and other senior members of
the RUF' for 'crimes against the people of Sierra Leone and for the
taking of United Nations peacekeepers as hostages.'[20] The Sierra
Leone Attorney-General and Minister of Justice, Solomon Berewa,
explained this about-face on the Lome agreement with a characteristic lack of irony:

1. After the atrocities of 6th January 1999, what every Sierra Leonean
wanted most was peace and reconciliation. If, as we had hoped, we had
achieved sustainable peace as a result of the Lome Agreement, Sierra Leoneans would have grudgingly settled for this and gone about mending
their shattered lives.
2. We needed a Peace Agreement with the RUF, which alone would have
enabled the international community to come here as they have now done
and to do things they are now doing.
3. We needed to have an agreement with the RUF on having permanent
cessation of hostilities. The need for a Peace Agreement at the time became obvious from the panicky reaction of Sierra Leoneans to a threat
issued in Lome by Cpl Foday Sankoh that he would call off the talks. I had
to make a radio broadcast from Lome to assure the Sierra Leone public
that there was every probability that the Peace Agreement would be concluded...
4. Most importantly, the RUF would have refused to sign the Agreement if
the Government of Sierra Leone had insisted on including in it a provision
for judicial action against the RUF and had excluded the amnesty provision from the Agreement.[21]

In response to President's Kabbah letter of request, the UN Security Council adopted the proposal as its own, and Secretary General
Annan promptly sent a planning mission to Sierra Leone to pursue
the matter. On 4 October 2000, on the basis of the findings of the
mission, Annan presented a report to the UN Secretariat contain-
ing proposals for action necessary to set up the Court.[22] A team of
UN experts was sent to Freetown by Annan in January 2002 to final-
ise details with the Sierra Leone government on the establishment

[20] UN, *Fifth Report of the Secretary General on the United Nations Mission in Sierra
Leone*, UN document S/2000/751, 31 July 2000, para. 9.
[21] Solomon Berewa, 'Addressing Impunity Using Divergent Approaches:
The Truth and Reconciliation Commission and the Special Court', *Truth
and Reconciliation in Sierra Leone* (Freetown: Unamsil, December 2001),
pp. 55–6.
[22] UN Security Council Resolution 1315, 14 August 2000; and *Report of the
Secretary-General on the United Nations Mission in Sierra Leone*, UN Document S/2000/915, 4 October 2000.

of the Special Court, and on the 16th of that month, the Statute for the Special Court for Sierra Leone and the Agreement between the United Nations and the Sierra Leone government on the Establishment of the Court were issued.[23]

Meanwhile work on the setting up of the TRC had resumed with a series of workshops, seminars and meetings involving civil society activists and human rights monitors emphasising its relevance for the longer-term stability of the country, and on 5 July 2002 the TRC was finally inaugurated in Freetown. That same month the Special Court also officially began work with the arrival in Freetown of a Prosecutor, David Crane (a former US army lawyer), and a Registrar, Robin Vincent (a former judicial official in Manchester, England).

The TRC, headed by an uncharismatic and little known Sierra Leonean Methodist Bishop, Joseph Humper, and with a limited budget (by the end of its first year of work, only $3.5 million of the $6.5 million pledged by donors had arrived), had a bumpy ride at the start. There were administrative problems, including allegations of improper hiring procedures for national staff and trouble raising funds, but by December 2002 there was evidence of more vigorous activities including serious tours of the country on a 'sensitisation' mission.[24] A more energetic and determined approach appeared to have been taken by the Special Court.

The Court, mandated to arrest and prosecute 'persons who bear the greatest responsibility for the commission of serious violations of international law and crimes committed under Sierra Leonean law,' including those 'leaders who, in committing such crimes, have threatened the establishment of and implementation of the peace process in Sierra Leone,' focused on crimes committed since 1996, which marked the signing of the Abidjan Accord. The limited timeframe was criticised in some circles, but it may not be as inhibiting and arbitrary as it appears. Many of the people who directed atrocities before 1996 continued to direct them into 2000; and in spite of brief spells in gaol it can be shown that Foday Sankoh, for example, was very much in control of the RUF throughout much of the conflict (he was under some kind of house arrest in Nigeria in May 1997, for example, when he broadcast a radio message—via telephone—calling on the RUF fighters to join mutinous soldiers in Freetown in Major Koroma's coup, an order they instantly obeyed).

[23] Both the Statute and the Agreement can be found at: http://www.sierra-leone.org/specialcourt/html.
[24] The International Crisis Group (ICG), *The TRC: A Fresh Start*, Freetown/Brussels, December 2002.

The Special Court is concerned less about the foot soldiers than about those in leadership or command positions, people who were in a position to have 'planned, instigated, ordered, committed or otherwise aided and abetted in the planning, preparation or execution of' war crimes. This may seem like a simple task. Sierra Leone is a small country and many people know, or think they know, who exactly were in command positions among the various rampaging militias that wreaked such havoc on defenceless civilians. The Special Court's mandate to focus on 'crimes against humanity', which are defined as crimes that constitute a pattern of 'widespread and systematic attack against any civilian population'—including such egregious offences as murder, enslavement, extermination of whole populations, sexual slavery, child recruitment for combat purposes, forced deportations or displacements, torture, rape and enforced prostitution—is part of the global effort to combat impunity even in once forgotten and irrelevant corners of the world. The beauty of Sierra Leone's Special Court is that it will be making use of both local and international resources in this effort, and it will be held, in time honoured tradition, at the actual scene of the crime.

The Court is run by a management committee comprising countries which contributed to it, and it will not be bound by UN or Sierra Leonean rules of employment. Both the Chief Prosecutor, an energetic former Pentagon judge advocate, and the President of the Court, Geoffrey Robertson, an English barrister, spoke of their determination to carry out their mandate in a determined and independent manner, and to 'follow the evidence wherever it leads'. Robertson, author of the critically-acclaimed and bestselling *Crimes Against Humanity*,[25] has been a leading advocate of the need for an international criminal court.

Among the judges are two Sierra Leoneans, and the rest are from other African states, Europe and North America. By September 2002 construction work on the Court's permanent building had started at the site once housing Freetown's juvenile prison at New England in Freetown. The building was completed and opened in March 2004. There is more than a little irony in this choice of site: the recently-ended conflict, which if you take away the element of resource predation and theft was more a case of organised mass delinquency than anything else, had, as we have seen, a special focus on children—as perpetrators and victims. The violence, while

---

[25] Geoffrey Robertson, *Crimes Against Humanity: The Struggle for Global Justice*, New York: New Press, 1999.

systematic, had an ecstatic millenarian quality—madness with a method.

The Court had a budget of $58 million (since increased to more than $80 million) and a mandate to run for three years. In an interview this writer had with David Crane during one of his 'sensitisation tours' of the country in November 2002 at Pujehun—a ravaged town in the south of Sierra Leone which was among the RUF's earliest targets—Crane said: 'The point needs to be made that the age of impunity is over. I take this job seriously and I want my constituency, which is the people of this country, to take it just as seriously. I am a family man and when I hear stories of atrocities and see evidence of such gratuitous attacks against children it only reinforces my determination to bring those responsible to justice.' But critics, who noticed the dominance of Americans on the Prosecutor's staff and other key positions in the Court, complained that the Court was driven by a US agenda to undercut arguments for the International Criminal Court, which the United States has so far opposed on the grounds that the institution will be used for politically-motivated trials of US peacekeeping soldiers or servicemen who have seen action in foreign countries.[26] Significantly enough, the Statute for the Special Court explicitly rules out prosecution of foreign troops, except if a request by the country sending the troops is made for such a prosecution. This rules out prosecution of Nigerian and other West African troops, some of them no doubt implicated in gross violations, including atrocities like summary executions, rape and looting. The US government only fuelled these corrosive suspicions when in March 2002 it reached an agreement with the Sierra Leone government committing the latter to an agreement not to surrender US soldiers to the International Criminal Court.

The Court's huge budget, compared with the badly under-resourced Sierra Leone judicial system, has also come in for criticism. Is the world only interested in the prosecution of a handful of notorious criminals while people in the country must continue to make do with a collapsed judicial system and the same venal petty officials who compounded the problems that plagued civil society in the country before, during and after the war?

Special Court officials have countered that the Court is independent of any government, and that it will leave a 'legacy' of transparent jurisprudence that will go a long way to destroying impunity

[26] Richard Dowden, 'Justice goes on trial in Sierra Leone', *Guardian*, 3 October 2002.

and the tendency for corrupt judicial practices.[27] But a wider fear about the impact of the Court's activities on the still-fragile peace surfaced dramatically in March 2003, with the indictment of an initial batch of seven people, including Foday Sankoh and a popular member of Kabbah's government, Hinga Norman, the putative head of the CDF and the former Minister of the Interior. Norman, regarded as a hero for leading the resistance against the RUF and its renegade SLA allies, was brashly arrested in his office, handcuffed and flown to Bonthe Island in the remote south of the country, where he was detained in a former holding facility for enslaved Africans on their way to the Americas through the Middle Passage. This humiliation sparked outrage in many quarters, and the former British High Commissioner to Sierra Leone, Peter Penfold, bitterly complained to British MPs and called for Norman's release. The former AFRC leader Johnny Paul Koroma, the RUF's Sam Bockarie, Issa Sesay, Augustine Gbao and several others were also indicted.

Koroma and Bockarie were out of the country at the time, fighting for Taylor's beleaguered regime in Liberia. The Special Court asked that President Taylor hand over both of them. Instead Bockarie was murdered and Koroma simply disappeared. There were claims that he was also murdered a few weeks after Bockarie's summary execution, but this has been disputed. Koroma had fled Sierra Leone (and his Parliamentary seat—he had been elected to Parliament in the 2002 General Elections) a few months earlier following allegations by the government that he was plotting another coup. No doubt Taylor was fearful that he would himself be indicted, as indictments of both men mentioned the crucial role he played in the formation and activities of the RUF.

In early June 2003, shortly after Taylor arrived in Accra for peace talks to end his country's ever-widening and never-ending civil war—talks sponsored by the African Union and the United Nations—the Special Court unveiled a long-sealed indictment accusing Taylor of bearing 'the greatest responsibility' for the decade-long war in Sierra Leone, and calling on the Ghanaian authorities to have him arrested and sent to Sierra Leone. However, the chagrined Ghanaian government, embarrassed at this request, ignored the indictment and sent Taylor back to Monrovia in a Ghanaian government plane. But the indictment clearly unsettled Taylor and helped destabilise his regime. He quickly offered to resign if he were the obstacle to peace. Nigeria's President Obasanjo offered

[27] Interview with Robin Vincent, Court Registrar, Freetown, June 2003.

him asylum and in August 2003 Taylor relinquished power and went into exile in Nigeria. The Special Court meanwhile insisted that it would pursue Taylor to Nigeria and had the Swiss authorities freeze his associates' bank accounts whose balances totalled nearly $2 million. Interpol declared Taylor a 'wanted man', with an international arrest warrant issued for him.

Only time will tell whether Taylor, the true mastermind of the brutal wars in the region, will finally be apprehended and brought to account for his catastrophic activities. Meanwhile, Foday Sankoh died in custody in Freetown on 30 July. Without him and Taylor, and with Bockarie and possibly Koroma also dead, four of the characters with prime responsibility for the carnage in Sierra Leone are not facing the Special Court. So the Court has been left with the far more benign and popular Norman as the most prominent figure to face trial. The likes of Sesay and Gbao, in spite of their records, were clearly largely marginal figures until late in the war, and both fade beside the charismatic figure of Norman. It is an irony that can hardly be lost on Sierra Leoneans—the man who fought to resist the murderous rebels will now be the main interest in the trial of those bearing the 'greatest responsibility' for the war.

There were other problems attendant upon the Special Court and the TRC. TRC commissioners were complaining privately after the Special Court indictments that their work was hindered by the activities of the Special Court. Disagreement between the two organs exploded in public in late 2003 after TRC officials disclosed that the Commission had been prevented by Vincent from taking testimony from Special Court detainees, particularly Norman. Norman's lawyers sued to have him allowed to testify in public, but the Special Court President Robertson ruled that Norman could only give evidence privately by sworn affidavit. Norman's lawyers rejected this offer. TRC officials also claimed that many former RUF, CDF and SLA personnel who would otherwise have testified to the Commission were reluctant to do so lest they implicate themselves or their friends. This was in spite of the fact that both organs had made public their commitment not to share information or data. But the TRC sessions were held in public (except where minors or in some cases rape victims were concerned) and broadcast live on radio, and in any case, the Commission's report was due to be submitted to the government in October 2003 (when it would then become public property),[28] by which time the Special Court had

---

[28] TRC Commissioners were hinting in July 2003 that they might ask for a six-month extension so they might cover more areas of the country. Pro-

just begun trials of those it had indicted. This is common knowledge across the country.

This writer took a trip with the TRC to Kono district in July 2003 and sat through over a dozen testimonies. Almost all those testifying were victims of rebel atrocities. The one individual with definite links to the RUF, a dispirited young man named Abdul Razak Kamara, spoke with irritating detachment, claiming to have been a 'peace activist' who happened to have been caught behind rebel lines and was made to play an important role in the RUF during the Lome peace talks. A fairly educated man who claimed to be from a chiefly family, Kamara was part of a three-man RUF team that visited President Taylor on its way to Lome. Yet he claimed in the commission not to have seen or participated in any serious acts of atrocity. When asked whether Issa Sesay, with whom he worked closely during the final stages of the disarmament, had committed atrocities, he said he never saw Sesay do so, except, he said, that Sesay had him (Kamara) severely beaten and he was now impotent as a result. Sesay, he said, did that to him because the RUF leader wanted to take his wife from him. However, he stayed with the RUF throughout the disarmament process. He was a great activist, he insisted, and he wished the Special Court well in its work. Only the Court would establish the truth about the atrocious activities of the RUF. He didn't know anything. The frustrated Commissioners listened to him calmly, asked him some questions which he answered with the same evasiveness, and let him go, smiling grimly to himself. Truth, justice and reconciliation, it seemed, were being actively redefined in post-conflict Sierra Leone.

---

vision was made for this in the Act setting up the Commission, and the extension was granted in September 1993. In fact, it was not until October 2004 that the TRC finally submitted its report—a 5,000 page document, including transcripts of testimony, mainly from victims (but also from some perpetrators).

BIBLIOGRAPHICAL NOTE

This book relies heavily on the author's own notes and observations, but also on contemporary newspaper reports and commentaries, as well as other published sources. Sierra Leone has a long tradition of lively newspaper journalism, beginning in 1801 when *The Sierra Leone Gazette and Advertiser* (West Africa's first newspaper) was launched. The war years, however, were an especially difficult period for journalists, with access to the amorphous and unpredictable rebels almost impossible. The climate of newspaper publishing in even relatively secure areas like Freetown was particularly tough: journalists were targeted by the fighting forces, and about a dozen were killed during the war years, almost all by the insurgent forces. Without access to reliable information and to the key players, newspaper reporting of the war was marked largely by sensationalism and sometimes outright fabrication, but some of the reporting and commentaries were good and insightful. The following Freetown-based newspapers were particularly useful: *Vision, Concord Times, New Citizen, Daily Mail, New Shaft, For Di People, Expo Times, Standard Times, Punch, Unity Now, Uniweek* and *Democrat.*

Although the war was largely under-reported by the Western media before the spectacular atrocities of 1999, the BBC showed a not always helpful interest throughout, and newspapers like the *Guardian, The Times,* the *Independent,* the *New York Times* and the *Washington Post* provided sometimes serious coverage. The London-based (now defunct) *West Africa* magazine was also a very useful source. The *Sierra Leone Web,* run by an ex-Peace Corps volunteer from Minnesota, was an invaluable source, and so was the Sierra Leonean email discussion forum *Leonenet.*

Early attempts by analysts and scholars to understand the war included the useful if little-known pamphlet by John Lansana Musa and Sorie Musa, *The Invasion of Sierra Leone: a Chronicle of Events in a Nation under Siege* (Washington, DC: Sierra Leone Institute Publications, 1992). Better-known attempts included Robert Kaplan's article 'The Coming Anarchy' in *Atlantic Monthly* (February 1994), the writings of scholars like Paul Richards (particularly *Fighting for the Rainforest,* the first book-length study of the war, which appeared in 1996), and essays by Ibrahim Abdullah, Yusuf Bangura, Ismail Rashid, Patrick Muana, Arthur Abraham, Jimmy Kandeh and the present writer. Full citations for these works are made in the text. The work of Partnership Africa Canada on the role of diamonds in the conflict did more than most to arouse the world's attention to the conflict.

Since 1999 a number of popular, tabloid-type books have been published on the war. The most useful of these are Teun Voeten's *How De Body?*

216

One Man's Terrifying Journey Through an African War (New York: Thomas Dunne Books, 2003), Ian Stewart's *Freetown Ambush: a Reporter's Year in Africa* (Toronto: Penguin, 2003), and Major Phil Ashby's *Unscathed: Escape from Sierra Leone* (London: Pan, 2003). Aminatta Forna's *The Devil that Danced on the Water: a Daughter's Memoir* and Michael Jackson's *In Sierra Leone* (Durham, NC: Duke University Press, 2004), though not dealing with the war *per se*, provide enormously interesting and insightful description and analysis of events that could help explain the war as well as providing pointers to the country's post-war future.

INDEX

Reno, William 29, 181
Revolutionary United Front
  (RUF): 1–2, 6–16, 46, 59–64, 89–
  92, 95–6, 101–3, 151–6, 157–9,
  162–5, 168–9, 170, 171, 175, 177,
  189–96, 201–7; campaign (1991–
  9, 2000–1) 1–2, 6–16, 59–69, 74–
  5, 76–89, 92–5, 103, 106–7, 117,
  120–38, 141–56, 162, 165–7,
  172–4, 177–8, 180–91, 199, 204,
  210, 215
Revolutionary United Front Party
  (RUFP) 193–4, 195–6, 197–8
Richards, Paul vii, 62n, 132, 136–8,
  143–5, 150–1, 181
Riley, Steve 99
Robertson, Geoffrey 211, 214
Roelf, Colonel 93–4
RUF, *see* Revolutionary United
  Front
Rwanda 144, 159, 160

Salim, Salim Ahmed 89
Samura, Daembaso 82–3
Samura, Sorious 131
sanctions 113, 115, 170, 175, 186
Sandline International 115
Sankara, Thomas 53
Sankoh, Foday 8, 39–48, 51–4, 59–
  63, 80, 85, 88, 90, 95, 96, 102,
  114, 116–17, 121, 126, 129, 133,
  136, 151–2, 174, 184, 195–6, 201,
  209, 210, 212, 213; government
  appointment and re-arrest
  (1999–2000) 3, 51, 157, 163–4,
  166–7, 170, 193, 194, 196
Sanyang, Kukoi Samba 52, 55
Sebo, Addai 12, 90
Segbwema 76
Senegal 159, 177
Sesay, Issa 148, 171, 174, 190, 200–
  1, 213, 214, 215
Sesay, Mohamed 135
Sewa, Fallah 87
Shamel, Hanneh 32
Sieromco 88–9

Sierra Leone Bar Association 36–7
Sierra Leone Broadcasting Service
  (SLBS) 41
Sierra Leone Peoples Party (SLPP)
  20, 25, 26–8, 34, 44, 45, 83, 194,
  195
Sierra Leone Produce Marketing
  Board (SLPMB) 33
Sierra Leone Selection Trust
  (SLST) 22, 25, 29–32
Sierra Rutile 88–9, 106–7
sobels 81–2, 88, 95, 96, 99, 102–3,
  105, 182
Somalia 144, 159
Sorogbema 66
South Africa 48, 91, 93, 124, 164,
  190, 207
Southern Province 33, 71, 86, 92,
  134
Special Court 16, 154, 167n, 194,
  200, 201, 207–15
Special Security Division (SSD) 29,
  50, 58, 120
Stevens, Siaka 4, 7, 21, 23, 25–35,
  41–3, 49, 85, 90, 103, 120, 195,
  196
Strasser, Valentine 4, 67, 68–9, 70–
  3, 79, 81, 91, 92, 93, 103, 133
student protests 43–4, 45, 111
Switzerland 190n, 214

Talibi, Mohamed 63
Tamaboros 82–3
Tarawalie, Sahr Momodu 199
Taylor, Charles 5, 6, 8, 11, 16, 52–
  60, 131, 143, 148, 151, 161, 167,
  170, 172, 176, 183–4, 187–90,
  200, 213–14
Telu-Bongor 86
Temne people 18, 19, 26, 119
timber 176, 184
Tolbert, William 53
Tongo Field 116, 193
Tonkolili 39, 83
Totangie, Khalilu 48
Toure, Sekou 20